T0116974

*f*P

BOOKS BY EDA G. GOLDSTEIN, D.S.W.

Ego Psychology and Social Work Practice

*Self Psychology and Object Relations Theory in
Social Work Practice (forthcoming)*

Borderline Disorders: Clinical Models and Techniques

Clinical Social Work with Maltreated Children and Their Families

SHORT-TERM TREATMENT AND SOCIAL WORK PRACTICE

An Integrative Perspective

EDA G. GOLDSTEIN, D.S.W.

MARYELLEN NOONAN, Ph.D.

THE FREE PRESS

THE FREE PRESS
A Division of Simon & Schuster Inc.
1230 Avenue of the Americas
New York, NY 10020

Designed by Carla Bolte

Manufactured in the United States of America

10   9   8   7   6   5

Library of Congress Cataloging-in-Publication Data

Goldstein, Eda G.
    Short-term treatment and social work practice: an integrative
perspective / Eda G. Goldstein, Maryellen Noonan.
        p.   cm.
    Includes bibliographical references (p.   ) and index.
    1. Social service.   2. Social case work.   I. Noonan, Maryellen.
II. Title.
HV40.G63   1999
361.3'2—dc21   98–21755
                                                                        CIP

ISBN 978-1-4391-9993-0

To our students

Contents

Preface and Acknowledgments

This book is about short-term treatment in social work practice. We hope it will provide social work students, practitioners, supervisors, and educators, as well as members of other disciplines who are interested in this modality, with an integrated and holistic person-situation framework that can guide assessment and intervention with a wide and diverse range of clients.

There is no consensus regarding the most appropriate or effective short-term intervention model for most problems. Moreover, most short-term approaches in the mental health field are geared to high-functioning clients, those who are experiencing a crisis, or those with specific and concrete problems. These models are ill suited for work with clients who have inadequate or impaired coping capacities, show more chronic difficulties, or need environmental resources and supports.

Social work theory and practice have a great deal to offer in guiding short-term approaches with a broad range of clients in today's practice arena. The social work profession has its own history of experimentation with innovative and efficient ways of intervening with troubled populations, and much of social work practice has been short term in nature. Drawing on social work's rich knowledge base and practice wisdom, this book sets out a comprehensive person-situation framework for short-term intervention that is relevant to today's practice needs.

Our interest in short-term treatment stems from our clinical, teaching, and consulting roles. We have used short-term approaches in our

Although ISTT is eclectic, it should not be equated "with some magpie collection" that assembles ideas haphazardly or in a hodge-podge manner (Perlman, 1957, p. xii). Rather, it reflects an attempt to put forth an organized, coherent biopsychosocial perspective that can serve as a guide for social work practice and its evaluation. Eclecticism allows one to draw on the strengths of a variety of approaches so long as they are consistent with social work's values and knowledge base (Siporin, 1975, p. 153).

Short-term approaches differ markedly in their duration. It has been suggested that both the practitioner's and client's attitudes toward time are more important than the actual length of treatment. Nevertheless, the realities of practice generally dictate that intervention take place within a specified time frame. The duration of intervention intended for ISTT ranges from 8 to 25 generally weekly contacts, although meetings may be spaced over a longer time frame. This allows for considerable latitude in the length of intervention that undoubtedly will influence treatment goals and process. In some settings, 25 sessions may seem like long-term treatment. We believe, however, that this range accurately reflects the varying span of brief intervention in today's practice arena.

The book consists of two parts. Part I provides an overview of the scope, evolution, and varieties of short-term treatment in the mental health field generally and social work practice specifically and discusses the theoretical concepts underlying ISTT and its major characteristics. The book then describes and illustrates the beginning, middle, and ending phases of ISTT and the 14 components of the practice framework in detail: (1) problem identification, (2) biopsychosocial assessment, (3) engagement, (4) planning intervention, (5) contracting, (6) implementing the interventive plan, (7) maintaining or altering the focus, (8) monitoring progress, (9) dealing with obstacles to change, (10) managing the worker-client relationship, (11) addressing termination and its implications, (12) reviewing progress and identifying unresolved issues, (13) resolving the worker-client relationship, and (14) referral and follow-up. Part II of the book discusses special issues in the application of ISTT to intervention with diverse problems and special populations. It contains chapters on crisis-oriented ISTT, clients with emotional disorders, nonvoluntary and hard-to-reach clients, family-oriented ISTT, and group-oriented ISTT.

We have tried to write in a hands-on, user-friendly style that makes use of our clinical, teaching, and supervisory experience. In most instances, the numerous case examples and excerpts that we have utilized throughout the book are based on our own practice and teaching. They have been disguised and edited and sometimes reflect composites of similar client situations rather than one case.

Writing a book is a challenging task, and the collaborative effort that this book entailed has been a source of stimulation, collegiality, and fun and enabled us to weather the painstaking aspects of the process. The senior author (E.G.G.) expresses gratitude to those who have shown interest in and enthusiasm for the book: Patricia Petrocelli has been steadfast in her support, and both friends and family members, including Norma Hakusa, Lucille Spira, Enid Ain, Dick Rizzo, John David Earnest, Mildred Goldstein, and Mervyn Goldstein, have been important sources of encouragement along the way.

The coauthor (M.N.) particularly thanks colleagues and mentors who in their interest and encouragement throughout the years have helped to bring this work to fruition. Brenda, Mitch, and Michael Scher, Diane Connolly, Diane Murphy, Karen Brumer, and William Noonan deserve a special note of thanks for their ongoing support, enthusiasm, and patience. Finally, many thanks are due to the students whose commitment to learning and dedication to their clients inspired this book.

Both of us express our appreciation to Dean Tom Meenaghan and Vice Dean Eleanore Korman at the New York University Shirley M. Ehrenkranz School of Social Work for their advice and assistance. We also acknowledge the contributions of the following colleagues at the school who participated with us in a study group on short-term treatment: Barbara Dane, Roberta Kabat, Joan Klein, Judith Mishne, Lala Straussner, Carol Tosone, and Alice Wolson. We sincerely appreciate the confidence, patience, and expertise shown by Philip Rappaport, editor of the Free Press. Finally, we are indebted to the late Shirley M. Ehrenkranz for her many years of commitment to and leadership of a school that has nurtured our professional growth, to our mentors who have shown the way, to our students and supervisees who have taught us sometimes more than we wanted to know about the realities of social work practice, and to our clients who have shared the details of their lives and their pain with us and who have shown courage and strength in trying circumstances.

Social work is a unique profession that has reflected a keen sense of mission and values throughout its history. We hope that this book will provide social workers and other helping professionals with a useful guide to short-term intervention and its evaluation and contribute to their efforts to relieve clients of their suffering and strengthen their functioning, feelings of efficacy, and sense of well-being.

THEORETICAL CONCEPTS AND
PRACTICE PRINCIPLES

Chapter 1

Short-Term Treatment: An Overview

M ental health professionals in a variety of disciplines are using short-term methods in their practice more than ever before. Although brief treatment always has been part of the therapeutic repertoire, it received little positive attention in mental health circles until the 1940s. The first wave of interest in short-term and crisis intervention occurred during and just after World War II as a result of several concurrent developments: efforts to make traditional psychoanalytic psychotherapy more efficient, experiences with soldiers under battle conditions, attempts to help soldiers and their families when the former returned to civilian life, and work with the victims of disasters and those undergoing stressful life events. Despite the interest in short-term approaches, they were not widely assimilated into mainstream mental health services at that time.

Even after the revival of interest in brief treatment that occurred in the 1960s, it continued to be relegated to a second-class status in comparison to long-term treatment among psychodynamically oriented clinicians. Showing a prejudice in favor of so-called deeper and more intensive treatments, which were thought to be essential for the achievement of personality change, many psychotherapists viewed short-term intervention as shallow and superficial (Shechter, 1997; Wolberg, 1965).

THE RISE OF SHORT-TERM TREATMENT

Numerous factors have contributed to the diminished status and use of long-term treatment and the increased use of short-term and crisis

3

intervention (Budman & Gurman, 1988; Parad & Parad, 1990b; Shechter, 1997). Beginning in the 1960s, optimism about the ability of mental health treatment to help people led to efforts to make treatment accessible to greater numbers of individuals at earlier points in the emergence of their difficulties and for help with problems in living, as well as severe emotional disorders. The short-lived community mental health movement, ushered in by the Community Mental Health Centers Act of 1963 during the Kennedy presidency, was heavily weighted toward emergency and brief treatment. Even psychodynamically oriented clinicians experimented with short-term treatment, and new interventive models proliferated, including those that were cognitive and behavioral.

Another contributing factor to the changing nature of treatment was the criticism of traditional forms of intervention on the part of numerous special populations who sought greater opportunities for self-expression, freedom from oppression, and respect for their diversity. Among these groups were those reflecting counterculture lifestyles, people of color, women, and gays and lesbians, who tended to perceive long-term, psychodynamically oriented treatment as a form of social control, a means of blaming the victim, and a way of labeling difference as pathological. Self-help, consciousness-raising, and rap groups, along with other types of alternative helping methods, gained popularity and eroded the dominance of more traditional therapies.

As mental health treatment became more available, individuals sought help for a host of concerns that previously would not have been thought to warrant treatment. Less motivated for long-term treatment, clients expected treatment to focus on more here-and-now, reality-oriented problems. Often they possessed more knowledge about treatment options and were more vocal in questioning the utility of seemingly ill-defined and open-ended approaches with unspecified goals.

The accumulation of findings from practice research also supported the use of short-term approaches since many studies failed to show that more open-ended treatments were superior to brief intervention (Koss & Shiang, 1994; Wells & Phelps, 1990). Moreover, the use of long-term treatment was associated with high dropout rates. For example, in one study, as many as 80 percent of patients in mental health clinics and family service agencies, who were offered more ongoing intervention, were seen for six or fewer sessions (Garfield, 1986). Thus, despite clinicians' stated preferences for long-term treatment, intervention turned out to be short term by default rather than by design (Budman & Gurman, 1988, pp. 6–7). Additionally, as Wells (1990, p. 13) notes, there is some evidence to show that even for those who actually received long-term treatment, improvement occurred early, with 75 percent of clients making considerable progress within six months.

The economic climate of the past several decades has been another major cause of the dramatic increase in the use of briefer forms of treatment. New, more cost-conscious and seemingly efficient forms of delivering mental health care have proliferated, and reimbursement for, allocation of, and accessibility to mental health services have been greatly curtailed and circumscribed. Social agencies and hospitals, which have been the mainstays of service delivery in their communities, have been forced to slash their budgets, rearrange their priorities, downsize their staffs, engage in reengineering their operations, and offer more short-term intervention, sometimes to the exclusion of other types of treatment. Practitioners in these settings, as well as those in private practice, are being forced to reexamine their customary and preferred ways of helping others.

For all the reasons cited, social workers, among other mental health providers, are using time-limited treatment with ever greater numbers of clients. Some practitioners are embracing this development enthusiastically, while others are resigning themselves to it out of necessity. On the positive side, short-term approaches may be highly responsive to what clients want and expect. Consumers seek or are mandated to seek help for a wide range of problems, many of which can be addressed appropriately by brief forms of intervention. For example, a young adult may enter treatment after the breakup of a relationship and may benefit from supportive work aimed at assisting him in dealing with issues of loss and blows to self-esteem. Similarly, a mother who seeks help in disciplining an acting-out youngster may be able to benefit from brief, educative work focused on parenting skills, and a truant adolescent boy may benefit more from a simple change in his school setting than from open-ended ongoing treatment of his personality problems.

Even if clients present with more complex treatment issues that might warrant a more open-ended approach, they may not want or be amenable to such intervention. Proceeding when the goals of the worker and client are divergent runs the risk of causing the client to withdraw from treatment. It is preferable to try to meet the client's expectations if possible, as illustrated in the following example.

Mrs. Pierce, a twice-divorced, recently remarried 40-year-old woman, came for help because of marital problems that were leading her to want to separate from her new husband. She recounted incidents in which he had ignored her needs and wishes and gave evidence of her concerns that he was seeing another woman. Although the worker accepted the client's view of her husband, she learned that Mrs. Pierce had a history of repetitive instances in which her suspiciousness of men's motives led her to distance herself from them and she thought that she was contributing to her unsuccessful relationships. Concerned that the client might leave her current husband, only to repeat her pattern again and again, the psychodynamically trained worker thought that it would be advisable for Mrs. Pierce to get help in understanding the origins of her long-standing feelings of distrust, her sense of inadequacy, and her fears of rejection so that she could modify her ways of perceiving and relating to her husband and other men. The client, however, expressed an interest only in getting help in summoning the courage to leave her spouse.

Recognizing that she could not involve the client in a more insight-oriented and modifying long-term treatment unless she saw its benefit, the worker explained the reasons behind her thinking that the client would benefit from looking into her characteristic relationship patterns. The client missed the next session. In the following meeting, in response to the worker's inquiry about her feelings after their last meeting, the client indicated that she was not going to return at all because she did not want to dwell on the past but she realized that the worker meant well and was probably right. She said that she did realize that she had made a mess of her marriages but needed help in extricating herself from her current relationship, adding that she felt too upset to deal with her other issues at the present time. The worker accepted the client's wishes to focus on her present concerns and abandoned her agenda.

Despite the rationale for briefer forms of intervention, many practitioners remain skeptical, if not overtly negative, about the proliferation of short-term methods. Although their opposition may reflect bias against brief intervention, many clinicians also believe that the current emphasis on short-term treatment is misguided and ill conceived as a result of philosophical, political, and economic reasons.

Whether viewed from a positive or negative perspective, the use of short-term approaches challenges practitioners to expand and change their attitudes about the nature of the treatment process, learn new interventive strategies, and address greater external demands for accountability.

SHORT-TERM TREATMENT MODELS IN
MENTAL HEALTH PRACTICE

There are three main types of short-term treatment models that are being used extensively in mental health practice: (1) the psychodynamic model, (2) the crisis intervention model, and (3) the cognitive-behavioral model. The table on pp. 20–21 compares the major characteristics of these models.

The Psychodynamic Model

The short-term psychodynamic treatment model consists of a variety of approaches that modify some of the basic assumptions of traditional psychoanalytic theory and treatment and embody more contemporary psychodynamic theories. Short-term psychodynamic psychotherapy generally is used with clients who have circumscribed problems that are embedded in either mild or moderate long-standing conflicts and maladaptive personality traits and patterns. Although their goals are restorative and supportive in some instances, most time-limited psychodynamic models aim at selective personality change and resolution of underlying conflicts. They have clearly defined selection criteria that favor highly motivated and well-functioning clients who have circumscribed problems and tend to exclude a wide range of individuals whose difficulties are more severe, pervasive, and chronic.

Despite the fact that each of the psychodynamic short-term models to be discussed below has somewhat different origins, goals, foci, selection criteria, and practice principles, they share common assumptions and features:

Common Features of Psychodynamic Approaches

1. The belief that early childhood experiences are a major contributor to adult dysfunction
2. The view that presenting problems generally are embedded in long-standing personality conflicts and patterns
3. The use of selection criteria such as a history of adequate adjustment, problems of acute or recent onset, strong motivation, and ability to relate easily
4. A quick and focused assessment
5. Setting of treatment goals that include either selective or more global personality change
6. The early establishment of a working alliance
7. A focus on core conflicts or relational themes that are manifested in the client's history and the treatment relationship
8. The utilization of active techniques such as clarification, confrontation, and interpretation
9. The use of time limits that can be negotiated flexibly in some instances

Although the classical psychoanalytic model has been associated traditionally with in-depth, long-term treatment aimed at restructuring the personality, many authors have commented on the short-term nature of Freud's early cases and the fact that initially psychoanalysis was not long term (Flegenheimer, 1982; Shechter, 1997; Stadter, 1996; Wolberg, 1980). Nevertheless, the techniques that are characteristic of Freudian psychoanalysis are geared to helping the patient undergo a controlled regression in which early memories and childhood experiences are explored. The patient's revival of important aspects of his or her relationships with significant others in early life in the treatment or transference to the analyst or therapist provides the basis for therapeutic work. The patient's distorted perceptions of the therapist can be analyzed and interpreted in order to help the patient gain insight into the nature of his or her problems and their roots. Traditionally, the analyst was to remain neutral, anonymous, and abstinent or nongratifying so as to maximize the patient's transference.

Interested in making psychoanalysis more efficient and available to a greater range of patients, Ferenczi and Rank (1925) were the first psychoanalysts to address the issue of time in the treatment process. Rank believed that setting and adhering to a time limit in treatment would prevent regression and force the patient to deal with reality. Ferenczi emphasized the importance of using active techniques, such as suggestion and direct advice, in order to maintain the client's level of functioning, help the patient focus on his or her difficulties, and foster motivation (Flegenheimer, 1982, p. 27). Ferenczi and Rank's views were radical for the time and were neither endorsed nor accepted by the psychoanalytic community. Their work fell into disrepute for some time.

Two decades later, Alexander and French (1946) published a pioneering book, *Psychoanalytic Therapy*, the first systematic presentation of short-term psychodynamic psychotherapy. As Koss and Shiang (1994, p. 665) point out, Alexander and French believed that psychoanalytic principles could be beneficial, irrespective of the length of treatment, and sought to adapt selective psychoanalytic techniques in order to "give rational aid to all those who show early signs of maladjustment" (1946, p. 341). Drawing on the earlier work of Ferenczi and Rank, they also questioned some of the basic assumptions of the traditional psychoanalytic approach: that depth of treatment was related to length; that brief treatment was temporary and superficial while the results of long-term treatment were stable and profound; and that it was necessary to prolong treatment in order to overcome the patient's resistance to change (Budman & Gurman, 1988, p. 2).

Alexander and French tried to avoid techniques that fostered regression and emphasized therapy over real-life experiences. Among the more directive and active techniques that they advocated were (1) the manipulation of the frequency of sessions in order to confront the patient's dependency on the therapist; (2) the utilization of temporary interruptions to determine the patient's reactions to termination; (3) emphasis on the patient's affective experience in the here and now, with attention to relevant historical material; (4) direct encouragement of the patient to face conflicts and problems and to put what he or she learned in therapy into practice; and (5) the therapist's assumption of a role that was diametrically opposed to the earlier parental roles in order to promote an emotionally corrective experience that would foster the patient's functioning and ability to engage in more satisfactory interpersonal relationships.

Like Ferenczi and Rank, Alexander and French were ahead of their time and provided the foundation for all later psychodynamic short-term approaches. Nevertheless, their work was controversial at best and minimized and denounced at worst within the psychoanalytic community. In social work, however, it found a more appreciative audience.

Following is a summary of the salient characteristics of the better-known and more recent psychodynamic short-term models.

MALAN'S INTENSIVE BRIEF PSYCHOTHERAPY. In two books based on his studies at the Tavistock Clinic in London, Malan (1963, 1976) outlined an approach to short-term treatment that relied heavily on the technique of classical interpretation of a central conflict or important aspect of the patient's psychopathology. His research indicated that change included not only symptom relief but also modifying basic and entrenched neurotic behavior patterns. The number of weekly treatment sessions ranged from 10 to 40, and the best results occurred when patients showed (1) high motivation for insight, (2) good ego strength, (3) the ability to formulate a specific focus, (4) the ability to establish a quick transference to the therapist, (5) favorable reactions to interpretation, and (6) the ability to deal with their emotional reactions to termination. The therapist's enthusiasm was considered a major factor associated with good outcome.

SIFNEOS'S SHORT-TERM ANXIETY-PROVOKING PSYCHOTHERAPY. Like Malan, Sifneos (1972, 1979, 1987) developed a short-term treatment model that used interpretation of a patient's oedipal conflict as it appeared in the transference to the therapist as the major tool of therapy. In order to help the client focus on the main problem area, Sifneos relied heavily on confrontation and other anxiety-arousing techniques, which often created anger and resistance that needed to be addressed.

The duration of treatment ranged from 7 to 20 weekly sessions. Sifneos's selection criteria were among the most stringent and exclusionary of all the short-term psychodynamic models and stressed the presence of numerous patient characteristics, including (1) above-average intelligence; (2) possession of at least one meaningful relationship in the past; (3) psychological mindedness; (4) ability to interact with the therapist in an affective manner; (5) motivation beyond symptom relief; (6) honesty, curiosity, and openness to self-reflection; (7) willingness to make accommodations and sacrifices; (8) receptivity to new ideas; and (9) realistic goals (Stadter, 1996; Wolberg, 1980).

Sifneos also proposed a brief treatment model, anxiety-suppressive therapy, for patients who showed weaker egos, impaired interpersonal relationships, and chronic difficulties. The goal was to reduce anxiety through more supportive measures, such as reassurance, advice giving, ventilation, environmental manipulation, persuasion, hospitalization, and medication (Wolberg, 1980).

DAVANLOO'S INTENSIVE SHORT-TERM DYNAMIC PSYCHOTHERAPY. Davanloo (1978, 1980, 1991) was another proponent of a highly confrontational and interpretive approach, which had definite selection criteria. Stadter (1996, p. 72) views this model as the most forceful and persistent of the short-term psychodynamic approaches. Davanloo himself referred to his methods as relentless. The model also is the most ambitious in that it aims for complete personality or structural change.

The evaluation process can take up to six hours, usually during the course of one day. The length of the treatment depends on the severity of the patient's problems and rate of progress and can vary from as little as 1 to as many as 40 sessions. The emphasis of the treatment is on uncovering unconscious conflict through systematic challenging and interpreting of resistances, making the therapy process highly intense and affectively charged. Discussion of termination is kept at a minimum.

MANN'S TIME-LIMITED PSYCHOTHERAPY. A unique approach to short-term treatment is found in the work of Mann (1973, 1991). Like Rank, Mann made a conscious use of time and the struggle around separation and loss in his short-term treatment model. His approach is highly structured, with a rigid adherence to time limits. The approach consists of a formulation phase followed by 12 sessions, which may be spaced at varying intervals. Selection criteria include patients who can rapidly establish a therapeutic relationship and possess an ability to tolerate loss.

After determining the central issue to be addressed in the treatment during the assessment period, the therapist gives the patient the formulation of the problem, even if it is at variance with the patient's stated complaint, and how the work will proceed. All treatment deals with the theme of separation-individuation as a basic universal conflict that influences the resolution of all later conflicts. Despite the patient's presenting problem, the formulation always relates to the patient's negative self-image, which Mann believes is linked to unresolved separation and loss issues in a patient's life. Because of the treatment's time limit, the therapist helps the patient deal with the establishment of a dependent relationship amid the reality of the impending separation and loss. Presumably the therapy provides the patient with a more optimal setting in which to master separation anxiety and achieve autonomy.

STRUPP AND BINDER'S TIME-LIMITED DYNAMIC PSYCHOTHERAPY. The work of Strupp and Binder (1984) began at Vanderbilt University and drew on the work of Sullivan (1953). Their model, along with that of Luborsky, was among the first psychoanalytic approaches to employ a treatment manual, thus making it easier to implement and study systematically. It was used with patients who showed a range of functioning and personality traits, including resistance, hostility, and negativity.

The duration of the treatment is limited but flexible and ranges from 25 to 40 sessions in instances where personality problems are mild rather than severe. In this model, intrapsychic conflicts are redefined as interpersonal in nature. The therapeutic process relies heavily on the therapist's empathic responsiveness to and ability to address the patient's cyclical maladaptive patterns of relating as they appear in the therapeutic interaction rather than on the use of technical interventions in creating change. Thus, no particular techniques are emphasized. The research findings generated in the use of this model have shed light on the importance of the therapist's personality in treatment outcome.

LUBORSKY'S SUPPORTIVE-EXPRESSIVE PSYCHOTHERAPY. Luborsky's (1984) model incorporated ego psychological theory and practice principles to a greater extent than other models. It emphasized both the supportive relationship between the therapist and patient and the technical interventions in facilitating change. Although Luborsky suggested screening out the most severely disturbed and antisocial patients, as well as those who had environmental problems, he believed that the model could be used broadly.

Like Strupp and Binder, Luborsky thought that the duration of treatment was related to the severity of the patient's problems. He recommended 25 sessions that sometimes were spread over time rather than occurring weekly. In more severe cases, Luborsky (1984, p. 67) indicated that as many as 40 sessions might be necessary. Treatment goals are individualized and are supposed to be consistent with what the patient perceives as his or her main difficulties and needs. The therapist employs the full range of psychotherapeutic techniques. A major component of the model is its focus on a patient's core conflictual relationship theme as it is reexperienced in the relationship with the therapist. A manual of procedures that Luborsky developed in conjunction with this his model has been used extensively.

OBJECT RELATIONS AND SELF-PSYCHOLOGICAL MODELS. As psychodynamic frameworks that differed from classical Freudian theory and psychoanalytic ego psychology have gained a wider audience, some theorists have begun to apply their principles to short-term treatment. For example, Stadter (1996) has drawn on object relations theories in his perspective, and Baker (1991) and Seruya (1997) have put forth a self-psychological model of brief treatment. Although similar in some respects to the other models discussed so far, these newer approaches are important in their alerting the practitioner to a different and broader range of past and existing factors that give rise to certain types of dysfunction than do either Freudian theory or ego psychology. They emphasize the importance of the therapist's ability to provide a holding environment and/or an empathic selfobject experience for the patient.

There are several important limitations associated with the use of psychodynamic approaches. First, as noted by Koss and Shiang (1994, p. 671), the majority of individuals who seek help from mental health settings do not meet their selection criteria and thus would not be considered suitable for brief treatment. This fact would not constitute so much of a problem if other types of treatment were readily available. Given the constraints of services, however, an exclusive reliance on a psychodynamic model may result in inappropriate treatment. A second problem in the use of psychodynamic approaches is that they are not suited to patients who are beset by environmental difficulties or seeking help with more concrete needs and immediate concerns. A third difficulty in using these models is that they often employ techniques, such as confrontation and interpretation, that may be contraindicated with some individuals.

The Crisis Intervention Model

Crisis intervention is a form of brief treatment, but not all short-term intervention is crisis oriented. Because all individuals, regardless of their particular personality and strengths, are potentially vulnerable to having their equilibrium disrupted by extremely stressful life events, crisis intervention can be used with a wide range of clients so long as they have been thrown into a state of crisis.

The crisis intervention model originated in part from the study and treatment of soldiers who developed so-called war neuroses and combat fatigue during World War II (Grinker & Spiegel, 1945). Psychiatrists and other mental health professionals, who were charged with the task of helping soldiers return to their battlefield assignments quickly, used emergency interventions that seemed to be effective in many instances, particularly when treatment occurred at or near the front lines. Treatment was based on the belief that soldiers could regain their equilibrium and return to active duty if they were given immediate, supportive help. It was observed that such prompt attention prevented regression, secondary gain, guilt, feelings of failure, stigmatization, and loss of peer support (Parad & Parad, 1990a, p. 13). Additionally, the return of soldiers to civilian life after the completion of their military service necessitated readjustment of both the veterans and their families. Many sought help for transitional difficulties that seemed to respond to brief interventions.

Concurrently, other investigators became interested in the reactions of individuals to disasters and stressful life events. Lindemann's classic paper, "Symptomatology and Management of Acute Grief" (1944), delineated identifiable stages of the grief process of the survivors of the tragic Coconut Grove nightclub fire in Boston, in which hundreds of individuals lost their lives or were injured. According to Lindemann, an important component of grief resolution is the survivor's ability to master various affective, cognitive, and behavioral tasks. He observed that people could resume and even improve their precrisis level of functioning after a crisis, or they could deteriorate. Lindemann believed that those who showed more maladaptive solutions to their grief could be helped to cope more effectively with their mourning through intervention, and he developed an interventive approach of 8 to 10 sessions.

Lindemann's work, along with that of Caplan (1964), led to more systematic study of how people cope with disasters and other stressful life events and to the establishment of community-based crisis intervention services. Caplan, in his work at Harvard University in the 1950s, was instrumental in the development of programs that provided early intervention to those experiencing acute situational stress in an attempt to facilitate crisis resolution and to forestall more serious problems.

In the 1950s and 1960s, crisis theory expanded greatly. One of the hallmarks of this period was a greater delineation of different types of crises—for example, those resulting from developmental and maturational stages, life and role transitions, and traumatic events. Others who contributed to this body of knowledge were Hill (1958), Janis (1958), Kaplan (1962, 1968), Langsley and Kaplan (1968), Lazarus (1966), Le Masters (1957), Parad (1971), Parad and Caplan (1960), Rapoport (1962, 1967), Selye (1956), Strickler (1965), and Tyhurst (1958).

Crisis theory is based on the assumption that an individual strives to maintain equilibrium through an ongoing series of adaptive measures and problem-solving techniques. A crisis represents an upset in that equilibrium in which the person's customary coping strategies are inadequate to deal with the task at hand. Although some crisis theorists suggest that all people who experience a similar event will respond in a similar manner, others have focused on the unique meaning that the individual attaches to a particular situation. For example, Jacobson, Strickler, and Morley (1968) differentiate between generic and individual intervention, the former focusing on the common reactions of all the people who experience the same event and the latter emphasizing the more unique reactions of each person. Although the active state of crisis is time limited, usually lasting four to six weeks, intervention can facilitate crisis mastery, prevent more maladaptive solutions, and allow for the reworking of underlying conflicts. It is crucial that crisis intervention be undertaken as near to the stressful event in time and proximity as possible. Due to the client's state of helplessness and vulnerability, he or she is more open to influence and change during a crisis.

Crisis intervention usually occurs in 4 to 12 sessions. The therapist attempts to convey an empathic understanding of the patient's state of disequilibrium and establish a working alliance with the patient. The therapist becomes a benign authority figure who provides a sense of safety and strength.

The goals of crisis intervention usually are limited to the resolution of the crisis, but this is not always a simple matter. For example, Langsley and Kaplan (1968, pp. 4–5) suggest a recompensation type of crisis intervention that helps the client return to his or her precrisis level of functioning and a limited psychotherapy model that deals with the underlying conflicts that have been reactivated. There may be instances, however, when it is not possible to help an individual resolve a crisis without dealing with these underlying issues since it is the triggering of these past conflicts and experiences that transformed the stressful current situation into an actual crisis.

Jacobson, Strickler, and Morely (1968) identify four levels of crisis intervention: (1) environmental, where the therapist serves as a referral source; (2) general support, involving ventilation, active listening, acceptance, and reassurance; (3) generic, in which the therapist deals with the common reactions that individuals who experience the same type of event are likely to show; and (4) individual, in which the therapist uses his or her understanding of the patient's personality dynamics to foster the development of insight into why the crisis event has been so disruptive.

The greatest strengths of the crisis model—its specificity and clear methodology for working with individuals who are experiencing a state of acute disequilibrium—become potential limitations in certain situations. Although all persons who seek help are uncomfortable in some way, most are not in a true state of crisis. Problems may have existed for a long time before the person seeks help, or they may be chronic. Sometimes individuals show a pattern in which being in crisis has become a way of life. In these and other instances, crisis intervention is not an appropriate model.

The Cognitive-Behavioral Model

Although behavioral and cognitive theories and treatment methods originated independently, in today's practice arena they overlap to a great extent and often are referred to as cognitive-behavioral approaches (Koss & Shiang, 1994, pp. 666–667). The cognitive-behavioral model focuses on modifying clearly defined ways of thinking and behaving and the current factors that are sustaining them rather than uncovering or exploring the past origins of the behaviors.

Not developed specifically as a short-term treatment, the cognitive-behavioral approach nevertheless is used frequently as a part of time-limited treatments, and results can be achieved in 12 to 20 sessions (Wright & Borden, 1991, p. 424). Cognitive-behavioral methods have been shown to be helpful in the treatment of anxiety disorders and phobias, obsessive-compulsive disorders, weight problems, smoking, somatic disorders, eating disorders, alcohol and drug abuse, and some aspects of schizophrenia (Goisman, 1997; Koss & Shiang, 1994). More recently, cognitive therapy has shown some promise in work with borderline personality disorders over a longer time frame (Beck, Freeman, & Associates, 1990; Heller & Northcut, 1996; Linehan, 1993).

The field of behavior therapy and behavior modification emerged after World War II and drew heavily on experimental psychology and social learning theory. Pavlov's work on classical or respondent conditioning, in which existing patterns of stimulus and response are associated with new stimuli to create new responses, and Skinner's experiments based on operant conditioning, in which rewards and punishments were used to create and modify behavior, were seminal (1953). Additionally, social learning or learning through observation, imitation, role playing, and rehearsal became an important part of the behavioral repertoire (Goisman, 1997, p. 4; Thyer & Myers, 1996, pp. 27–28). Other major contributors to the behavioral model were Wolpe (1958, 1969) and Lazarus (1971, 1976).

Cognitive treatment had its roots in the work of Adler (Adler & Ansbacher, 1956) and gathered renewed interest through the development of Ellis's (1962, 1973) rational emotive therapy and the later cognitive therapy of Beck (1976). In the 1970s, behaviorally oriented clinicians and researchers began to incorporate aspects of cognitive theory into their work (Craighead, Craighead, Kazdin, & Mahoney, 1994). As Thyer and Myers (1996, p. 29) point out, cognitive theorists accepted many aspects of behavioral theory but stressed additional elements that they felt were essential to understanding behavior and planning treatment, such as the importance of the cognitive representation of events rather than the events per se and the role of cognition and thinking in determining behavior and emotions.

Behavior therapy emphasizes the consistent implementation of techniques with the goal of altering self-defeating or maladaptive behaviors and undesirable traits. The primary foci of the treatment are (1) identifying target behaviors, that is, those that need to be changed; (2) the antecedents of the behaviors; (3) the consequences of the behaviors; and (4) the interactions of both the antecedents and consequences of the behaviors (Bandura, 1976). Efforts are made to reinforce new behaviors and to modify, punish, or extinguish maladaptive behaviors through systematic desensitization, respondent and operant conditioning, flooding, and observational learning.

Cognitive therapy attempts to modify the patterns of thinking that are at the root of dysfunctional behavior and troubling emotions by (1) correcting misconceptions, unrealistic expectations, and faulty ideas; (2) modifying irrational thoughts that relate to the self; (3) improving problem solving; and (4) improving self-control and self-management (Fischer, 1978, pp. 177–178). The therapist helps the patient bring into focus the thoughts, beliefs, and ideas that are creating and maintaining his or her problems. The approach is reality oriented and educational. It uses such techniques as clarification of thinking, reeducation, and homework assignments.

Cognitive-behavioral therapies are well suited to addressing specific and circumscribed target symptoms, traits, and behaviors that the individual is highly motivated to change. Although there is some indication that these techniques can be used to modify certain ways of thinking and behaving in those who show more deep-seated personality problems, generally they are not as helpful in dealing with complex individual, interpersonal, and person-environmental difficulties. Further, the exclusive focus on altering thinking and behavior overlooks more dynamic aspects of the person and often leads to a mechanical application of technique.

SOCIAL WORK PRACTICE MODELS AND
SHORT-TERM TREATMENT

Social workers are part of a unique profession and are particularly well suited to serve clients in the current climate. From the profession's inception, they always have been on the front lines in working with clients from diverse backgrounds and with clients who faced problems in living as well as more severe and persistent personality and environmental difficulties. Moreover, much of social work practice over the years has been short term in nature.

Social workers intervene with clients presenting a staggering array of problems in a variety of facilities and in private practice—for example, Vietnam veterans and their families; persons with HIV-related illnesses and their caregivers; survivors of physical and sexual abuse and other types of trauma; individuals suffering from mental illness and other forms of emotional disorder; substance abusers; victims and perpetrators of child abuse and other forms of domestic violence, rape,

Comparison of Psychodynamic, Crisis, and Cognitive-Behavioral Short-Term Treatment Models

	PSYCHODYNAMIC	CRISIS	COGNITIVE-BEHAVIORAL
Nature of problems	Embedded in early childhood developmental deficits and conflicts and long-standing personality patterns	Resulting from developmental and maturational stages; life transitions; traumatic events; and disasters	Self-defeating or maladaptive behavior; undesirable traits; distorted and irrational thinking
Selection criteria	Problems of recent nature; history of adequate adjustment; strong motivation; can relate easily	Person in crisis	Broad range of circumscribed target symptoms, traits, and behaviors
Goals	Symptom reduction; selective or global personality change; sometimes support	Restoration of equilibrium; sometimes resolution of underlying issues	Change of maladaptive behavior and distorted patterns of thinking; enhanced problem solving, self-control, and self-management
Focus	Core conflicts, relational theme, and developmental issues	Immediate crisis; sometimes insight into underlying issues	Maladaptive behavior; undesirable traits; irrational and distorted thinking
Techniques	Active use of clarification, confrontation, and interpretation; some reliance on empathy and support	Ventilation, active listening, acceptance, support, reassurance, education, and referral	Systematic desensitization; respondent and operant conditioning; flooding; observational learning; role playing; education; homework assignments; logical discussion; self-monitoring; rehearsal

Nature of relationship	Establishment of positive working alliance; focus on transference and countertransference	Benign authority and establishment of positive working alliance	Expert authority or educator
Nature of change	Insight and supportive relationship	Restoration of coping mechanisms; ego support and ego mastery; sometimes insight	Behavioral reinforcement; modification of distorted thinking; learning new ways of behaving and thinking; role modeling
Duration of treatment	12–40 sessions	4–12 sessions, sometimes longer	12–20 sessions, sometimes longer
Limitations	Excludes many people who need help; does not address person-environmental problems; techniques may be detrimental	Excludes those who are not experiencing acute disequilibrium	Does not address more complex personal, interpersonal, and person-environmental problems; ignores certain dynamic aspects of person; can be mechanical

and crime; individuals and families coping with death, divorce, physical illness, disability, aging, unemployment, homelessness, and other types of life crises; and those struggling with family difficulties, interpersonal, school, and occupational problems, and life cycle transitions.

When social work originated in the nineteenth century as a result of the activities of the Community Organization Society and, later, the settlement houses, the focus of intervention was the person in interaction with his or her environment. Early caseworkers, or friendly visitors as they were called, as well as settlement house workers attempted to help those in lower socioeconomic circumstances, many of whom had recently emigrated to the United States. They confronted problems that were immediate, sometimes concrete, and often related to family, situational, environmental, and cultural issues.

The Early Diagnostic Model

As social work became professionalized, Mary Richmond's pioneering book, *Social Diagnosis* (1917), became the foundation of casework practice. Relying on a medical model, Richmond advocated an exhaustive study process. Only after a formal diagnosis of the client's problem was made could treatment be implemented. In keeping with Richmond's emphasis, the "diagnostic school" or "differential" approach emerged in the 1920s, taking its name from the fact that it regarded diagnosis as the foundation of all intervention. This model developed in the aftermath of World War I, which brought social workers in hospitals and clinics into greater contact with psychiatric principles and practices. During this period, Freudian theory, which emphasized the role of intrapsychic conflict in causing client problems, gained acceptance among a large segment of social caseworkers, particularly in the northeastern United States. It seemed to explain why it was so difficult for clients to change certain behaviors and their seeming resistance to intervention (Hollis, 1963, pp. 7–23).

Many practitioners adopted the Freudian view that it was necessary to modify clients' underlying conflicts in order to help them improve their current functioning, and they incorporated psychoanalytic techniques into their practice. The focus of treatment shifted away from the more here-and-now, concrete manifestations of clients' problems and their environmental component to emphasize the personality dimensions of the clients' difficulties and their childhood origins. Because the process by which a client developed insight into the true nature of his or her personality difficulties and altered their basic patterns of functioning was time-consuming, treatment became lengthier. For a time, diagnostic casework and individual long-term psychotherapy seemed to be synonomous.

The Functional Model

In response to what some have argued were excesses in the use of the diagnostic model during this early period (Hamilton, 1958, pp. 11–37; Meyer, 1970, pp. 36–53), a schism developed between the diagnostic caseworkers and those who called themselves functional caseworkers. As early as the 1930s, Robinson (1930) recognized the importance of time as a propelling factor in treatment, and she, along with Taft (1937, 1950), made it a central component of functional casework practice.

Taft and Robinson rejected Freudian theory and the diagnostic casework approach associated with it because they felt it was too pathology oriented in its view of clients' problems, robbed them of taking responsibility for change, created undue dependence, and led to an unrealistic, never-ending process of exploration of the past (Yelaja, 1974, pp. 151–152). They drew instead on the theories of Rank, who viewed individuals as more active and creative in seeking health, capable of changing themselves and their environment within the limits of their capacities, and able to use relationships to move toward their life goals (Smalley, 1970, pp. 90–91). In fact, Robinson stressed the use of relationships as a major force in helping to empower the client to make necessary changes. Further, she viewed the client, rather than the worker, as having the major responsibility for his or her life.

As described by Yelaja (1986, pp. 52–53), the functionalists rejected the concept of diagnosis as it was being used at the time and the need for in-depth and time-consuming exploration of the client's personality difficulties. In large part, the agency's function organized and directed the interventive process. Workers attempted to engage clients in a relationship process designed to release the client's own power for choice and growth. The use of time was a crucial factor in functional casework since it presented the client and worker with the need to accept constraints and endings. The helping process was partialized and linked to the client's use or rejection of the agency's services within a specified time limit. This focus on time led to greater attention to the present and a more conscious use of the phases (beginning, middle, and ending) of the helping process. The functionalists viewed the ending phase, which involved separation from the worker, as a major force in helping the client take responsibility for his or her own life. The functionalists believed that the client would benefit from and become more self-actualizing, empowered, and self-sufficient as a result of this process, irrespective of his or her particular problem.

Like the diagnostic model, functional casework had its critics, many of whom argued that it created rigid conditions, ignored the client's view of the problems, misused agency and worker authority, and engendered a relationship struggle between worker and client in which the client's problems were lost.

Ego Psychology and the Evolving Diagnostic (Psychosocial) Model

At the end of the 1930s (although it became more significant in the post–World War II period), ego psychology gained recognition in the United States and had an important impact on social work practice (Goldstein, 1995a; Woods & Robinson, 1996). Followers of the diagnostic school used ego psychological concepts to help correct what some considered to be the model's narrow intrapsychic focus, reliance on psychoanalytic techniques, lack of specificity of goals, and open-ended nature. In 1940, Hamilton published the widely used *Theory and Practice of Social Casework*, which put forth the principles of the evolving diagnostic approach. Hamilton began to use the term *psychosocial*, which was incorporated by Hollis, who was responsible for continuing and expanding the model after Hamilton's death (Hollis, 1964, 1972; Hollis & Woods, 1981; Woods & Hollis, 1990).

Among ego psychology's contribution were (1) its more optimistic and humanistic view of human functioning and potential; (2) its view of environmental and sociocultural factors as important in shaping behavior; (3) its focus on clients' rational, problem solving, adaptive capacities, and strengths; (4) its conception of development as a lifelong process; (5) its expanded view of change processes to encompass learning, mastery, corrective relationship experiences, and environmental supports rather than only insight; and (6) its view that it is possible to enhance, sustain, or modify functioning without reworking the client's underlying personality difficulties (Goldstein, 1995a).

Diagnostic caseworkers used ego psychological concepts to reconceptualize the casework process. Some of the desired modifications included (1) shortening of the study phase; (2) assessing clients' ego functions, including their strengths and the degree to which the external environment was creating obstacles to successful coping; (3) focusing on more current issues, particularly the degree to which clients were coping effectively with major life roles and tasks; (4) appreciating the key developmental issues affecting the clients' current reactions and addressing them in the interventive process where feasible; (5) attending to goal setting, greater structuring of the interventive process, and more active focusing; (6) classifying types of intervention more clearly (for example, supportive, experiential, insight or modifying, environmental modification); (7) expanding interventive procedures to include more supportive and environmental measures; (8) recognizing the importance of the helping alliance between client and worker; (9) emphasizing the reparative, enhancing, and sustaining impact of the casework relationship; and (10) using crisis, short-term, and long-term methods (Goldstein, 1995a; Parad, 1958; Parad & Miller, 1963).

During the 1940s and 1950s, there were many attempts to define the goals and techniques of social casework, differentiate social casework from psychotherapy, and enlarge its range of application (Austin, 1948; Cockerill & Colleagues, 1953; Garrett, 1958; Hollis, 1949, 1964, 1972; Stamm, 1959; Towle, 1949, 1954). In codifying and refining the psychosocial approach, Hollis described and studied a group of techniques that can be used flexibly in the interventive process. In addition to those used primarily with the individual, including sustainment, direct influence, exploration-description-ventilation, person-in-situation reflection, pattern-dynamic reflection, and developmental reflection, Hollis also classified environmental intervention according to the type of resource employed, the type of communication used, and the type of role assumed (provider, locator, creator of a resource, interpreter, mediator, or aggressive intervener) (Goldstein, 1995b).

Those involved in the evolution of the psychosocial approach have shown an openness to new knowledge over the years and a willingness to discard ideas that are not useful. Nevertheless, it has remained associated with its earlier and more psychoanalytic and long-term thrust. It is beyond the scope of this chapter to discuss all the reasons for this. It can be said, however, that although many social workers incorporated important changes in the model, others either did not understand how to use these newer ideas in their direct practice, or they continued to be invested in using the more traditional approach.

The Problem-Solving Model

Efforts to assimilate ego psychological concepts and emerging cognitive and social science theories also led to a distinctive problem-solving casework model developed by Perlman (1957). Among the factors motivating her work were a desire to heal the split between the diagnostic and functional caseworkers and a wish to offer correctives for practices that she viewed as dysfunctional and believed were responsible for long waiting lists, high dropout rates at family agencies and mental health clinics, unfocused and lengthy treatments, and the pathologizing of clients.

Although Perlman viewed herself as diagnostically oriented, she also saw the value of many of the principles of the functional school (for example, partialization and attention to the phases of the helping process) and incorporated these into her approach. In her seminal book, *Social Casework*, Perlman evolved a casework model based on the premise that all human living is effective problem solving. She described the casework process as a series of problem-solving operations that were carried out within and given impetus by the client-worker relationship.

Perlman (1957, p. 17) referred to the ego as the problem-solving apparatus of the personality system. Interested in cognitive theory, she emphasized rational thinking processes. Drawing on Erikson's (1959) views of the life cycle and White's (1959) theory of competence, Perlman thought of the individual as always striving toward growth and having an inherent thrust for self-actualization. Her optimism and belief in the positive impact of current relationships and experiences played an important role in her understanding of the casework process.

Two major contributions of the problem-solving model were its sharp focus on the client's presenting problem and its recognition of the importance of partialization in deciding how to intervene. The process consisted of three phases: the beginning phase of the work centering on understanding the facts of the problem; the middle phase focusing on engaging the client's thinking and feelings about the problem and establishing a focus; and the third phase including ongoing discussions of options, alternatives, and consequences of actions and emphasizing decision making and doing.

Unlike the diagnostic approach, which required a period of study and diagnosis before treatment could begin, the problem-solving approach stressed the importance of immediate engagement in which the client is supported and sustained and encouraged to think and talk about the various aspects of the problem and begin to explore possible solutions. Assessment of the client's motivation, capacities, and opportunities (Ripple, 1964) occurred simultaneously.

Although Perlman's model achieved considerable success in many circles, it failed to overcome the division between the diagnostic and functional caseworkers, both of whom criticized Perlman for abandoning too many important features of their respective approaches.

The Crisis Intervention Model

During a period in which there was an expansion of knowledge in the social sciences and experimentation with new practice models, Golan (1978) brought together much of the burgeoning crisis theory literature discussed earlier in the chapter. In *Treatment in Crisis Situations*, she put forth a crisis model specifically geared to social work practice. Additionally, Parad (1965) and Parad and Parad (1990b) compiled numerous important articles that applied crisis intervention to a broad range of special populations.

According to Golan (1978, pp. 62–63), the crisis situation encompassed a total sequence of events, "from equilibrium to disequilibrium and back again," and contains five components: (1) the hazardous event, (2) the vulnerable state, (3) the precipitating factor, (4) the state of active crisis, and (5) the state of reintegration or crisis resolution. Assessment must include an understanding of the nature of the crisis, the individual's precrisis level of functioning, the coping capacities of the individual or family, and the presence of inner and outer resources.

Rapoport (1970, pp. 297–298), another important social work crisis theorist, described the minimum goals of crisis intervention as (1) relief of symptoms, (2) return to previous level of functioning, (3) understanding of what precipitated the crisis, and (4) identification of the remedial measures that clients can take or that are available through community resources. She also indicated that the more ambitious goals of connecting current stresses with past life experiences and conflicts and helping the client develop new coping mechanisms might be undertaken when the client's personality and social situation were favorable and the opportunity existed.

Practice principles of the crisis model include (1) time-limited interventions, (2) worker flexibility, (3) high level of worker activity, (4) circumscribed specific goals, and (5) the identification of tasks to be mastered. The interventive process emphasizes ventilation, clarification, reassurance, direct influence, supporting strengths, and the mobilization of inner and outer resources.

The crisis intervention model has been used increasingly among social workers and occupies a crucial role in social workers' armamentarium of approaches. However, it has a restricted range of application and cannot be relied on exclusively.

The Task-Centered Model

The task-centered approach (Epstein, 1980, 1992; Reid & Epstein, 1972) had its origins in research conducted by Reid and Shyne (1969) in which planned short-term treatment of an unspecified nature, consisting of 8 to 12 interviews over a three-month period, was compared to more open-ended and extended treatment at the Community Service Society in New York. The findings showed that clients who received short-term intervention did as well in a briefer period of time as did those receiving continued service. A major component of intervention that differentiated the two forms of treatment was the degree of worker activity, which was much greater in the short-term process.

In *Task-centered Casework* (1972), Reid and Epstein presented a more structured and systematized model of short-term treatment that drew on problem-solving, cognitive, and crisis theories. Like those who used crisis intervention, Reid and Epstein believed that the client's presenting request for help usually reflected problems in living and a temporary interference with customary problem-solving abilities. Further, they argued that the client would seek to restore his or her equilibrium and that time limits would accelerate the helping process.

The task-centered approach has a number of important features: (1) the delineation and use of a problem topology, (2) a stress on the worker and client's coming together in identifying the goals and focus of intervention; (3) the organization of the helping process around specific client tasks, and (4) the specification of modes of intervention (Reid & Epstein, 1972, p. 25). Diagnosis centers on target problems rather than personality functioning, treatment goals are specific and limited, and the treatment process encourages clients to carry out a specified course of action related to the client's own perception of the problem and its possible solution. The relationship process is de-emphasized in favor of more specific case planning and technical interventions.

Originally, Reid and Epstein enumerated certain target problems or areas that they felt were amenable to task-centered practice, including (1) interpersonal conflict, (2) dissatisfaction in social relations, (3) problems with formal organizations, (4) difficulties in role performance, (5) problems of social transition, (6) reactive emotional distress, and (7) inadequate resources. In addition, they felt that clients must recognize and show motivation to work on the problem, that the problem must be solvable, and that it must be limited in scope (pp. 42–53). Later, Epstein envisioned an even more inclusive approach, suggesting that all problems are appropriate for task-centered intervention and that the worker's responsibility is to help the client define target problems and specific foci that can be addressed by means of the model's techniques (Epstein, 1992, p. 103).

The task-centered approach underwent considerable testing and development during the 1970s and 1980s (Epstein, 1992, pp. 114–115). In *Brief Treatment and a New Look at the Task-Centered Approach* (1992), Epstein outlined a more methodical, detailed, and prescriptive approach to the model and described four sequential but overlapping steps: Step 1, in which the client's target problems are identified; Step 2, in which the contract (the agreed-on goals, focus, tasks, scheduling of interviews, and time limits) is established; Step 3, in which problem solving, task achievement, and/or problem reduction are implemented; and Step 4, in which termination occurs. Although time limits were established at the beginning of treatment, they could be modified by mutual agreement between worker and client.

The task-centered approach, used widely in social work, is more suited to work with very concrete and specific problems and highly motivated clients. Some criticisms of the model include its almost total lack of attention to personality functioning and dynamics in assessment, its narrow and mechanical application in goal setting and intervention, its simplistic view of human problems and their amelioration, and its limitations in work with more complex difficulties.

The Cognitive-Behavioral Model

When psychodynamically oriented treatment came under attack in the 1960s, some social workers embraced cognitive and behavioral theories, which view patterns of thinking and behaving as leading to problems in functioning. Although each of these models has a distinctive focus, in that the cognitive approach tends to be educative, centering on altering the ways clients think and behavioral intervention emphasizes the client's overt behavior, the models overlap and share common characteristics: (1) a systematic assessment in which presenting problems are redefined in terms of current thoughts, observable behaviors, and environmental factors that are contributing to the problem; (2) a clear prescription for how to correct distorted thinking and self-defeating behavior, create new ways of perceiving the self and others, and develop more desirable behaviors and skills; and (3) the use of objective measurements of progress and outcomes.

These models do not make use of time in the interventive process explicitly, but the duration of treatment tends to be short term. Often intervention takes place in 25 to 30 sessions or more. In fact, the seeming rapidity with which positive outcomes were attained was a controversial issue when the models were first used (Wilson, 1981, p. 131). Cognitive-behavioral approaches tend to envision the worker as an expert who is going to direct the change process. It advocates the use of more active rather than reflective techniques—for example, education, direct influence, logical discussion, rehearsal, homework assignments, behavioral reinforcement, self-monitoring through the use of record keeping, and a variety of other techniques aimed at modifying concrete behaviors and irrational or distorted ways of thinking.

Like the task-centered model, cognitive-behavioral approaches have been shown to be effective in addressing very specific types of target problems and symptoms with clients who show strong motivation. Their limitations center on their narrow focus and range of applicability.

The Ecological Perspective and Life Model

Attempting to correct for what they perceived as casework's lip-service attention to the environmental component of client problems and continuing reliance on psychodynamic theory and psychotherapeutic techniques, a number of authors proposed that general systems theory become an overarching framework that would provide a distinctive and unifying conception of social work practice (Bartlett, 1970; Gordon, 1969, pp. 5–11).

In an effort to go beyond general systems theory's more theoretical, mechanistic, and abstract characteristics, Germain (1979) and Germain and Gitterman (1980) used concepts from ecology, ego psychology, particularly the work of Erikson (1959) and White (1959), and theories of stress and coping in evolving their ecological perspective.

Germain redirected attention to the transactions and mutual and reciprocal impact of people and their environments in the process of adaptation. She regarded adaptation as involving either the individual's attempts to change himself or herself in order to cope more effectively with the environment or efforts aimed at making the environment more responsive to people (Germain, 1991, p. 17). Germain also emphasized the "goodness of fit" between people and environments as essential to individuals' well-being and viewed problems as stemming from the "discrepancies between needs and capacities, on the one hand, and environmental qualities on the other" (Germain & Gitterman, 1980, p. 7).

In keeping with the ecological perspective, Germain and Gitterman (1980) put forth the life model, which provided an alternative to a disease-oriented approach. It assessed clients' problems in three interrelated areas of living: (1) life transitions and traumatic life events, (2) environmental pressures, and (3) dysfunctional interpersonal relationships. The life model advocated interventions directed at improving the quality of the person-environmental fit.

The life model aims to release the potential for growth, health, and adaptive social functioning and to make the social environment more responsive to human needs, goals, and capacities (Germain & Gitterman, 1986, p. 628). It focuses on strengths rather than pathology and combines a focus on helping the individual with an emphasis on organizational and social change. Thus, it encompasses both micro- and macrosystems intervention.

Although not developed as a distinctively short-term model, the life model can be used on a short-term basis. The assessment process is ongoing and interactive rather than constituting a clearly defined diagnostic phase conducted solely by the worker. In the interventive process, the life model stresses (1) the mutuality of contracting between client and worker with respect to problem definition, objectives, planning, and action; (2) engaging the client's decision making and cognition and enhancing the sense of self-direction, self-esteem, and competence; and (3) the importance of mutuality and authenticity in the client-worker relationship in order to promote the client's competence and reduce social distance and power differentials (Germain &

Gitterman, 1986, p. 632). In the area of techniques, the life model is not prescriptive; it is thought to be composed of common and generic practice skills directed at improving the person-environmental fit.

As an alternative to the psychosocial model of practice, the life model has gained considerable adherents, particularly in academic social work circles. It has been criticized, however, as abstract and difficult to use, minimizing the personality system in assessment and intervention, leading to more superficial interventions, and creating a new division between more clinically oriented social work and "real" social work (Goldstein, 1996).

The Proliferation of Practice Models

When direct practice reasserted its importance in the 1970s and 1980s after being eclipsed by a focus on macrosystems intervention, the awareness of the pressing needs of clients for individualized services led to many new theoretical developments and practice models. In addition to those already discussed, psychodynamic theory expanded to embrace newer developments in ego psychology, object relations theory, and self psychology, which are more interpersonal and transactional in nature; couple and family approaches became popular; group treatment gathered more adherents; more affirmative and empowering models for work with women, people of color, and gays and lesbians were put forth; empirically based practice models were advocated; and practitioners began to experiment with hypnosis, biofeedback, gestalt techniques, and other newer forms of intervention. A popular social work text cites over 25 different frameworks for practice and does not include some of those that have developed since (Turner, 1996). For example, some social workers have integrated more spiritually oriented approaches into their work, and newer models such as the narrative and social constructionist approaches have emerged, both of which take a radically different stance than do traditional frameworks.

This proliferation of social work practice models has expanded the repertoire of helping approaches but also has led to fragmentation and polarization. Each model has a special emphasis and lens through which it views clients and tends to be put forth as the "correct" model.

Although all the models have important applications and advantages, each has limitations, and no one single model is good for all situations. Consequently, the exclusive use of one model does not do justice to the range of client needs and problems and to the complexity of practice.

SUMMARY

This chapter has reviewed the scope and evolution of short-term treatment and discussed the main characteristics, strengths, and limitations of short-term approaches in the mental health field and of social work's major interventive models. As short-term methods are being used with a broad range of clients who display increasingly varied levels of functioning, motivation, coping capacities, and environmental stresses and supports, there is a need for an integrative approach to short-term intervention that is consistent with social work's values and person-environmental focus and is appropriate to the realities of practice with diverse populations of clients. Evolving such an integrative short-term interventive framework provides the opportunity to reaffirm social work's historical foundations and to draw on the wealth of theoretical and practice developments that have taken place during the past century.

Chapter 2

Theoretical Perspectives and
Major Characteristics

Integrative short-term treatment (ISTT) draws on selected concepts from ego psychology and other contemporary psychodynamic theories, crisis theory, cognitive-behavioral theory, and ecosystems theory in constructing its perspective on human behavior and maladaptation. This chapter first discusses this view and then describes the major characteristics of the interventive framework.

THE VIEW OF THE PERSON

ISTT prizes the uniqueness of the individual. Although the framework uses general principles that govern all human development, it recognizes that each individual's personality organization and interaction with others and the world forms a distinct constellation. This configuration is composed not only of externally observable behaviors but also of the particular subjective meaning that the person gives to his or her experience.

The person is a holistic being in that emotions, thoughts, and behaviors are interconnected in a complex fashion and cannot be isolated from one another. The individual must be viewed in terms of his or her existing capacities and life circumstances, past experience, and future goals and expectations.

People have complex and varied needs. When basic needs for survival, safety, and security are met, other needs emerge, for example, for mastery, competence, autonomy, belonging, connection, intimacy, generativity, and meaning. The individual is in large part dependent on the family, the environment, and society to provide the conditions that facilitate the meeting of these needs.

The developmental process is lifelong and biopsychosocial in nature. The interdependence of heredity, constitutional, psychological, interpersonal, environmental, and cultural factors during development form the individual's personality, which reflects potentialities, customary traits, characteristic patterns, and areas of strength and vulnerability. The personality develops through the environment's gratification of and responsiveness to the individual's needs, desires, talents, and capacities; identifications and internalizations of others; learning; mastery of developmental tasks; effective problem solving; and successful coping with internal needs and environmental conditions, expectations, stresses, and crises.

Individuals are active, adaptive organisms who are capable of affecting their surroundings, rather than merely passive respondents to environmental influences. Although innate drives and unconscious motivations propel behavior, people are capable of rational, conscious, problem-solving activities in the service of adaptation. Adaptation involves a reciprocal relationship between the individual and his or her environment. The individual is able not only to adjust to external conditions (autoplastic adaptation) but also to change those conditions to suit his or her needs better (alloplastic adaptation).

The term *coping capacities* refers to the equipment and talents that a particular person brings to life transactions in the process of adaptation. An individual's coping capacities must be understood in relation to the social and environmental context that impinges on the individual. People always are in transaction with some aspect of their social environment, which provides the conditions that produce stress or obstruct successful coping.

The personality is organized around heredity and constitutional factors, physical health, drives, ego functions and cognitive capacities, the superego, internalized object relations, and the self structure. Personality development occurs throughout the life cycle and can be viewed from a variety of lenses. Further, gender, sexual orientation, ethnicity, race, class, and religion and spirituality are important influences on the personality, behavior, and one's view of the world.

Heredity and Constitutional Factors

Although the environment plays a major role in shaping the personality, there is increasing evidence that a person is born with certain biological traits and potentialities, such as temperament, intelligence, coordination, talents, predispositions to certain illnesses, and even selected personality traits and vulnerabilities. Some of these innate characteristics appear in the first months of life and influence the infant's experience of the world and interactions with caretakers, who must be attuned to the infant's particular needs, response patterns, temperament, and, later, emerging talents and capacities. Some infants and children show an early tendency toward actively and persistently reaching out to the environment in order to get their needs met. It is possible that inborn features of the personality may be responsible for the resilience that some children and adults show in the face of traumatic or depriving life circumstances.

Physical Health

An individual's physical health exerts an important influence on personality development and interactions with others. Some (by no means all) aspects of an individual's well-being may be determined by hereditary and constitutional factors. Some children are more vulnerable than others to infection and childhood illnesses and may show early symptoms of severe health problems or physical disability. Maternal nutrition and health during pregnancy and substance abuse are important factors in determining a child's health status. The degree to which the caretaking and social environments nurture good health, prevent injurious accidents, and provide available medical care are crucial to a child's physical well-being. Children who suffer from physical illnesses or disabilities may experience a variety of burdens, including separations from their family, feeling different from and sometimes stigmatized by their peers, having to adhere to special procedures, acquiring a particular role in the family, and difficulties in school attendance or learning. Moreover, a child's health status can have long-lasting reverberations on his or her self-concept.

Drives

Although there are differences of opinion about the exact nature of the
forces that motivate behavior, most theorists agree that biological
drives are important determinants of the personality. Theorists differ
with respect to (1) whether drives are libidinal and aggressive in nature
or whether there also is a separate drive toward mastery and competence; (2) whether the aim of drives is tension reduction or whether infants are born with an innate push toward relating to others; and (3)
whether drives are the major factors influencing personality development or a part of a larger constellation of biopsychosocial influences.
There are compelling reasons to see the personality as encompassing all
of these elements. The strength of the drives differs from person to person. The drives themselves come under the control of the person's ego
during the developmental process, although conflict and other difficulties around drive expression and gratification can occur all through life.

Ego Functions

The ego is that part of the personality that mediates between the individual and the environment. Ego functions are the means by which
the individual copes with and adapts to the world. Bellak, Hurvich,
and Gediman (1973) identified 12 major ego functions:

> *Reality testing*, in which there is an accurate perception of the exter
> nal environment, one's internal world, and the differences be
> tween them.
> *Judgment*, in which there is a capacity to identify certain possible
> courses of action and anticipate and weigh the consequences of
> behavior in order to take action that achieves desired goals with
> minimal negative consequences.
> *Sense of reality of the world and of the self*, in which the world and the
> self are experienced in accurate ways, such as feeling the world

and one's connection to it are real or feeling a sense of bodily in-tactness or a firmness of boundaries with others.

Regulation and control of drives, affects, and impulses, in which there is an ability to modulate, delay, inhibit, or control the expression of impulses and affects (feelings) in accord with reality and an abil-ity to tolerate anxiety, frustration, and unpleasant emotions such as anger and depression without becoming overwhelmed, impul-sive, or symptomatic.

Object (or interpersonal) relations, in which there is the capacity for mature and reciprocal interpersonal relationships.

Thought processes, in which secondary process thinking, which is characterized by being goal directed, organized, and oriented to reality, replaces primary process thinking, which is characterized by wish fulfillment. Secondary process thinking is associated with the reality principle—the ability to postpone instinctual gratification until reality conditions are appropriate. In contrast, primary process thinking is associated with the pleasure princi-ple—the tendency to discharge instinctual impulses immedi-ately without considering reality.

Adaptive regression in the service of the ego, in which there is an ability to permit oneself to relax the hold on and relationship to reality, to ex-perience aspects of the self that are ordinarily inaccessible when one is engaged in concentrated attention to reality, and to emerge with increased adaptive capacity as a result of creative integrations.

Defensive functioning, in which the individual develops unconscious, internal protective mechanisms that enable him or her to ward off the painful experience of anxiety or fear that arises from cer-tain impulses or situations.

Stimulus barrier, in which the individual is able to maintain his or her equilibrium, level of functioning, or comfort despite increases or decreases in the level of stimulation to which he or she is exposed.

Autonomous functions, in which certain ego functions such as atten-tion, concentration, memory, learning, perception, motor func-tions, and intention have a primary autonomy from the drives and thus are conflict free.

Mastery-competence, in which the individual is able to and has the feeling that he or she can interact with the environment successfully.

Synthetic/integrative function, in which the individual is able to fit all the disparate aspects of the personality into a unified structure that acts on the external world (Goldstein, 1995a).

Within the same individual, certain ego functions may be better developed than others and may show more stability; that is, they tend to fluctuate less from situation to situation or over time, and are less prone to regression or disorganization under stress. Further, even in individuals who manifest ego strength, regression in selected areas of ego functioning may be normal in certain types of situations, for example, illness, social upheavals, crises, and role transitions, and do not necessarily imply ego deficiencies. The same individual can have highly variable ego functioning, although in cases of the most severe psychopathology, ego functions may be impaired generally.

An assessment of the various ego functions provides a composite picture of the ego strength that an individual brings to interactions with others and with the social environment. Further, the observing ego, that is, the ability to observe one's behavior, is another crucial aspect of ego functioning. Additionally, there are other qualities and characteristics, which may be innate or the result of development, that contribute to a person's coping capacities, for example, humor, persistence, and resilience.

Although contemporary views of the importance of cognitive processes arose from a different system of thought than did conceptions of the ego and rely on a different set of assumptions about the significance of thinking in personality development, it can be argued that the ability to think, process information, problem-solve, and other cognitive processes are important aspects of ego functioning.

The Superego

The superego is a name given to that part of the personality that contains the conscience, which guides a person's sense of right or wrong, and the ego ideal, the standard to which one aspires. A person's superego reflects parental and societal values, morals, and prohibitions. Superego functioning exists on a continuum. Some people have an overly developed superego, while others have little sense of conscience. A person with a mature superego does not hold to certain values or standards of behavior in a rigid, mechanistic way that limits his or her ability to allow themselves gratification. They are able to consider the nuances and subtleties of life and determine their actions accordingly. An individual who has little superego may behave in ruthless and violent ways, show no concern for others, and not experience feelings of guilt.

Defenses

All people use defenses, but their exact type and extent vary from individual to individual. Defenses are part of the ego's repertoire of mechanisms for protecting the individual from anxiety by keeping intolerable or unacceptable impulses or threats from conscious awareness. Common defenses include (Laughlin, 1979; Goldstein, 1995a):

Altruism, in which satisfaction is gained through self-sacrificing service to others or through participation in causes as a way of dealing with unacceptable feelings and conflicts.

Asceticism, in which there is a renunciation of certain pleasures in order to avoid the anxiety and conflict associated with impulse gratification.

Denial, in which there is a lack of acknowledgment or nonacceptance of important aspects of reality or of one's own feelings, impulses, thoughts, or experiences.

Displacement, in which unacceptable feelings about one person or situation are put onto another person or situation.

Intellectualization, in which unacceptable feelings and impulses are warded off by thinking about them rather than experiencing them directly.

Isolation, in which the feelings associated with particular content or the ideas connected with certain feelings remain out of awareness.

Projection, in which unacceptable thoughts and feelings are attributed to others.

Rationalization, in which logical, convincing reasons are used to justify certain ideas, feelings, or actions so as to avoid recognizing their unacceptable underlying motives.

Reaction formation, in which an unwanted feeling or impulse is replaced by its opposite.

Regression, in which there is a return to an earlier developmental phase, level of functioning, or type of behavior in order to avoid anxieties.

Repression, in which unwanted thoughts, feelings, impulses, and experiences remain out of awareness.

Somatization, in which unacceptable impulses or conflicts are converted into physical symptoms.

Splitting, in which two contradictory states such as love and hate are compartmentalized and not integrated.

Sublimation, in which an unacceptable impulse is expressed in a socially acceptable way.

Turning against the self, in which angry impulses toward another person (alive or deceased), who also is loved and feared, are not experienced directly but instead are turned inward, leaving the person depressed or self-destructive.

Undoing, in which there is an attempt to make reparation for or nullify an unacceptable or guilt-provoking act, thought, or feeling.

Because defenses operate unconsciously, the person is not aware of using a particular defense. All defenses falsify or distort reality to some extent. When a person uses defenses in a flexible rather than rigid fashion with minimal distortion of reality and the person is able to function well without undue anxiety, the defenses are said to be effective and adaptive. The same defense, however, can severely limit a person's ability to perceive reality or cope effectively, and thus may be maladaptive. For example, a certain amount of denial of the possible outcomes of surgery may be helpful in enabling a person to pursue a risky procedure, whereas the presence of massive denial of the seriousness of a health condition may result in avoidance of necessary medical attention.

An individual does not deliberately seek to maintain his or her defenses, but because they serve a protective function, efforts directed at modifying defenses usually are resisted by the individual. This resistance, however, creates obstacles to achieving the very changes that the person would like to make. Although it may seem desirable to try to lessen or modify certain maladaptive defenses in a given individual because they interfere with effective coping, any effort of this sort will arouse considerable anxiety. In many instances, defenses should be respected, approached with caution, and sometimes strengthened. Under acute or unremitting stress, illness, or fatigue, the ego's defenses, along with the other ego functions, may fail. When there is a massive defensive failure, the person becomes flooded with anxiety. The result can be a severe and rapid deterioration of ego functioning, and in some cases the personality becomes fragmented and chaotic, such as in a psychotic episode. When defenses are rigid, an individual may appear exceedingly brittle, taut, and driven; his or her behavior may seem increasingly mechanical, withdrawn, or peculiar.

Object Relations

Through the process of internalization—that is, the act of taking in what was once external and making it part of one's internal life—the person acquires basic attitudes toward the self and others as a result of important interpersonal experiences early in life. When these inner representations accurately reflect both the good and bad aspects of the self and others and are subject to modification in the face of new experiences, the person usually is able to develop and maintain a positive self-image and engage in satisfactory interpersonal relationships. Sometimes, however, these basic attitudes are quite negative, one-sided, and rigid to the point of overriding other, more realistic perceptions. They are quite powerful. The person remains loyal to these internal self objects and representations. For example, a man who believes he is not intelligent may hold to this view regardless of evidence to the contrary. And a woman who has been sexually molested in childhood may view all men as potential abusers and feel easily victimized by a man's sexual interest in her. Thus, for individuals who suffer from impaired internalized object relations, scripts of the past dominate current interactions with others and make the maintenance of self-esteem and achievement of satisfying interpersonal relationships difficult. A person also may have a tendency to repeat in current life experiences that he or she had with early objects.

An alternative way of viewing these basic internalized attitudes toward the self and others is to see them as resulting from the ways in which individuals learn to think about themselves and the ways in which they process information cognitively rather than as a function of what they have taken in at an affective level from their interactions with significant others. The different emphases of object relations and cognitive theories are complementary, however, because it is possible and useful to view affective and cognitive processes as interrelated aspects of the personality that shape behavior.

The Self

The self can be understood not only as a product of what the person internalizes from others but also as an innate and separate structure of the personality that has its own developmental line. According to Kohut (1971, 1977), the self needs empathic selfobjects—that is, those who perform vital functions for the child that he or she cannot do for himself or herself. There are at least three main types of selfobject needs: (1) the need for mirroring that confirms the child's sense of vigor, greatness, and perfection; (2) the need for an idealization of others whose strength and calmness soothe the child; and (3) the need for a twin or alter-ego who provides the child with a sense of humanness, likeness to, and partnership with others (Elson, 1986). When the caretaking or selfobject environment provides for the selfobject needs of and responds in an attuned way to the innate potentialities of the nuclear self, the self flourishes, becoming strong and cohesive. A person is able to strive toward self-realization and self-esteem, which, despite some transient upheavals, remains positive and stable even in the face of life's blows. In contrast, when the self structure is weak and vulnerable as a result of unattuned, neglectful, or traumatic caretaking, both the self-concept and self-esteem regulation become impaired. The person may be at risk for experiencing severe disruptions in functioning and sense of well-being or may show chronic difficulties in performing in keeping with his or her talents and capacities.

The Developmental Process

Many theorists view personality development as undergoing a series of stages, the specific nature of which differs depending on the particular framework employed. For example, in writing about drive development, Freud (1905) described the oral, anal, phallic, latency, and genital psychosexual stages, each of which centers on a particular bodily zone that gives rise to pleasure or frustration. Erikson (1950, 1959) saw ego development and identity formation as resulting from the mastery of psychosocial tasks and crises during eight successive stages of the life cycle: trust versus mistrust, autonomy versus shame and doubt, initiative versus guilt, industry versus inferiority, identity versus role confusion, intimacy versus distantiation and self-absorption, generativity versus stagnation, and integrity versus despair and disgust. Although the resolution of each stage is described in terms of the achievement of positive and negative tasks that culminate in a sense of ego identity, in any individual, the achievement of the core developmental task posed by each stage may lie anywhere on a continuum from best to worst outcome.

According to Mahler (Mahler, Pine, & Bergman, 1975), the stages by which the individual moves from nonrelatedness to attachment to major achievements in the areas of separation, individuation, ego development, and internalized object relations are delineated by the separation-individuation process. In the autistic phase, the child is thought to be in a preattachment phase; in the symbiotic phase, the infant begins to show the capacity to invest in another, who is perceived as a "need-satisfying object" and as lacking a separate identity; in the differentiation subphase at about age 4 or 5 months, the infant's attention shifts from being inwardly directed within the symbiosis to being more outwardly directed, and the infant begins to separate self-representations from representations of the caretaker (the object); in the practicing subphase, the separation of self and object representations and the individuation process accelerates as the infant's own autonomous ego functions assume more importance; in the rapprochement subphase, there is a back-and-forth movement between autonomy and dependence, increasing ability to be on one's own, alternating with increased fears of separation and loss of the object, and a tendency to see the self and others as all good or all bad; and the road to object constancy, in which the child again seems able to be on his or her own without undue concern about the mother's whereabouts as object constancy is achieved, which implies the capacity to maintain a positive mental representation of the object in the object's absence or in the face of frustration.

There are other formulations of the development of internalized object relations that are less tied to specific stages that center on the quality of the child's relational experiences with the caretaker. They tend to emphasize how either "good enough" mothering or failures in the caretaking environment result in the growing child's acquisition of crucial capacities and basic attitudes toward the self and others (Klein, 1948; Fairbairn, 1952, 1954); Guntrip, 1969, 1973; and Winnicott, 1965). These theorists argue that once more negative views of the self and others develop, they exert a strong hold on the individual's personality and interactions with others and are not easily modified.

Stern's (1985) research revealed self-development as evolving as a consequence of complex interpersonal transactions that are not time bound to specific phases. He views self-potentialities as innate and delineated four "domains of relatedness": the sense of emergent self, the sense of core self, the sense of subjective self, and the sense of verbal self.

Finally, Piaget (1951, 1952), a cognitive theorist, focused on the sequential stages of intellectual development: sensory-motor stage from birth to age 2; the preoperational stage from 2 to 7 years; the stage of concrete operations from ages 7 to 11; and the stage of formal operations from 11 to 15 years.

Adults may show ongoing or acute problems related to developmental issues stemming from any or all of these stages. Further, because growth is possible throughout the life cycle, adulthood is affected not only by the past but also by the present and future.

Gender, Sexual Orientation, Cultural, and Other Types of Diversity

The tendency to view personality from a narrow perspective has led to insufficient attention to the unique development, experiences, characteristics, and strengths of women, gays and lesbians, people of color, and other individuals who are diverse with respect to class, ethnicity, religion, and lifestyle. Most traditional theoretical formulations have not taken these factors into account. For example, feminists have critiqued psychodynamic theories for using male development as the prototype for understanding women. People of color, members of ethnic minorities, and gays and lesbians have been among those who have pointed out the bias that they feel is inherent in traditional formulations of human development and views of maladaptation. They have argued persuasively that practitioners' expectations of what is normal and appropriate behavior and labeling of certain types of attitudes and behavior as pathological are the results of stereotypic, inaccurate, and negative views of different types of diversity.

Another important area that has tended to be overlooked in traditional formulations is the way a person gives meaning to his or her life, sometimes through religion or spirituality (Sermabeikian, 1994). Often a person's spiritual beliefs, which may or may not be tied to religious convictions and affiliation, are a major source of strength.

Knowledge about different populations is accumulating rapidly and is gradually being integrated into contemporary perspectives on personality development. There is now much greater appreciation of and respect for cultural and other types of diversity and for the importance of spirituality. Nevertheless, this process is evolving. Therefore, it is important to question what may be stereotyped and erroneous attitudes and beliefs and to individualize each person in the context of his or her total experience.

THE SOCIAL ENVIRONMENT

The concept of the social environment encompasses the individual's concrete physical surroundings; the family; the social network, which includes resources and services in the immediate neighborhood or community; the culture; and the society, which involves policies, programs, values, and attitudes. The social environment provides the conditions that produce stress or obstruct successful coping.

The Physical Environment

An important aspect of the social environment that affects an individual is the actual physical surroundings in which he or she lives, such as the size, condition, and location of a dwelling and the physical state of the street, neighborhood, and local community. In addition to the concrete and practical role that surroundings play in meeting one's needs or facilitating or obstructing effective coping, the physical environment has psychological meaning to the individual. It comes to represent how one is viewed and valued by others and can boost or diminish self-regard. For example, living in an overcrowded, poorly heated and ventilated, rodent-infested apartment in a dilapidated building that is inhabited by drug addicts and located in a neighborhood in which violence is commonplace undoubtedly will lead to health problems, disease, fear, accidents, and even death. Moreover, in many instances, such surroundings will contribute to a basic sense of insecurity, lack of safety, poor self-esteem, feelings of neglect, and a pessimistic and fatalistic outlook. Yet despite containing undesirable and stressful features, most communities possess their own unique strengths and supports. Not everyone who grows up amid stressful environmental conditions reflects the same personality.

The Family

The family system is a major potential support system. Its major responsibilities are to nurture, protect, guide, and socialize the individual. It is common to differentiate between an individual's family of origin, that is, the family in which a person is born and raised, and the family of procreation, the family that a person creates through marriage, other types of partnering, and childbearing. The family of origin both shapes personality development and exerts a powerful influence on the family that one acquires later in life. Sometimes family patterns exist that can be traced back several generations.

Who is considered to be family in any particular instance has to be understood within the context of an individual's cultural background and lifestyle and changes in society that have produced and recognized different types of family constellations. For example, single-parent, extended-kinship, blended families, as well as gay and straight domestic partnerships that do not involve marriage per se, are common family types.

There is not one correct way of being a family. Every family has a unique way of organizing itself in order to adapt to the environment, and each has its own strengths. Families differ in the following: characteristics, structure, division of labor and tasks; identification with their own culture, and assimilation into the dominant culture; management of generational, sexual, and other types of internal boundaries; external boundaries; provision of nurturance, protection, guidance, and socialization; management of feelings, intimacy, sexuality, dependence, autonomy, conflict, verbal and physical aggression, money, pleasure and recreation, spirituality, and separation-individuation; role modeling; performance of major social roles; openness to new inputs and external influences; and financial and other types of material resources and supports.

The Culture

Although not all families identify with their own cultural origins, they are a product of, influenced by, and carriers of their particular background. Their cultural origins often result in the perpetuation and transmission of traditions, mores, values, attitudes, child rearing practices, personality traits, and other behaviors. A person's cultural identification also provides a crucial sense of belonging, safety, and security.

When a person enters a new and unfamiliar environment, it is important that he or she attempts to maintain his or her cultural traditions and ties. Sometimes, however, these efforts result in the person's not learning the mores of or participating in the surrounding culture and in feelings of isolation. There are many instances in which adults and children who have emigrated feel caught in a conflict between two cultures. Conversely, there are families who may feel ashamed of their cultural origins and attempt to leave their traditions and history behind in an effort to assimilate to a new and more valued environment.

The Social Network

Every person interacts with a different set of informal interpersonal relationships and activities and more formal community organizations, institutions, and resources that can facilitate or impede effective coping. People differ in how well they are able to establish meaningful connections with others, such as friends, acquaintances, neighbors, and co-workers. Sometimes this depends on the opportunities available to them, and at other times it may reflect a person's difficulty in reaching out to or getting along with others. Some people are quite isolated, while others seem involved in a rich array of interpersonal activities and supports.

In addition to their more informal relationships, people come into contact with more formal systems in the community—for example, schools, health settings, places of worship, social welfare organizations, the court system, occupational settings, and therapeutic and support services. The availability and quality of these aspects of the social network vary widely, and people differ with respect to their knowledge about, access to, and willingness and ability to use the resources within their community. Some agencies do not make it easy for people to use their services. The application process and eligibility requirements are confusing and unwieldy; hours of operation are restricted; there is insufficient staff; staff do not speak the language of the applicants; policies may be rigid and insensitive to the consumer; the physical conditions of the setting may be uncomfortable, unwelcoming, and run down; privacy may be minimal; and staff attitudes may be judgmental, punitive, and biased.

The Society

People are affected by the values, laws, policies, and attitudes of the society at large. For example, the degree to which the society values the family, children, women, older persons, people who live in poverty, those who are mentally or physically ill or disabled, immigrants, people of color, and other minorities sets a national tone that gets filtered down to citizens in various ways. It is reflected in laws, social policies, the availability of vital resources, and the ways in which people show respect and behave toward one another. Racism, sexism, and discrimination against certain segments of the populations who are different, disenfranchised, or socially undesirable has insidious effects on many levels. In addition to limiting opportunities, equity, and social justice, they divide people and may engender feelings of profound rage, despair, alienation, low self-esteem, retaliation, and even violence to the self and others.

THE NATURE OF PROBLEMS

The problems that people experience when they seek help voluntarily or are mandated to do so can stem from five areas: (1) the social environment; (2) life events and circumstances; (3) interpersonal relationships; (4) hereditary, constitutional, and health factors; and (5) personality characteristics, patterns of relating, and vulnerabilities. A particular problem may stem from more than one source, or problems may exist in multiple areas. They may be acute and of recent origin, chronic and long-standing, readily amenable to intervention or deeply entrenched. In many instances, difficulties may be caused by a lack of fit between the person and the environment. For example, a young boy who displays learning problems may demonstrate more serious performance difficulties in a class or school in which teachers are not attuned to his special needs.

The Social Environment

Insufficient or inadequate resources with respect to employment, financial remuneration and security, housing, medical care, education, physical safety, and recreation often create enormous hardships and psychological stress. Such deficiencies in the environment contribute to problems in learning; educational failure; diminished opportunities for establishing purposeful social roles, fulfilling one's potential, and deriving gratification and satisfaction from life; depression, hopelessness, low self-esteem, feelings of powerlessness, and poor physical and mental health; and even violence and antisocial behavior.

Society itself may contribute to an individual's problems as a result of the existence of laws and social policies that are not equitable or sensitive to the needs of certain populations; the lack of necessary resources for particular groups and geographic areas; and the tolerance or stimulation of bias, discrimination, oppression, and violence toward people of color, immigrants, members of certain ethnic and religious backgrounds, women, gays and lesbians, older persons, children, the mentally ill, and others.

Life Events and Circumstances

Current stressful life circumstances and events are major sources of problems that individuals face. These include developmental and role transitions throughout the life cycle such as adolescence, midlife and aging, marriage, divorce, unemployment, homelessness, immigration, and relocation; traumatic crises such as death, illness, rape, battering, incest, and other acts of violence; and actual disasters such as floods, fires, hurricanes, plane crashes, and terrorist attacks. These occurrences challenge people's coping capacities, upset their equilibrium, and can result in severe deterioration in functioning.

Interpersonal Relationships

Interpersonal problems such as parent-child relations, couple and family conflict, social isolation, and difficulties with friends, peers, co-workers, employees, employers, and teachers are frequent areas of difficulty for which individuals seek help. Sometimes these problems are themselves a reflection of external factors such as unemployment, scarcity of resources, immigration, stressful events, and oppressive attitudes or conditions. In other instances, they may result in a clash of life cycle stages, conflicting or poorly understood needs, faulty communication, and more entrenched, maladaptive patterns of relating to others.

Heredity, Constitutional, and Health Factors

Individuals may experience problems that stem from hereditary and constitutional factors and physical and mental illness. For example, neurological impairment, physical disabilities, and cognitive deficits may create special needs and vulnerabilities or may limit an individual's ability to cope effectively. A person who has had a heart attack or an individual who has had a history of manic-depressive episodes and repeated hospitalizations may experience disabling fears about the future.

Personality Characteristics, Patterns of Relating, and Vulnerabilities

An individual's personality characteristics, internal conflicts, impaired ego functioning and cognitive capacities, dysfunctional patterns of relating to others, low self-esteem, and self and identity disturbances may result in symptoms; interpersonal conflict; problems in pursuing educational, occupational, relationship, and life goals; identity problems; destructive and self-defeating behaviors; and general feelings of anxiety and depression. Moreover, childhood sexual and physical abuse and neglect, familial substance abuse and violence, illness and disability, parental divorce, and death may have long-standing effects on the personality.

THE PRACTICE SETTING

The assessment of the client, the nature of the client's problem, and a decision about possible solutions should determine the nature of intervention. In actual practice, however, it often is the goals, structure, policies, and resources of the practice setting that determine how the client's difficulties are perceived and addressed. In today's practice arena, it often is the case that the agency expects the client to comply with its requirements rather than fit itself to the client's needs for service. This state of affairs stems from three main sources: (1) philosophical beliefs about the appropriate nature of treatment and the process of change; (2) fiscal considerations that affect staffing, the nature, length, and frequency of service, and reimbursement; and (3) the agency's need to meet the standards of accrediting bodies. Because of these factors, differential treatment may not be available at a particular agency, and there may not be another community facility that can serve the client. In some instances, the agency may offer services that can be detrimental to the needs of the client, as might be the case when a very distrustful client is required to undergo invasive procedures like drug testing or acupuncture.

The social work practitioner who is employed in an agency or is in private practice may be faced with certain dilemmas and constraints in his or her efforts to help clients. Although it is expected that a social worker respects and implements the policies of and works within the structure of the setting in which he or she is employed, it may be necessary for the practitioner to be more active in advocating for the client within the setting, to help the client to access needed resources and services, and to work toward altering or expanding agency policies and service arrangements in order to meet the client's needs more effectively. Further, because a client may have several workers or be known to many agencies, collaboration and coordination are essential components of the interventive process.

In the private practice environment, the need to provide a rationale for the client to access insurance benefits and obtain permission for the number of contacts for which the insurance provider will reimburse may require thoughtful and creative planning, good working relationships with case managers, and considerable advocacy. Clients in private practice also have needs for a range of social work services, may be involved with other professionals and thus necessitate close collaboration, and may need help in connecting with community resources.

WORKER ATTITUDES

There are four key attitudes that the practitioner needs to possess in order to engage in ISTT.

Help Is Possible in a Limited Period of Time

Practitioners must hold the conviction that clients can make improvements in their lives within a limited time frame. Clinical experience shows that clients seek help for a variety of problems that are responsive to short-term intervention. Some (although by no means all) of the situations that are amenable to brief treatment include:

1. Those in which clients' usual manner of functioning is disturbed and they are overwhelmed and unable to cope. They may benefit from short-term treatment that attempts to restore their previous level of functioning.

2. Those in which clients lack necessary information and resources or need advice and guidance in order to deal with certain aspects of their current life situation. They may benefit from an approach that provides education, enhancement of problem solving, and mobilization of resources.

3. Those situations in which clients' presenting problems are rather limited in scope and situational in nature. They may respond well to a brief, supportive approach that emphasizes their here-and-now functioning.

4. Those in which clients show strong motivation and ego strength and have problems that reflect long-standing underlying difficulties. They may be able to make significant changes in a highly focused, intensive short-term approach that attempts to modify and restructure selected aspects of the personality and patterns of relating to others.

5. Those in which clients present with impairments in their personality functioning. They may be able to make use of a supportive approach that is aimed at developing or enhancing particular ego functions, problem-solving capacities, coping mechanisms, object relations, and self-esteem.

6. Those in which clients show multiple and chronic internal and external problems. They often can be helped to manage their day-to-day lives more effectively by means of partialized and circumscribed interventions aimed at helping them create a better fit between their social environment and their coping capacities.

The Nature of Help Is Multidimensional

It is necessary for practitioners to examine and sometimes redefine their conceptions of what constitutes help. Help is not the same as cure, nor does it necessarily involve changing the client's personality, meeting all of an individual's needs, helping him or her with all problems, or completely altering his or her personality and life situation. Help can be defined as any activity that attempts to alleviate discomfort, stress, or suffering or to improve some aspect of the client's functioning or life situation.

There are many ways of achieving these goals: providing an atmosphere in which the client can share his or her feelings and concerns and obtain encouragement, support, and guidance; linking the client to necessary resources or opportunities; restoring, maintaining, or enhancing his or her personality functioning; helping the client to modify some aspect of his or her personality functioning; or by improving or altering the environmental circumstances. Thus, the nature of help varies from client to client and situation to situation.

The Focus and Nature of Change Are Multifaceted

It is important for practitioners to widen their views about what is to be changed and the nature of change itself. Because problems may be caused and perpetuated by multiple factors, change efforts might be directed at the person or the environment, or both. In many situations it might be preferable to intervene by making modifications in a person's life situation rather than by attempting to change the individual's thinking or behavior. Further, when change efforts are focused on the person, fostering insight and self-awareness are not always essential. There are other mechanisms by which change occurs, including enhancement of coping skills, ego support and ego building, correction of distortions in thinking and ways of perceiving the self and others, learning and positive reinforcement, ego mastery, corrective emotional experiences, and role modeling.

Short-Term Treatment Has Its Own Unique Characteristics

The duration of ISTT ranges from 8 to 25 contacts. Although meetings often are held weekly, flexibility in their spacing may be indicated. For example, clients in crisis may need to be seen more often, and there are situations when greater intervals between sessions may enable clients to practice and consolidate changes. Ideally, the exact number of sessions and their frequency should be based on client needs and treatment goals, but realistically, agency policy and financial reimbursement often determine these parameters. Because there is a clear time difference between 8 and 25 meetings, the goals and process of the treatment vary accordingly.

Practitioners who engage in the integrative approach to brief treatment must understand the special features of the interventive framework and develop the knowledge and skills necessary to implementing this approach.

MAJOR CHARACTERISTICS OF ISST

ISTT has 10 major distinguishing characteristics:

1. The conscious use of time
2. A high level of worker activity
3. Quick engagement
4. Rapid assessment
5. Partialization and focusing
6. Flexibility of approach and technical interventions
7. Differential use of the worker-client relationship
8. Emphasis on client strengths and capacities
9. Collaboration, linkage, and advocacy
10. Acceptance of the limitations of treatment

The Conscious Use of Time

The awareness on the part of both worker and client that treatment must occur within a particular time frame has numerous consequences:

the need to establish and maintain a clear structure and focus; the enhancement of motivation to work on the problem; the expectation that some aspect of, but not necessarily all of, the client's difficulties can be resolved within a circumscribed period; the setting of realistic and attainable goals; the fostering of client autonomy because the client cannot rely on the worker's presence indefinitely; the experience of mutuality between worker and client because it is necessary for teamwork to occur; and a greater conscious delineation of the beginning, middle, and ending phases of intervention because termination is anticipated from the outset of the process.

High Level of Worker Activity

Because of the time-limited nature of the treatment process, the worker must be active from the beginning of the interventive process in structuring the treatment, engaging the client, identifying the problem to be addressed, setting goals, focusing intervention, and monitoring progress. This requirement should not be interpreted as license to impose one's agenda on the client. Rather, it necessitates that the worker strike a balance between being attuned to and responsive to the client and assuming responsibility for directing the process. This balance can best be achieved through the worker's ongoing explanation of the nature of the interventive process, exploration of the client's feelings about and reactions to the treatment and the worker, and active involvement with the client in decisions about how to work on the problem.

Quick Engagement

Engagement is an affective and cognitive process. On the affective level, the worker attempts to create an environment in which the client feels accepted, understood, listened to, and respected. Engagement is fostered by the worker's sensitivity and responsiveness to the client's stated need. On the cognitive side, the worker tries to enlist the client's view of the problem, attempts to alleviate it, and sets expectations about what is needed or what would help. In relating to the client on these two levels, the worker facilitates the client's motivation and collaboration in working on the problem.

Rapid Assessment

Assessment involves an understanding not only of the presenting problem but also of the client's personality, life situation, and all the systems with which the client interacts. A comprehensive evaluation is necessary because problems and their solution often are multifaceted and complex. Assessment is the means of determining (1) the nature of the client's presenting problem and possible underlying difficulties; (2) what in the past or current person-situation configuration is contributing to the individual's problems; (3) what is interfering with problem resolution; (4) what aspect of the problem is most amenable to change; and (5) what internal and external resources are available to help in resolving the problem.

In order to carry out this assessment, the worker needs to be guided by the client's view of the problem while at the same time using his or her professional knowledge and skill to survey selectively what might be relevant to the client's problem and its solution. The areas of inquiry include the client's constitutional and hereditary endowment; cultural, racial, and ethnic background; personality strengths, capacities, and limitations; motivation; family and interpersonal influences; and environmental resources, supports, and deficits.

Partialization and Focusing

Partialization, a key principle of the interventive process, makes the work more manageable and less overwhelming to both worker and client. Because clients may present with multiple or long-standing problems, the process of setting goals and establishing a focus necessitates prioritizing with respect to what is most immediate or most amenable to change or resolution. Sometimes the selection of a circumscribed aspect of the total problem constellation may be indicated. Likewise, breaking the problem down into smaller elements engenders hope and a sense of greater control. Further, the achievement of modest goals engenders feelings of mastery and enhances motivation.

Together the worker and client establish clear goals, which they must keep in the forefront. The worker helps to maintain the focus, but this is not always an easy task because new concerns may arise or become more pressing throughout the course of treatment. The worker needs to show flexibility in addressing other issues that arise even if they initially seem unrelated to the identified problem or stated goals. The worker's task is to determine whether a particular line of discussion is connected to the treatment focus, whether goals need to be redefined, or whether it is necessary to bring the client back to the main problem.

Flexibility of Approach and Technical Interventions

Because help can be provided in a variety of ways, the choice of approach should be based on both the nature of the problem and the client's capacities rather than on the worker's preferred way of working. This versatility requires that the worker be knowledgeable about and skillful in using a diverse set of interventions. For example, in some situations, the worker might decide that environmental intervention rather than ego building is most appropriate even though the client shows impairments in ego functioning. With other clients, the worker might incorporate elements of both cognitive and psychodynamic models into the interventive process. In still other instances, the worker might use a psychodynamic approach exclusively.

There is a wide variety of techniques that can be used effectively in working with clients, and flexibility in their use is indicated. Techniques, such as sustainment, ventilation, and exploration are always employed to some degree in most situations; techniques such as confrontation, interpretation, homework assignments and tasks, role playing, and rehearsal may be used selectively, if at all.

Differential Use of the Worker-Client Relationship

The worker-client relationship is the vehicle through which the practitioner provides help (Perlman, 1957), and thus it is important for the worker to engage the client actively in a positive working relationship from the outset. The worker tends to use himself or herself as a benign authority, who has the expertise to help the client, or as a collaborator, who involves the client in joint problem-solving activities. The relationship often is essential to instilling a sense of hope and fostering motivation.

Short-term treatment emphasizes the more realistic rather than transferential aspects of the interactions between worker and client. Empathy, warmth, genuineness, acceptance, active listening, and the provision of a safe "holding" environment are the main ingredients used to establish and maintain the worker-client relationship. Respect for diversity in all its forms and a genuine interest in learning about the client's particular background and life experience is vital to helping the client feel understood and valued.

The worker may use himself or herself either with the client directly or on behalf of the client by functioning as an auxiliary ego for clients who are overwhelmed or unable to act in their own best interests; providing support and encouragement; facilitating problem solving; educating the client; acting as a role model; helping the client to access and use other resources; intervening in the client's environment; advocating for the client; and helping the client modify maladaptive personality patterns and ways of relating to others.

The worker monitors the quality of the relationship by eliciting the client's input on the work they are doing together. Negative reactions to the worker's interventions are explored and addressed because it is important that the positive relationship be maintained.

Often certain characteristics of either the worker or the client or their interaction make it difficult for a positive working relationship to be established and maintained. For example, a suspicious client or one who has had numerous negative experiences with authority figures may have difficulty trusting the worker; or a worker who is not sensitive to a client's cultural background and style of relating may alienate the client. The worker's responsibility is to acknowledge these difficulties and strive to overcome or surmount them.

Emphasis on Client Strengths and Capacities

ISTT embodies a strengths perspective (Weick, Rapp, Sullivan, & Kisthardt, 1989). It is especially important for the worker to search out, identify, and work with the client's strengths and capacities in order to bring them to bear on problem resolution in a timely fashion. It is not always easy to maintain a strengths perspective when clients are beleaguered by severe personality or environmental problems. At the very least, however, the fact that clients seek help is a strength on which to build. Even clients who display long-standing and severe problems nevertheless may be motivated to relieve some aspect of their discomfort. Additionally, even individuals who show pervasive impairments in ego functioning may exhibit some areas of intact functioning. For example, an adolescent boy may have poor impulse control but exhibit a good capacity to understand the consequences of his actions. The worker might help him to focus on the possible ramifications of his behavior, thereby helping him to gain some control over his behavior.

Collaboration, Linkage, and Advocacy

The worker not only draws on the client's strengths and capacities but also marshals outside resources during the interventive process. Often the worker must reach out and involve others who can be of assistance to the client, including the family, peers, entitlement programs, self-help groups, and community agencies and services. Intra- and interprofessional collaboration and work with others in the client's social network often are needed in linking clients to vital resources and support systems. In some instances, the client will need an advocate to help him or her obtain what is needed. Collaboration, linkage, and advocacy have their own distinctive set of skills that must become part of the worker's repertoire.

Acceptance of the Limitations of Treatment

There are many benefits to short-term treatment, particularly those that result from being able to help the client make a circumscribed change or attain some resolution of a pressing problem within a brief period of time. There also are some potential limitations for both worker and client as a result of the short-term nature of the interventive process.

Because not all of the problems that the client may evidence can be alleviated, it is important that worker and client accept the concept of partialized goals and focus on what is most amenable to change. This task may be difficult when the client's problems are in many areas or are rooted in long-standing personality patterns and/or entrenched environmental deprivations and assaults. In such cases, the worker may feel that he or she is not doing enough to help the client, fear that the client's problems will reoccur, and believe that more can be achieved through further treatment. It has been shown that sometimes clients are more satisfied with the outcome of short-term contact than is the worker (Mayer and Timms, 1970). In addition to both worker and client's being able to recognize and appreciate what has been accomplished, it also is important to bear in mind that even small gains may lead to further growth, that work continues after treatment ends, and that clients can seek help again later.

Although the short-term nature of the approach enhances autonomy and mastery, a second possible limitation surrounds the issue of separation and loss because the treatment process is designed to come to an end at a specified time. Both worker and client may wish to prolong the contact because of the meaning the relationship has to each, the feelings that are aroused in the process of separation, or the wish to experience the satisfaction and gratification of the beneficial outcomes of the work. Because all of life involves separation, the experience of having to end the treatment relationship provides the client and the worker with an opportunity to rework prior losses and master the feelings associated with endings.

SUMMARY

This chapter has discussed ISTT's view of the person, the social environment, the nature of problems, and the practice setting. It highlighted the importance of the worker's positive attitudes about the distinctiveness, nature, and effectiveness of short-term intervention. Then it presented an overview of the 10 major characteristics of ISTT. The following chapters explicate these principles further and show their application to a variety of client problems and situations.

Chapter 3

The Beginning Phase: Part I

The beginning phase of ISTT consists of five components: (1) problem identification, (2) biopsychosocial assessment, (3) engagement, (4) selection of goals and foci, and (5) contracting. In practice,
these processes often occur simultaneously and reinforce one another.
Since they possess their own unique properties, however, each will be
discussed separately. This chapter describes and illustrates the first two
components, problem identification and biopsychosocial assessment, in
which the worker elicits the client's presenting problem and possible
underlying problems and undertakes a more comprehensive assessment.

COMPONENT 1: PROBLEM IDENTIFICATION

In ISTT, problem identification and biopsychosocial assessment are pivotal features of the interventive process since they form the basis of goal
setting and treatment planning. They begin immediately in the initial
contact with the client. By the end of the first meeting, the worker should
have some beginning understanding of the client's problem and what is
contributing to it, the capacities and strengths the client possesses that
can be used in working on the problem, and the external resources that
may need to be mobilized to help the client. The completion of a more
comprehensive but focused biopsychosocial assessment, described later in
the chapter, generally requires at least one more visit. It must be kept in
mind, however, that assessment is a continuous activity as new information becomes available or as the client's situation changes.

Because of the demands of time, the problem identification and assessment process is challenging. The worker needs to balance the act of seeking crucial information with the need to be attuned to the client's pace and style of relating or risk alienating, confusing, or losing the client. Although the engagement process will be discussed separately in Chapter 4, it nevertheless is important to keep in mind that the establishment of a relationship and the assessment process go hand in hand and mutually affect one another. Additionally, it is helpful for the worker to possess a healthy curiosity about the uniqueness of the individual and his or her situation.

The need for a rapid evaluation necessitates that the worker actively explore the main areas in the client's life and background that shed light on the presenting problem. The worker does not adhere to a set pattern of questioning but instead responds flexibly to what the client presents, keeping in mind the uniqueness of each person and the situation. For example, with a recently homeless client, the worker would inquire not only about the circumstances that led to the homelessness but also about the client's health status, educational and vocational skills, and family and interpersonal supports, since these usually are important areas in such cases. If the client exhibits suspiciousness in response to the worker's questions, it would be imperative for the worker to acknowledge the client's reaction and refrain from probing into what appear to be sensitive topics until establishing more of a relationship with the client. Alternatively, if the client indicates that he or she is having suicidal thoughts, the worker's exploration of the nature and severity of this ideation should take precedence over asking about other issues.

In carrying out the evaluation of the client, the worker focuses on five interrelated facets of the client's situation: (1) the presenting problem, that is, the reasons for which the client is seeking help; (2) the degree to which there are additional or underlying problems related to the presenting problem; (3) the factors in the client's past and current biopsychosocial situation that are contributing to or perpetuating the problem; (4) the client's motivation to work on the problem and expectations of the helping process; and (5) the client's internal capacities, strengths, and external resources that can be mobilized in order to help the client.

Understanding the Presenting Problem

The worker begins by actively eliciting (1) a description of the problem for which the client is seeking help, including its history, background, implications, and consequences; (2) the client's feelings about and reasons for seeking help, particularly whether the client is there voluntarily or involuntarily; (3) the client's efforts to resolve the problem; and (4) the client's ability to consider the causes of the problem and possible solutions.

EXPLORATION OF THE PROBLEM. The worker takes an active stance in exploring the client's view of the problem, feelings about the problem, its consequences and implications, and its history and background. An effort should be made to get as full a picture of the client's perceptions of and feelings about the problem and current situation as possible. Since the client's primary concern generally is to relieve whatever is causing discomfort regardless of the problem's origins, it usually is essential to stay with the here and now of the client's concerns initially rather than delve too quickly, if at all, into the client's past.

It is helpful for the worker to develop skill in asking questions that guide and focus the exploration. All too often, less experienced workers either allow the client to drift or do not know how to deepen and expand the inquiry. One way of keeping the process on track is for the worker to paraphrase what the client has said, a tactic that encourages the client to continue talking. Sometimes it is useful to employ open-ended questions, such as, "Can you say more about that" or "What was that experience like for you?" The worker must learn to recognize and address comments and areas that require elaboration. For example, if a client says that something is fine, the worker can inquire, "What made it fine?" And if a client reports being angry, the worker can ask a series of questions: "What type of situation makes you angry?" "Is there anyone in particular who makes you angry?" "How do you show your anger?" "How do you get over your anger?" If a client finds these queries confusing or has difficulty responding, the worker can overtly acknowledge the client's reaction and seek to understand it, educate the client as to why it is important to explore certain areas, or try to determine, with the client's input, what would make it easier for the client to talk to the worker.

As the client responds to the queries, the worker takes note of the nonverbal cues that emanate from the client—facial expression, body language, tone of voice, eye contact, and posture. These features of the client's presentation are likely to reveal important feelings that the client is experiencing. It is useful too for the worker to recognize that people communicate on both manifest and latent levels. Although accepting the client's statements at face value is a good principle generally, there may be a discrepancy between what the client says overtly and what he or she really thinks or feels. For example, a client may indicate verbally that she does not need anyone to help her but actually may be feeling that others cannot be trusted or will disappoint her. It often is difficult initially to understand the client's latent communication until the worker has a more complete understanding of the client.

As the client describes the problem, the worker asks the client to consider and think about the implications, consequences, and possible factors contributing to their difficulties. Hollis (1964) calls this person-in-situation reflection because it relates to what is happening in the here and now. Since clients differ in their ability to think about themselves, it is essential to pose reflective questions in a sensitive, nonjudgmental way. For example, with a man who feels that his employer is treating him unfairly and has a history of frequent job loss, the worker might say, "Sometimes when there is a problem between two people, both parties play a role. Even though your boss sounds quite difficult, have you thought about whether there is any way in which you might be contributing to the problem?" Similarly, in the instance of a woman who complains that her children do not listen to her and tells the worker she screams at them regularly, the worker might comment, "Clearly your children upset you when they don't listen. Have you thought about why this might be?"

After obtaining all of the information related to the client's current situation, the worker engages in an exploration of the background of the presenting problem and related issues. In order to do this, it is helpful if the worker again asks specific and relevant questions. For example, if a male client seeks help because he is experiencing distress after a marital separation, the worker would ask about not only the nature and duration of his disturbance but also what led to the separation, how it has affected his life, and what the marriage was like. Additionally, the worker might ask about the incidence and effects of past separations and losses and how these were handled in order to see if there are similarities between current and past events or whether the current separation is stimulating feelings related to earlier occurrences. This exploration also could lead the worker to inquire about the client's parents' marriage, particularly if the worker learns that there has been a history of parental separation, divorce, or death. In this manner, the worker develops an understanding of how the client's presenting problem is linked to his or her prior experiences.

Based on this line of questioning into the presenting problem and its background, the worker tries to establish an initial impression about where the problem is located. It is useful for the worker to consider the degree to which the client's presenting problem is a function of the conditions and impact of the social environment or a lack of necessary resources; life events, roles, and developmental tasks; interpersonal relationships; hereditary, constitutional, and health factors; or personality characteristics, patterns of relating, and vulnerabilities (Goldstein, 1995a).

FEELINGS ABOUT AND REASONS FOR SEEKING HELP. It always is important for the worker to explore the client's feelings about and reactions to seeking help since the nature of the feelings about this matter will influence the client's participation in the interventive process. Many clients may feel hopeful about asking for or needing help from another person, but others may feel frightened, embarrassed, ashamed, or resentful. The worker also needs to understand what is prompting the client to ask for assistance at this particular time. For example, it is important to know whether the client is going through a crisis caused by a traumatic event, role change, or life transition; experiencing ongoing or chronic problems that are worsening or having new consequences; encountering a reemergence of older problems; or facing an anniversary, birthday, or other event that triggers the client's greater sense of distress or decision to reach out for help.

Clients also differ in whether they are seeking assistance of their own volition. Some clients are voluntary in the sense that they have decided that they need assistance; some come primarily because others have suggested it; and still others are mandated to be involved in some type of intervention and face serious consequences if they do not follow through. When clients are mandated to obtain treatment because of serious problems about which others are concerned, they may appear indifferent about their problems, show resentment at having to be involved with the worker, or exhibit suspiciousness and fear about the consequences of their participation in the helping process.

Those who refer clients often have essential information about the client and situation. Although the worker may have been in communication with the referral sources before seeing the client, the worker can arrange such contact later with the client's permission. Sometimes there is a discrepancy between the client's and referral source's views of the problem. The reasons for these differences always must be explored. In some instances, the referring individual or agency may not have an accurate picture of the client or may not be operating in the client's best interests. Alternatively, clients may not understand or acknowledge the nature and seriousness of their problem.

THE CLIENT'S ATTEMPTS TO RESOLVE THE PROBLEM. The worker attempts to elicit information about the ways in which the client has attempted to deal with the problem. For example, some individuals consistently try to find solutions, and others ignore or minimize problems or engage in wishful thinking that the problems will melt away. Some individuals have shown considerable resourcefulness and creativity in attempting to cope with highly stressful circumstances, sometimes to the point of exhaustion, while others display a lack of knowledge about available resources or have given up. The information that the worker obtains about this aspect of the client's functioning is an important indicator of his or her ability to deal with problems.

THE CLIENT'S CAPACITY FOR SELF-REFLECTION. The evaluation of the degree to which the client is able to identify his or her role, if any, in contributing to the problem and possible courses of action that might alleviate it is another significant client characteristic. There are clients who are not responsible in any way for their problems and need help either in accessing needed supports and resources or in coping more effectively. Some clients, however, may be contributing to the problem, and an awareness of this role may enable the client to assume greater responsibility for bringing about a solution. A client who has some realistic sense of what might help to resolve the problem can be supported in his or her actions. In contrast, in cases in which a client feels a lack of control over life or that others are to blame for the problems, the worker may need to focus on helping the client develop some sense of his or her own ability to alter the situation.

Determining Additional and Underlying Problems

The presenting problem may be of recent origin, highly circumscribed, or related to a lack of resources or difficulty locating or accessing services. Thus, it may constitute the only difficulty to be addressed. In these instances, problems usually are most amenable to change, and intervention can be more straightforward and readily implemented.

The client's problem, however, may be an aspect of a different but related difficulty or a manifestation of more deep-seated personality, interpersonal, or environmental issues that are influencing the client at the time. Moreover, the client may be experiencing multiple problems. The fact that related, underlying, or additional difficulties exist does not necessarily mean that these become the focus of intervention in ISTT. It does imply that the worker must determine the degree to which these problems are causing or perpetuating the presenting problem and thus must be addressed.

The following three examples show clients who presented with similar financial concerns, but in each case, a detailed assessment revealed significant differences in the impact of the contributing factors to their problems and thus led to different interventive strategies.

THE ROBINSON CASE

Mrs. Robinson, a separated 35-year-old mother of two school-age children, was referred to the social worker at her union because of increas-

ing preoccupation and inefficiency on the job. The union provided eight free counseling sessions for their employees. In her first interview, she told the worker that she was having serious financial problems and felt overwhelmed. The worker learned that the client's money difficulties seemed to begin six months earlier, shortly after her husband, who had always managed the finances, left the household and stopped giving money to her. Although it appeared that her income was sufficient if she made some adjustments in her spending, Mrs. Robinson continued to live as she had prior to the separation. She had never lived on her own previously and had little experience with financial matters. The balances on her credit cards were mounting, and she could no longer make the monthly minimum payments. As a result, she was receiving threatening telephone calls from creditors and was behind in her rent payments.

Exploration revealed that Mrs. Robinson had thought of trying to get a second job on weekends but did not have anyone with whom she could leave her children. She reported that her friends, although emotionally supportive, were in no position to help with the children or finances. In addition, her mother had died one year earlier, and her sister was going through a difficult divorce. The worker learned that Mrs. Robinson's father died when she was a young child, and her mother supported the family on her social security pension and part-time work. The client felt that she should be able to carry on in a similar manner.

Mrs. Robinson told the worker that she had a difficult time coping with the separation from her husband and her mother's death but was mainly preoccupied with her dire financial situation. She also was concerned about her children's reactions to the loss of their father but had little energy to address their feelings. She kept hoping that the problems would straighten themselves out and that the children would get used to their father's being away.

Discussion

In examining all the facets of Mrs. Robinson's presenting problem, it appeared that multiple issues were impinging on her ability to deal with her finances effectively: her reactions to the loss of her mother and husband, her lack of experience in handling money, her concerns about her children, and the demands on her time and energy. The worker also speculated that Mrs. Robinson's husband's departure had reawakened feelings related to the early loss of her father. Nevertheless, the worker concluded that the client's financial difficulties were primary and that they could be addressed without dealing with these other issues. Consequently, the worker planned to use the eight sessions to help Mrs. Robinson take control of her finances by working out a payment plan with her creditors and landlord, learning how best to allocate her funds, and finding ways of reducing expenses.

THE SIMON CASE

Mrs. Simon, a 15-year-old, widowed, recovering alcoholic with seven years of sobriety, sought help from a local family service agency that offered 10 treatment sessions. Depressed and anxious, she told the social worker that she had allowed her finances to get out of control and was deeply in debt. Mrs. Simon had attended Debtor's Anonymous for several meetings, but despite her best intentions, she found herself continuing to spend money impulsively on clothing that she did not really need.

The worker ascertained that overspending had been a long-standing problem for Mrs. Simon that would periodically culminate in significant debt, with which she coped by withdrawing money from savings from a small inheritance. This fund was all but depleted. She also had borrowed money from her sister and friends. The client herself wondered if she was doing the same thing with money as she had done with alcohol.

In discussing the other aspects of her life, Mrs. Simon indicated that she had been in a relationship with a man for several years who was inconsistent, withholding of money and affection, and unreliable. She often felt disappointed, ignored, and unappreciated. The worker began to wonder if the client was buying clothes as a means of coping with her uncomfortable feelings, as she had done when she was drinking heavily.

In exploring Mrs. Simon's relevant history, it came to light that she came from a strict, religious, working-class family in which material possessions were scarce and disparaged and her emotional needs were neglected. She envied other girls who, while also coming from families with modest incomes, nevertheless seemed to have more clothes, jewelry, attention, and closeness with their parents. She moved away from her family when she graduated from high school and supported herself before marrying her husband, who died suddenly after they had been married ten years. It was then that Mrs. Simon's drinking escalated.

Discussion

Although Mrs. Simon's presenting problem was depression and anxiety related to overspending, it became clear to the worker why the client was having difficulty using the money management approach of Debtor's Anonymous to control her spending. Not buying clothes made her feel too deprived and more agitated. The worker also recognized that similar to her experiences in her family of origin, Mrs. Simon was in a relationship that was not meeting her emotional needs and showed a history of problematic object relations. The worker wondered if clothes were a substitute for love and affection and whether the client's excessive spending was a way of giving to herself to compensate for feelings of deprivation and as a means of coping with her disturbing feelings.

The worker concluded that the most efficient way to help Mrs. Simon at this time was to enhance her ego functioning by helping her to identify the purpose that buying clothes served for her in the present without a full exploration or attempt to address her early feelings of deprivation; focus on her needs and how and when these were frustrated in her interactions with her boyfriend and others; and find alternative and more appropriate ways of coping with her feelings and making herself feel better.

THE HOFFMAN CASE

Mr. Hoffman was a 52-year-old resident of an adult home for chronically mentally ill individuals able to live in the community. He was referred to the social worker attached to the residence because of his inability to manage his monthly social security disability checks. The worker learned that when Mr. Hoffman received his checks, he would eat all of his meals in restaurants rather than shop and cook for himself, and he also would attend cultural events. After 10 days, he had spent all of his money and would request additional funds from the setting in order to manage until his next check.

Mr. Hoffman explained to the worker that he could not adjust to having to live on a limited income and felt that he was more educated, cultured, and refined than the other residents in the home. He added that he was accustomed to good food and fine restaurants and thought it was beneath him to have to prepare his own meals. The worker noted that Mr. Hoffman looked quite disheveled and was attired in the same outfit in which she had seen him on other occasions. She ascertained that Mr. Hoffman spent all of his time alone and was very disparaging and critical of the other residents and staff, who did not seem to like him.

Although reluctant to speak about his history, Mr. Hoffman shared that he was the only child of Jewish immigrants who lived an isolated life in a small apartment in a borough of New York City. He dropped out of high school, never worked, and lived at home with his parents, rarely leaving the apartment. He spent his time reading and watching television; his mother cooked all of his meals, washed his clothes, and cleaned his room. This state of affairs continued despite his father's death 10 years earlier and ended when his mother passed away a year earlier. The landlord called Adult Protective Services because the rent had not been paid, and the neighbors complained of a foul odor coming from the apartment.

This history led the worker to inquire about Mr. Hoffman's daily living skills, which she learned were minimal. He showered infrequently, had no schedule, rarely did the laundry, did not even know how to boil water, let alone cook, and had never written a check. Although Mr. Hoffman seemed unconcerned about these matters, the worker was struck by the contrast between his inflated way of speaking about himself and his actual way of living. The worker speculated that the client was protecting his feelings of inadequacy, vulnerability, and fear by assuming an air of superiority. It seemed clear to the worker that Mr. Hoffman's difficulties with his finances were only one part of a larger constellation of problems that included not only his lack of

*skills but his need to preserve his fragile self-esteem by means of a fa-
cade of grandiosity.*

Discussion

*Despite Mr. Hoffman's obvious need for concrete help in developing fi-
nancial management and daily living skills and with his underlying in-
securities, the worker understood that he was not ready to accept
simple interventions offered by the agency, such as hygiene, nutrition,
shopping, cooking, and money management classes or address the reasons for his reluctance to involve himself in such activities. Since he related to her as a competent and benign parental figure, she decided to
try to build on their relationship. She offered him the opportunity of
meeting with her in order to figure out a way for him to continue par-
taking of some of the "pleasures" that he sought without jeopardizing
his finances and to use his intellect to find activities that might boost his
self-esteem and build his skills.*

These three examples show that even in a short-term approach, it is
important to determine all of the factors related to the client's presenting problem. An accurate assessment leads to more appropriate and
differential interventions.

In order to ascertain what additional or underlying issues, if any, are
relevant to the presenting problem, the worker engages in a variety of
tactics. For example, the worker needs to consider the meaning or purpose that certain behaviors have to the client since dysfunctional behavior often serves important functions in preserving the client's sense of self
or relationships with others. Another line of inquiry is the exploration of
whether the client has ever experienced similar problems or feelings. One
might ask the client, "Has anything like this ever happened before?" or
"Have you ever felt this way before?" or "Does this experience remind you
of anything?" The worker also might ask if the client has other problems
that are affecting or related to the current problem. These questions can
assist the worker in determining whether the presenting problem represents a discreet occurrence or a pattern of difficulties.

In some instances, clients may not be aware of, do not make the
connection to, or do not wish to disclose underlying or additional fac-

tors. Or because they do not think along these lines, do not trust the worker, or may feel ashamed, they do not volunteer information that sheds light on these matters. It may be necessary for the worker to formulate questions that stimulate the client's thinking about and reporting of significant data. The worker uses knowledge of human behavior and the developmental process and the impact of the social environment to guide the exploration.

The following example illustrates how the worker elicited important information that established some of the underlying factors in the client's presenting problem.

THE MAY CASE

Mrs. May, a married, 48-year-old professional woman with two adolescent children, sought help because she was highly conflicted about whether to separate from her husband in order to pursue a relationship with Mike, with whom she had been having an affair for eight years. Although unhappy with his wife, he was not encouraging Mrs. May to leave, as he was comfortable with the situation as it was.

Mrs. May described her husband as kind and a good provider but as having been depressed and needy since they married 18 years earlier. She yearned for Mike, whom she described as exciting and charming. She was preoccupied with thoughts of divorcing her husband and marrying Mike and spent considerable time and energy devising ways to be with him. She was disturbed by his being flirtatious with her female colleagues, his continuing to see numerous women friends, and his practice of bar hopping rather than staying home when they were not together. She worried that if she left her husband, Mike would return to his wife or find someone else, but she could not give him up.

Mrs. May sought help because as time went on and Mike did not take a move to leave his wife, she became increasingly depressed. She told him she needed him to take some action, whereas he stated that he wanted her either to stay with the husband or leave him if she truly wanted to end the marriage but not to leave because of him. Thus, a stalemate existed. Exploring the client's dilemma, obsessive thoughts, and paralysis yielded little insight into why the client was so stuck. The worker shared with the client the fact that sometimes the past influences the present and that she wanted to ask her some questions that might shed light on what other factors might be affecting the dilemma.

The worker first asked the client if yearning for someone who was unavailable reminded her of anything she had experienced earlier in her life. The client was not able to relate to this query. Then the worker drew on her knowledge that people tend to re-create significant family-of-origin experiences in their current intimate relationships. She explored the client's relationship to her parents and their relationship with one another.

The worker learned that the client's current situation was not the first time that she had yearned to be with someone whom she idealized and found to be stimulating while remaining with a depressed partner. She reported having had a charming, vibrant, elusive, and successful father to whom she felt close. He nevertheless was unavailable to her while paying attention to her female friends. Even as an adolescent, she used to yearn to spend more time with him and wished that he would make her feel special. She felt unattractive and uninteresting compared to her friends. The client did not feel close to her mother, whom she described as critical, aloof, and depressed. The father died suddenly of a heart attack when the client was 17. She felt abandoned and left to the care of the mother. This traumatic loss left her with unfilled needs for the father and resentment at the mother's emotional detachment.

In response to the worker's question about whether Mike resembled the father whom she had loved and lost, the client acknowledged that she found Mike, who was not particularly handsome, attractive initially because of his mentoring of her occupationally, that he seemed strong in her eyes, and that she felt safe with him. In contrast, her husband's depression made him seem weak to her and reminded her of her mother.

Discussion

If the worker concludes that additional or underlying problems must also become the focus of intervention, then it is necessary to educate the client about the fact that there often are connections between past *experiences and current difficulties and that dealing with such issues may be essential to resolving the present difficulties.*

In the case of Mrs. May, the worker suggested that one of the likely reasons that the client was feeling so stuck was that her current problems, although very real, were being influenced by her earlier experiences with her parents, particularly her relationship with her father and the impact of his death and that these earlier relationships needed to be discussed. When Mrs. May asked what difference this made, the worker said that it was sometimes necessary to understand and deal with unresolved issues from the past in order to relieve current difficulties.

Sometimes the problem for which the client seeks help can be a symptom associated with a psychiatric syndrome, such as anxiety, suicidal thinking, problems in concentrating, intrusive thoughts and memories, compulsive behavior, somatization, or difficulties controlling drinking, spending, or eating. Likewise, there are times when the client's presenting problem is indicative of a serious difficulty about which he or she is ashamed, fearful, or reticent to divulge, such as substance abuse, domestic violence, or sexual abuse. In order to assess the client's true difficulty, it is necessary for workers to have an understanding of the overt symptomatology of a variety of major disorders, including the range of DSM-IV classifications (APA, 1994) and to be knowledgeable about and able to recognize the sometimes subtle manifestations of these syndromes. With a correct assessment, the worker is in a better position to determine and offer the best course of treatment or assist the client in obtaining the help he or she needs.

THE NICHOLS CASE

Mr. Nichols, a 28-year-old bank teller, was referred to the social worker at his company's employee assistance program because of attendance problems, lateness, moodiness, and problems with co-workers. In talking to the worker, the client acknowledged these difficulties but was quick to add that he was going to improve. He seemed eager to please but was vague in his explanations of why he was having problems or discussing his life outside the workplace.

Knowing that sometimes bank employees are fearful of disclosing any information that might jeopardize their jobs, the worker explored whether Mr. Nichols had such concerns. He denied this initially and said he felt that he was getting his life under control. Having recognized that some of Mr. Nichols's behaviors might suggest an alcohol or drug problem but not wanting to be confrontational about a sensitive subject, the worker said, "What I am going to say may not apply to you, but some of the difficulties you are having are common when people drink a lot or use drugs. We have a lot of experience working with these kinds of problems since many excellent employees find themselves in this kind of predicament. We're here to be helpful, not to judge or be punitive."

Mr. Nichols seemed to relax visibly and acknowledged that he sometimes had a few beers to help him sleep at night. Aware that it was likely that the client was minimizing his alcohol use in order to see her reaction and to save face, the worker commented, "I'm glad you felt able to tell me about that. I wonder if there are other times when you take a drink to help you relax?" The client responded hesitantly, "I guess I do drink a little more than I should."

COMPONENT 2: BIOPSYCHOSOCIAL ASSESSMENT

The previous discussion shows some of the important features of the assessment process and highlights how the worker arrives at problem identification. What follows is a comprehensive guide for further elucidating significant aspects of the client and his or her situation and the internal and external resources available for problem resolution.

Biopsychosocial Assessment Guide

I. The Person
   A. Heredity and constitutional factors
   B. Physical health and substance use
   C. Internal capacities and coping mechanisms

1. Drives
2. Ego functions
    a. Reality testing
    b. Judgment
    c. Sense of reality of the world and the self
    d. Regulation and control of drives, affects, and impulses
    e. Object relations
    f. Cognitive functioning and thought processes
    g. Adaptive regression in the service of the ego
    h. Defensive functioning
    i. Stimulus barrier
    j. Autonomous functions—mobility, motility, memory, intelligence, perception
    k. Mastery and competence
    l. Synthetic and integrative functioning
    m. Observing ego
3. Superego functioning
4. Defenses
5. Object relations
6. Self-structure
7. Strengths
8. Attitude toward seeking help
9. Motivation

D. Developmental tasks
    1. Psychosexual stages
    2. Psychosocial stages
    3. Separation-individuation phases
    4. Object relations, self, and cognitive stages
E. Gender, sexual orientation, ethnic and cultural background, and other types of diversity
F. Sense of meaning or spirituality

II. The Social Environment
A. Physical surroundings
    1. Housing
    2. Neighborhood and community conditions

    3. Schools, hospitals, places of worship, prisons, social agencies, and other facilities

B. Family

    1. Structure and development

        a. History and membership

        b. Type of family (for example, nuclear, extended, kinship, single parent, blended, gay or lesbian)

        c. Life stage

        d. Roles and tasks

        e. Internal and external boundaries

    2. Patterns and style of communication

        a. Direct or indirect

        b. Covert or overt

        c. Stated and unstated rules

    3. Cultural background and degree of acculturation

        a. Values and religious beliefs

        b. Mores and child-rearing practices

        c. Identifications

        d. Degree of acculturation

    4. Relationship to others and to the community

    5. Environmental conditions, stressors, and resources

    6. Strengths and problem-solving capacities

    7. Attitudes toward help

    8. Motivation

C. Social network in neighborhood and community

    1. Formal organizations

    2. Informal groupings

    3. Interpersonal relationships

    4. Services and resources

D. Cultural context

    1. Values and religious beliefs

    2. Mores and child-rearing practices

    3. Identifications

    4. Degree of acculturation

    5. Attitudes toward seeking and receiving help

E. Society
   1. Attitudes including racism, sexism, homophobia, ageism, and other forms of discrimination and bias
   2. Legislation and social policies toward the poor, physically and mentally disabled, children, elderly, immigrants, and other disenfranchised or oppressed groups
   3. Practices of social institutions

This guide is meant to be used selectively. The worker need not engage in a systematic inquiry into every aspect of the client's life and situation or take a complete history in a formal sense. Nevertheless, it always is necessary for the worker to engage in a more comprehensive evaluation of the client's ego functioning since even when the problem is located in the social environment, the client's capacities affect his or her ability to deal with external stressors and to locate and access environmental resources. In clients whose problems are related to or caused by impaired ego functions, intervention may be focused on strengthening those capacities that are most relevant to helping the client.

Many of the areas outlined are illuminated as the client shares his or her story and the worker selectively explores what the client already has touched on. The worker's developing impressions of where the problem is located guides the focus and depth of exploration. Carrying out an ego assessment in ISTT requires that the worker be knowledgeable about how ego functions are manifested in the client's current situation, including the client's interactions with the worker. Additionally, the worker gathers important data about the client directly by means of selective questions and indirectly from the client's demeanor and presentation.

As the client relates information about his or her situation, the worker pays attention to the client's style of communication and behavior; affect regulation, thinking, and cognitive processes, impulse control, frustration tolerance, reality testing, judgment, sense of mastery and competence, self-concept, and object relations; and ability to consider the causes of his or her difficulties and possible solutions. For example, the worker evaluates whether the client is able to talk in a coherent and logical fashion or is vague, tangential, or fragmented; overwhelmed, depressed, anxious, angry, detached, or withdrawn; realistic and appropriate in attempts to deal with the problem or avoidant, impulsive, and involved in magical thinking; moody, emotionally labile, inappropriate, or constricted; self-denigrating or grandiose; and able to engage in stable and mutually gratifying relationships or isolated, avoidant, dependent, or involved in stormy interactions with others.

In observing the client's behavior and demeanor in the interview situation, however, the worker must be cautious about making premature judgments about the client's capacities without obtaining additional supporting data. Initial impressions of the client's ego functioning should be validated or modified based on further exploration of the client's history, relationships with others, and ability to function in the real world.

Additionally, as Goldstein (1995a, p. 211) points out, the worker has an impact on how the client behaves in the interview. Thus, the worker's attitudes, interventions, or insensitivity may stimulate clients to react in ways that do not necessarily reflect their characteristic personality traits or patterns. A client also may react to the worker as a symbol of authority or a representative of a society that is viewed as oppressive, discriminatory, or threatening. For all of these reasons, workers must strive to understand both their own and their agency's impact on the client.

The following example illustrates the negative consequences of the worker's judgmental response to the client, about which she remained unaware.

THE MCGRAW CASE

Ms. McGraw, a 22-year-old single clerical worker who resided with her parents, was referred to the social worker at the hospital where she sought medical attention following a rape. In the initial meeting with the worker, the client explained that she had been dating Ben, a young man in her neighborhood, for six months when he abruptly broke off their relationship. A few weeks later, he called to invite her to go to a local club with him and his male cousin, who was visiting from another city. She agreed, and as they were walking down the street, the cousin suggested that they explore an abandoned building that looked interesting. Once they all entered the building, the cousin tried to kiss her. She pushed him away. Becoming angry, he persisted despite her protests and raped her while Ben stood by. Afterward, she ran out of the building and when she arrived home, her parents, upon seeing her disheveled appearance and disturbed state, took her to a nearby emergency room.

The worker immediately began to question the client pointedly about why she had gone with Ben and his cousin in the first place, why she went into an abandoned building with them, and whether she had considered the possible consequences of her actions. The client began crying and said she felt confused and guilty. The worker said she could understand that the client felt guilty, and it was important to discuss why she exhibited such poor judgment. Although the client returned, she indicated that she was doing so only to please her parents. She refused to take her coat off and was reluctant to talk. Other than learning that the client's daily functioning had deteriorated, the worker was not able to glean any additional information.

The worker interpreted the client's responses as indicative of the client's denial of her role in the rape. When the client began to speak of suicide in the next meeting, the worker sought help from her supervisor. Noting what appeared to be the worker's judgmental and somewhat angry attitude toward the client, the supervisor asked the worker if she had spent any time helping the client express her feelings about the rape. The worker acknowledged that she had omitted this step since she wanted the client to grapple with her poor judgment. The supervisor wondered if the client was reacting strongly to the worker's lack of empathy with her plight and to her confrontational style, which could be making the client feel misunderstood and guilty.

Although the worker remained unconvinced, she was willing to try a different approach because of the client's worsening condition. The worker began the next session by stating that she felt she had been on the wrong track and had not really explored how awful the rape experience was for her and how betrayed she felt by her former boyfriend.

The client looked surprised and sat back in the chair. When the worker encouraged her to say more about her feelings about the rape, she began to talk about how much she had trusted Ben.

There are other situations in which the worker misunderstands and misinterprets certain features of the client's presentation, which are the product of his or her cultural background and lifestyle. A worker who does not appreciate the values, mores, communication patterns, child-rearing practices, ways of dealing with feelings, intimacy, money, sex role expectations, family ties, and so on of particular populations runs the risk of defining certain client behaviors and attitudes as pathological, as illustrated in the following example.

THE ARTURO CASE

Ms. Arturo, a 27-year-old mother of two small children, was referred for help by the educational evaluator at the board of education, who was concerned about her apparent distress at learning about her son's speech problem. In inquiring about how Ms. Arturo's husband was dealing with the child's difficulties, the worker learned that the client had not yet told her husband about the true nature of their son's problem because of her fear that he would blame her. She knew he was having casual affairs with other women and worried about his spending more time away from her.

When the worker asked how Mrs. Arturo had been coping with the news about her son and her concerns about her husband, the client said she had talked with her mother, with whom she was very close. The mother told her to minimize the son's problem when she spoke to the husband, merely indicating that she was going to take him for some tutoring and that she should not worry so much about her husband's activities since he was a good provider and always came home to her, adding, "That's the way men are." The mother also revealed that Ms. Arturo's father had done similar things, as did her brothers, and that they always stayed with their wives since they valued family above all else. The client was reassured by her mother's advice but came for help because she was very worried about her son and wanted to do everything she could to improve his condition.

As the worker tried to explore the client's feelings about her hus-band's affairs, the client changed the subject back to her son. The worker thought that this indicated Ms. Arturo's resistance. She also believed the client to be too dependent on and compliant with her mother and husband.

In her regular meetings with her supervisor, the worker shared her assessment of the client and her plan of focusing on the client's depen-dence and passivity. The supervisor was concerned about the worker's conclusions because she felt that the worker was making assumptions about the client for which there was little evidence; that the worker had not considered sufficiently the client's cultural background and its atti-tudes toward fidelity and marital relationships; that the client was not presenting her marital problems as her concern at this time; and that the worker was too quick in locating the client's deficits rather than rec-ognizing and supporting her strengths.

Determining Client Motivation

Motivation involves a desire or willingness to work on some aspect of a problem. Clients differ with respect to what component of their problem they are willing to address and in their level of motivation. Although the worker's role in facilitating the client's motivation will be discussed in Chapter 4, it is important to bear in mind that the worker's attitudes and behavior affect this important ingredient of the interventive process. When clients exhibit a low level of mo-tivation, the worker must try to understand the reasons and try to instill or mobilize the client's willingness to engage in the helping process.

Some of the factors that influence the client's motivation are his or her degree of discomfort and hope; voluntary or mandatory status; prior experiences with seeking assistance; expectations about the help-ing process; and ability to invest time, energy, and resources in resolv-ing the problem.

DISCOMFORT AND HOPE. Client motivation is fueled by both the "push of discomfort" and the "pull of hope," since discomfort alone may lead to indifference or resignation (Perlman, 1979, pp. 186–87). The degree of discomfort and hope that a client experiences as a result of his or her problems varies considerably and depends on the nature and severity of the problem, the effects of his or her expectations of and basic outlook on life, the influence of the client's background and experience, and the impact of the client's self-concept and feelings of worth. Common variations include clients who are uncomfortable but have a fatalistic orientation and are accepting of whatever occurs in life, sometimes attributing this to God's will or the natural order of things; those who feel distress but expect little from life and resign themselves to feeling that nothing can or will ever change or feel powerless to alter their circumstances; clients who feel discomfort but believe that they should handle their problems themselves or are ashamed to admit problems to others; those who are optimistic about the possibility of change; clients whose situation seems intolerable or feel desperate and have little hope but are willing to try some avenue that holds out the possibility of relief; clients who suffer from low self-esteem or an irrational sense of guilt, feeling that they do not deserve better for themselves; those who seek relief from their discomfort but because of their feelings of impotence and inadequacy expect others or their situation to change; and those who are uncomfortable not so much because of a problem itself but because of its negative consequences, as might be the case with a man who is at risk of being incarcerated unless he enters a rehabilitation program for his substance abuse even though he is not overtly unhappy about his drug use.

In these and other situations, the worker must try to locate the client's discomfort and mobilize his or her sense of hope.

VOLUNTARY OR MANDATORY STATUS. Whether a client is voluntary or involuntary is likely to affect motivation. Voluntary clients at least initially are coming because they want something to change. Nevertheless, they may show ambivalence about making changes because of what these represent. They may fear the unknown, feel more secure with what it is familiar, or be afraid of the consequences of change. Additionally, in some situations, if the worker is not able to offer the immediate relief that the client seeks or redefines the problem to be addressed in terms of the client's need to modify some aspect of his or her behavior, the client's motivation may wane.

Involuntary clients, who are mandated or told to seek treatment by others under the threat of some dire consequences, often begin with little motivation and sometimes seem to hold on to their position in order to protect themselves from encroachment. If the worker can identify some positive gain for the client in working on a problem, the client's motivation may be enhanced.

PRIOR EXPERIENCES WITH SEEKING HELP. Another important factor that affects clients' motivation is their past experiences in seeking help. Positive experiences are more likely to result in the client's willingness to reach out, whereas negative experiences often will impede their help-seeking efforts. Social workers sometimes are associated with those who have power and control over the client's life and thus may be feared, resented, or viewed with antagonism. As will be discussed further in Chapter 4, the client's past experiences with the helping process need to be understood and addressed.

EXPECTATIONS OF THE HELPING PROCESS. Clients bring different expectations to the helping process about what they want with respect to relief or solutions and the nature of the process. For example, clients vary with respect to whether they want symptom relief, access to resources, advice, information, and guidance; sympathetic listening and acceptance; encouragement and support; someone who will help them in problem solving, interpersonal conflict resolution, and self-understanding; immediate relief or a more reflective process; or an authority who will unilaterally solve the problem or a more mutually participatory process. Many clients do not have a clear understanding of what to expect or what is expected of them. The worker needs to elicit the client's expectations and address how and if these can be met through the interventive process.

ABILITY TO INVEST IN THE HELPING PROCESS. Participating in helping efforts requires an expenditure of time and energy and can pose certain inconveniences. Not all clients are in a position to take time off from work or from their family responsibilities, nor do they have the emotional resources, financial means, or social supports to make use of services. Agencies may be difficult to reach geographically or may have limited and inconvenient hours of operation. These are very real factors that affect the client's motivation and must be considered in formulating the interventive plan.

Internal Capacities and External Resources

A final aspect of the assessment process is the worker's evaluation of the client's capacities, strengths, and external resources that can be brought to bear in the helping process. In ISTT, it is particularly important for the worker to search these out in order to facilitate intervention. Even clients who show severe impairments in their ego functioning may exhibit certain qualities such as perseverance, humor, sensitivity, and intelligence, which the worker can draw on to assist the client. For example, in assessing a male substance abuser who drinks when he is upset, the worker's observation that the client is intelligent, has good reality testing, is self-reflective, and is able to invest in activities such as reading can be helpful in efforts to help him find better ways of coping with his disturbing feeling states, lack of impulse control, and frustration tolerance. Moreover, clients who feel isolated from others and have few social supports may not be aware of or know how to access potential resources that exist in the community. In the case of a single parent who seeks help for her latency-age daughter who displays withdrawn behavior and spends a great deal of time alone after school, the worker's assessment of the mother's genuine interest in helping her daughter and the child's overall level of reasonably good functioning in school and at home suggest the utility of an environmental intervention initially. The identification of and help in accessing an after-school program at a local community center might be useful in helping the child to socialize with peers, and assisting the mother in contacting a support group for single parents might be beneficial in enabling her to feel less isolated.

SUMMARY

This chapter has stressed the importance of the worker's active and focused inquiry about the client's problem, all the systems that may be contributing to it, and the inner and outer resources that can be used in helping the client. It described the problem identification and biopsychosocial assessment components and suggested guidelines for carrying these out.

Chapter 4

The Beginning Phase: Part II

E ngagement is the process by which the client and the worker develop a working relationship. It is facilitated by the manner in which the worker approaches and interacts with the client. The worker's ability to relate sensitively to the client influences the client's willingness to share information and explore problems in greater depth.

A crucial aspect of ISTT is the worker's ability to assist the client in moving from being a seeker of help to becoming an active participant in the interventive process. Additional components of the initial phase are planning intervention and contracting in which the worker and client mutually decide the goals and focus of intervention based on the assessment process and arrive at an agreement about their work together.

COMPONENT 3: ENGAGEMENT

In ISTT, the worker's ability to establish a relationship with the client is intrinsic to the helping process because clients are more likely to ac-cept advice and guidance, consider and attempt to try out new ways of thinking, feeling, and behaving, take risks, and modify aspects of their usual ways of coping and relating to others when they have a meaning-ful connection to the worker. The engagement process begins when worker and client first have contact with one another.

By the end of their first meeting, both worker and client should experience a beginning sense of connection because something meaningful has occurred between them. The worker should have some grasp of the client's problem, who the client is, and what his or her life is like and feel that he or she can be of assistance; and both client and worker should feel a willingness to struggle together on the client's behalf. Ideally the client should feel understood and that there is some hope that together the worker and client will establish an effective means for addressing the client's difficulties.

Although the exploratory, clarifying, and sometimes reflective procedures used in assessment also foster engagement to some degree, there are other techniques that also are important. Thus, the worker encourages ventilation, shows empathy, offers appropriate reassurance and encouragement, acknowledges and validates the client's feelings, and provides information about the interventive process. The worker often needs to demonstrate his or her willingness, desire, and ability to help the client in very real ways. The worker selectively offers advice and guidance, provides concrete assistance, accompanies the client at times, advocates for the client, or helps the client to access additional services. These techniques will be described more fully in Chapter 5.

It is not only the techniques that the worker employs but the worker's manner of relating that contribute to successful engagement. The worker attempts to (1) establish a facilitating climate or environment, (2) be where the client is, and (3) mobilize, release, or build on the client's motivation.

Establishing a Facilitating Climate

There are three main ingredients of the workers' activity that promote a facilitating environment: his or her attitudes and characteristics, the clarification of the worker's role and agency function, and an emphasis on client self-determination and confidentiality.

WORKER ATTITUDES AND CHARACTERISTICS. The worker strives to engage the client rapidly by actively joining with the client. In ISTT, the worker must actively, consciously, and purposefully attempt to engage the client from the outset by exhibiting certain attitudes and behaviors that are common to all forms of intervention. It is erroneous for the worker to assume and act as if the working relationship will develop automatically over the course of time. Instead, he or she needs to demonstrate interest in what the client has to say, respect for the client, and a desire to be of help. Moreover, by conveying acceptance, genuineness, empathy, and warmth, the worker encourages the client to share his or her thoughts and feelings. These qualities also instill a sense of safety and security, help clients to feel understood, and demonstrate what clients can expect from the worker in the interventive process.

In addition to these general characteristics, there are four specific attitudes that are necessary to engaging the client in ISTT: the worker must convey (1) that the client can be helped in a short period of time; (2) that small changes or gains are significant; (3) that all clients possess strengths that can be used in the helping process; and (4) that although the worker takes an active and directive stance, the helping process remains one of mutuality rather than one driven by the worker's agenda or based on the worker's input alone. The worker's ability to convey these attitudes to the client early in the interventive process engenders hope and a sense of control; reduces anxiety, discouragement, and aloneness; and creates an expectation of active participation as the following excerpt illustrates.

THE NEVENS CASE

In the initial contact with Mrs. Nevens, a mother on welfare who was referred because of her "attitude" on the job, the worker elicited the client's feelings of resentment about being required to work in a menial job for which she was receiving a minimum wage and her discouragement about ever being able to make more money or receive additional training. Toward the end of their meeting, the worker said, "I can see how discouraged you are feeling about having to go to work for such a low salary and with so little to look forward to and how it is difficult for you to hide your feelings on the job. It is important that you have been able to go to work despite how you feel, that you want to better yourself, and that you are attempting to make the best of this situation. It's true that this job is not too rewarding and that it is going to take time for you to get to the place where you want to be. There are things that we can do together in the short run to help you to manage and tolerate this situation so that you will be in a better position to move on in the future. If we can help you find a way of staying with this job for now, you will be able to establish a consistent and reliable work record that makes you more likely to get a better job."

CLARIFICATION OF THE WORKER'S ROLE AND AGENCY'S FUNCTION. All too often workers assume that clients already know what social workers and the setting can do for the client. Because clients frequently lack knowledge or are misinformed about what social workers do and how agencies can be of assistance, the first step in engaging the client is for the worker to explain his or her role and the agency's function, that is, the ways in which the worker and the setting can help the client. This clarification gives the client needed information and also is a way of showing respect for the client.

The worker's explanation of his or her role and function should be simple and specific. With a client hospitalized for a medical problem, the worker might say, "My name is Mary Richards, and I'm a social worker. Often when people are hospitalized, they have concerns and worries about their condition, their families, or what will happen after they leave. My job at the hospital is to try to understand how things are going for you here. So I'm here to talk about the needs, worries, or concerns that you may have. I'll also be available to talk about and help you with your discharge."

Sometimes clients seek help from a setting that is not able to provide what the client needs, or the worker may not have the expertise necessary to help the client. If such circumstances occur, it is incumbent on the worker to locate the appropriate resources or assist the client in doing so.

CLIENT SELF-DETERMINATION AND CONFIDENTIALITY. In seeking help, clients may present with misperceptions about the helping process. For example, some clients, particularly those who are mandated, are fearful of having others impose their will on them. Others may wish for the worker to be a parental figure who will take over and unilaterally solve their problems. Still other clients may be anxious about becoming too dependent on the worker. In these and other instances, it is important for the worker to acknowledge the client's self-determination and facilitate the client's use of his or her own strengths and capacities in the helping process. Even in situations in which the client's capacity to act in his or her own interests is impaired, the worker still tries to maximize the client's self-determination to the extent possible.

The discussion of self-determination needs to be attuned and individualized to each client. With a client who seems anxious about becoming dependent, after exploring the client's fears and empathizing with them, the worker might say, "I can see that it is important for you to feel that you will be making your own decisions, particularly in the light of what you have told me. Let me assure you that I am here to point things out, make suggestions, and help you in the ways that you want or need rather than to tell you what to do or take over. The final decisions are yours."

Another example of how to deal with self-determination can be seen with a mandated client who feels forced to come for help. In this instance, the worker needs to acknowledge the client's feelings and lack of self-determination while trying to maximize client choice to the extent that this is possible. If the client displays anger at being coerced into getting help, the worker might comment, "It is understandable that you resent being forced to come here. Unfortunately, your concern that there will be serious consequences to your refusing help is realistic, and it is understandable that you feel resentful. It may seem that you do not have any choices, but you have come today and do seem worried about your situation. Maybe together we can find some way of helping you with what has been happening in your life. You do have some choice in how we use our time together."

Although confidentiality of the worker-client relationship is a basic principle of the interventive process, it involves complex considerations because one cannot nor should one necessarily promise total confidentiality in all circumstances in today's practice arena. There are limitations to strict adherence to this principle in many situations, such as those in which clients are at risk of hurting themselves or others, including child abuse and neglect. In addition, some settings require workers to monitor clients' attendance at sessions or abstinence from substance use. In other instances, workers are expected to make reports or testify about clients' functioning in order for them to obtain custody of their children, obtain parole, or be discharged from court-mandated treatment. What is most important in such instances is that the worker clearly articulate the parameters of confidentiality at the outset so that the client is informed of the implications of what he or she tells the worker.

Being Where the Client Is

The worker's ability to "be where the client is" is an important practice principle in all social work intervention. It reflects the worker's ability to stay with the client's communications and affective state, to be attuned to the meaning of the client's comments, and to individualize the client. Because of the pressures of time in short-term intervention, there may be a tendency to move too quickly. ISTT requires the worker to balance the need for being active, focused, and timely in interventions with the need to respect the client's pace and manner of relating. In order to implement this principle in the initial phase, the worker not only elicits the client's problem but also relates to his or her feelings about and expectations of the interventive process and individualizes the client with respect to his or her personality, situation, and background.

RELATING TO THE CLIENT'S FEARS, HOPES, AND EXPECTATIONS. Clients differ in their feelings about seeking help and their expectations of the interventive process. Many clients may feel hopeful about asking for or needing help from another person, but others may experience fear, embarrassment, shame, or resentment. Because of the potential of these feelings to impede engagement, it is necessary for the worker to recognize, explore, and address them.

Although many clients can speak directly about these reactions, others are reticent about sharing their thinking or feelings openly. Sometimes clients who have had negative experiences with authority may view the social worker as a representative of such figures. Their perceptions will affect how they relate to the worker and what they expect from the process. In such instances, it is important for the worker to explore the client's previous experiences, acknowledge their impact, and accept that the client will not readily alter his or her view even when the worker is well meaning. The worker consistently attempts to be sensitive to the client, provide the client with a more positive relationship than those in the client's past, and refrain from being provoked or retaliatory when the client continues to show distrust or hostility.

THE BAXTER CASE

Mr. Baxter, a 24-year-old single, former construction worker, who was seriously injured in an accident, was referred to the social worker at the hospital's rehabilitation unit because of his unwillingness to cooperate with his physical therapy program and his belligerent attitude toward staff.

In meeting the worker, he became angry at her attempts to learn more about his situation and yelled at her to leave him alone. The worker replied, "You certainly are upset at my being here, but I just want to be of help to you." Mr. Baxter retorted, "You're just like everyone else that comes in here. You're not interested in me. You just want to ask your questions, but you don't care what I want." When the worker asked the client what he meant by his statement that she was just like everyone else, Mr. Baxter went on a tirade about the doctors and nurses at the hospital when he first arrived. He described how they treated him as if he was not a person, taking his blood, waking him up in the middle of the night, making him wait for medication, and never asking him what he wanted or how he felt. The worker attempted to empathize with Mr. Baxter, but he became more accusatory, saying, "I've had social workers before. They took me away from my mother and only made my life worse." The worker maintained her composure and responded, "I know you won't believe my telling you that I really am interested in being of assistance and that I will listen to you and be sensitive to your needs. All I ask is that you give me a chance and we'll see how it goes."

Not expecting the worker's calm, validating, and concerned response, Mr. Baxter looked surprised and became quiet. When the worker asked what he was thinking, he said, "I don't believe you, but what else can I do laying in this bed?" The worker then asked Mr. Baxter to tell her more about what it had been like having to lie in bed all the time. The client angrily screamed, "What do you think it's like?" The worker commented, "I guess that was a pretty stupid question," to which Mr. Baxter replied, "All I think about is whether I'll ever be able to get out of here on my own two feet."

Clients' expectations of and hopes for the interventive process may be realistic or unrealistic. When the client's expectations and hopes are unrealistic, the worker must strive to build a bridge between what the client wants and what the worker is able to provide. This can best be achieved by first relating to the client's wishes, irrespective of their appropriateness. Without exploring and understanding what clients want, the worker runs the risk of preceding without their full participation because clients cannot move forward until they feel accepted and understood.

THE GRANT CASE

Mr. Grant, a psychiatric inpatient, expressed a wish to be discharged immediately despite the continuing presence of psychotic symptoms. In exploring this expectation, the worker learned that the patient hated taking his prescribed medication because of its side effects and had been noncompliant with the treatment regimen. In exploring the specific nature of the side effects of the medication, the worker learned that the client was most uncomfortable about feeling "in a fog" because this made him feel that a foreign substance was taking over his body and he felt disconnected from himself. The worker empathized with how uncomfortable and frightening these experiences could be and acknowledged Mr. Grant's wish to be off medication and to go home. The worker added that he wanted to help the client be discharged, and the quickest way to make this happen was to help him tolerate the medication by finding possible ways of handling the side effects. The client only wanted to discuss leaving the hospital.

Realizing that he was premature in his attempt to push the medica-

tion regimen, the worker focused on the client's experiences in the hospital and his feelings about and plans for discharge for the rest of the session. Mr. Grant told the worker that he wanted to live with his parents
and was angry that they would not accept him back until he acted better. In exploring what "better" meant, the worker learned that when
Mr. Grant was on medication, his behavior was more acceptable to the
family. Although the worker empathized with the client's frustration
about his parents' attitude, he clarified the client's dilemma, saying,
"On the one hand, you don't want to take the medication because of the
way it makes you feel, but you also want to go home and your family
won't allow you to be discharged because of the way you act when you
are not on the medication." The client reluctantly agreed at least to discuss the medication issue.

Because many clients do not have a clear understanding of what to
expect from the worker or the process, the worker also can educate the
client about the nature of the interventive process that the worker en-
visions and attempt to elicit the client's willingness to proceed. For example, with a client who has never been involved in any type of
treatment process previously and does not know what he or she is supposed to do or what to expect from the worker, the worker might say,
"In order for me to help you, I need to understand what problems you
are facing, when they started, how they are affecting you and others in
your life, and what you have tried to do about them so far. Then together we can try to figure out what we can do to help you with your
difficulties, including identifying what, if anything, is getting in the
way of your resolving them."

Sometimes the expectations of client and worker are at variance. In
this case, the worker needs to establish whether it is possible for the
worker and client to come to an agreement about what the process will
entail. In making this determination, the worker first should examine
his or her own ideas about what is best for the client and modify them
if indicated, based on the client's needs and wishes. For example, there
may be workers who expect clients to talk spontaneously and fully
about their situations without direction. Should such a worker encounter a client who is unable to meet this expectation and seems anx-

ious and uncomfortable, it might be necessary for the worker to become more active in asking questions, encouraging the client's participation, and thereby alleviating the client's anxiety. If the worker remains inflexible, it is likely that the client will feel such distress that he or she will not return.

Sometimes an agency or worker is unable to offer the particular service or practice modality that the client is seeking. In such instances, it generally is preferable to refer the client to a suitable facility or provider rather than try to convince the client to accept the help available. It is inappropriate and unethical, however, for a worker to refer a client to another setting or worker merely because he or she does not like the person or because the client does not live up to the worker's expectations.

INDIVIDUALIZING THE CLIENT. In order to engage clients effectively, it is important for workers to recognize, respect, and respond sensitively to the various ways clients may approach the interventive process based on their class, gender, race, ethnicity, religion, or sexual orientation. These factors can affect how the client interacts with the worker, the degree to which the client is willing or able to share information, and the expectations that the client has about his or her participation in interventive efforts.

For example, male clients from cultures that emphasize male strength and bravado may have difficulty showing their vulnerability to a female worker; clients from backgrounds in which authority and privacy are valued highly may be reluctant to raise concerns or question the worker; and clients who belong to stigmatized or oppressed groups or have experienced discrimination may hold back important details about themselves because of their fears of being judged or rejected. In instances like these, the worker may need to acknowledge the client's mores, values, cultural background, lifestyle, reality-based fears, and the difference in certain characteristics, such as age, gender, and race, in order to establish greater comfort and trust.

A gay male client who is having conflict with his live-in partner of many years but is reticent and fearful about discussing the nature of his relationship with a worker at a local mental health clinic may become more open if the worker wonders aloud if the client's hesitancy in speaking has anything to do with concerns about being judged by the worker. A middle-aged woman whose husband has died recently and seems questioning of a young worker's ability to understand her pain and help her may be more forthcoming if the worker acknowledges the differences in their age and life experience directly.

The worker's attempt to understand the client's background and unique characteristics through asking relevant questions in itself conveys sensitivity and respect. This individualization of the client guides the ways in which the worker approaches clients and responds to their communications. Consequently, flexibility on the worker's part rather than an adherence to a single style of relating is important.

Engagement is fostered by the worker's use of words and expressions that are accessible to the client. The worker should avoid using language that might be unfamiliar to the client. For example, in an initial meeting, an inexperienced worker tried to learn more about a client's suicidal thoughts by asking if she had any "fantasies" about hurting herself. Each time the worker questioned the client about her fantasies, the client denied that she had any. At the end of the meeting, the client seemed reluctant to leave, and when the worker inquired about this, the client said she was having "daydreams" about cutting her arms. The worker was frustrated because of this late revelation and became aware that the client had not understood her use of the term *fantasies* only when her supervisor pointed this out.

In cases in which there is a more pronounced language barrier between client and worker and a translator is necessary, the worker must not only explore the client's feelings about the need for and presence of another person, but also must use other means besides words to relate to the client. Additionally, there are clients who come from backgrounds where the expression of thoughts and feelings is discouraged. It then behooves the worker to offer an explanation for why he or she is asking about such matters.

Mobilizing, Releasing, and Enhancing the Client's Motivation

Clients are propelled to seek help in order to relieve their discomfort and may show a high degree of motivation to do whatever it takes to accomplish this. In many instances, however, the client's wish to relieve his or her pain is not always accompanied by the willingness or ability to do what is required. Starting with the distress that the client experiences, the worker's task is to mobilize, release, and build the client's motivation to do the work necessary to resolve the client's difficulties. In order to accomplish this, the worker first needs to acquire an understanding of and address what is impeding the client's motivation. This task may require that the worker be able to help the client identify some positive benefit from their work together. For example, a mother who is experiencing a severe grief reaction to the death of her daughter may express the wish to feel better but also is unwilling to talk about her daughter, saying, "What's the point of talking? Nothing can bring her back." The worker acknowledges the intense pain that the mother is experiencing as well as the fact that she is right that talking will not return the child to her but also adds, "It may be impossible for you to imagine ever feeling better, but talking to someone can help you feel less alone."

Sometimes helping the client see intervention as beneficial means presenting it as the lesser of two evils. For example, a male client shows motivation to receive vocational services but must also concurrently see a worker for the purposes of discussing his experiences in the program, his ongoing needs, and plans for the future. He does not want to be involved in this process but may reluctantly comply if the worker accepts his feelings about this requirement, helps him understand that in seeing the worker, the client will be able to receive the services that he wants, and explains that the agency has found that clients who are seeing a worker are more likely to complete the program successfully.

The client's motivation is affected by the imposition of reality factors that impede his or her ability to become involved in regularly scheduled appointments. The worker should make every effort to accommodate to the client's situation rather than always expect the client to accommodate to the setting. The degree to which a worker or setting is understanding of and responsive to clients' needs often will make a difference in whether they are able to engage in the helping process.

COMPONENT 4: PLANNING INTERVENTION

The assessment process leads the worker to an understanding of the client's significant problem areas, what factors in the client's personality or situation are contributing to or impeding the resolution of the problems, and what inner strengths and outer resources can be used in ameliorating the client's difficulties. Based on this assessment, the worker and client arrive at a plan of intervention in which they establish goals, that is, what they will try to accomplish, and a focus, what they will work on.

In ISTT, the worker is guided by the belief that achieving even limited goals can bring relief to clients and improve their functioning. Although it may be possible in some cases to set realistic and meaningful goals and to select a focus even in the first meeting, generally this will take as many as three sessions. In planning intervention, the worker engages in several key activities.

Partializing the Problem

Often clients are overwhelmed by their difficulties and do not know where to begin in order to help themselves. Sometimes they have only a vague and general notion about what is wrong. Further, problems often are multifaceted and complex, and the client may exhibit more than one problem. For all these reasons, the worker needs to help the client break the problem down into manageable parts, a process called *partialization*. This process includes prioritizing the different problems or elements of the problem in terms of their immediacy and significance. Partializing in this way reduces the client's feelings of paralysis and confusion and provides them with some sense of control and hope.

THE TYLER CASE

Ms. Tyler, a 45-year-old divorced bookkeeper, was referred to the social worker at the clinic to which she accompanied her elderly father for his routine medical appointments. One of the staff observed that she was crying in the waiting area. In talking with the worker, Ms. Tyler was quite emotional and tended to ventilate about all of the difficulties she was experiencing in trying to care for her father while dealing with the mounting pressures on her job. In addition to her father's increasing physical deterioration and dependence, he was belligerent and accusatory and repeatedly called her at work. Her employer was becoming impatient with these interruptions and with the client's preoccupation. Ms. Tyler kept saying that she did not know what to do but felt she could not go on much longer working and trying to care for her father at home. She valued her job and did not want to quit, nor could she afford to do so. Clearly overwhelmed, the client reported feeling anxious, exhausted, and depressed; had feelings of worthlessness, resentment, and guilt; had difficulty getting up in the morning; and was isolated from friends. An only child, she had no other family supports.

The worker's first priority was to help the client feel less overwhelmed. After exploring and acknowledging the various components of the client's difficulties, the worker said, "You are experiencing many stresses, but it is important to keep in mind that you do not have to solve everything at once and that together we can deal with the situation one step at a time." Because the client had no time to herself and was greatly fatigued by all of her responsibilities, the worker observed, "Not having any time for yourself and having to be with your father so many hours seems to be a major problem. Perhaps that's where we can begin." The client was relieved at this suggestion but also expressed her guilt about wanting time for herself. She also did not know how to manage her father's calls to the office. The worker indicated that these problems were related and that she could help the client with them.

Determining Goals and Foci

After viewing the whole constellation of problems that the client presents, the client's capacities, strengths, and resources, and the client's expectations and motivation, the worker and client establish specific goals. In order to do this, the worker selects those aspects of the client's difficulties that require immediate attention and seem most amenable to influence or change. Other considerations in this choice are what the client is motivated to work on and finding some aspect of the problem that allows the client to experience some sense of accomplishment. This is especially important when clients' problems are longstanding, or they feel overwhelmed and powerless. The client's ability to take even some small steps in alleviating his or her difficulties engenders confidence and increases motivation.

Ms. Tyler, the client described previously, showed a number of problems that needed attention. She and the worker agreed that the first goal of intervention was to relieve some of Ms. Tyler's actual caretaking responsibilities by finding someone in the community who could spend several hours a day with her father. The worker thought that easing the client's burden might reduce some of the client's distress and increase her ability to deal with other aspects of her situation. The client was motivated to work on this goal because of her wish to have some time for herself. At the same time, it was necessary to help the client with her feelings of guilt and resentment toward her father and to discuss ways in which she could limit and manage his calls.

The worker and client identified certain steps that would help to bring about the goal. Ms. Tyler agreed to call her father's physician and her church pastor to inquire about possible caretakers. The worker volunteered that she would check contacts at the clinic and call the local visiting nurses' association. In their meetings together, the worker and client discussed the pros and cons of different options, Ms. Tyler's fears that her father would reject outside help, her current interaction with her father and ways to deal with his demands, and her feelings of responsibility and resentment.

Although it took a month to locate a part-time aide for her father and to put the plan in place, Ms. Tyler felt energized by doing something about her situation, less burdened, and more able to assert herself with her father, particularly in limiting the amount of time she spoke to him from work. It then became possible to address her isolation through locating a support group for caretakers and encouraging her to form outside relationships.

In some instances, the decision about what to work on will involve helping the client with his or her underlying problems. In most cases, however, this will not be necessary, as shown in the following two brief examples.

Murray, a bright 10-year-old boy, was referred to the school social worker because of his disruptive and acting-out behavior in the classroom. He was in danger of being removed from school. As a result of her assessment, the worker determined that the likely contributors to Murray's problem in school were mainly his poor impulse control and judgment. She also learned that his acting out first appeared after his parents had separated three months earlier and that they overtly disparaged one another to Murray.

The worker concluded that these underlying and contributing factors, while significant, should not be addressed immediately and might be discussed later if the current situation improved. Because Murray was in jeopardy of being expelled from school and upset by this possibility, the worker decided on the goal of helping him to remain in school by focusing initially on assisting him to control his anger and improve his judgment. She thought she could make a difference rather quickly in this area and evaluated Murray as having the capacity and motivation to work on these aspects of his behavior. The worker planned to meet with his teacher in order to gain her interest and cooperation in helping Murray.

Sue Ellen, a teenage single mother, sought help from the social worker in the high school she was attending because she was conflicted about what to do when she graduated in two months. She lived with her father and stepmother, who wanted her to attend college. She was more interested in obtaining employment and securing an apartment for her and her daughter so that she could devote herself to caring for the child.

The worker's assessment led her to conclude that Sue Ellen's decision to have and care for a child was related to early abandonment by her own mother and the girl's wish to make up for her past loss. She was concerned that this underlying issue might lead Sue Ellen to make an uninformed decision. She also recognized that it would be futile to try to help Sue Ellen gain insight into this important issue in the light of her stated request and the constraints of time. Instead, the worker and client agreed on the goal of helping Sue Ellen come to a firm decision about her immediate plans at the end of the school term; in order to do this, they would focus on discussing the pros and cons of the various options she was considering.

In these cases, the workers' assessments led them to conclude that it was not essential to deal with the underlying and contributing aspects to Murray's and Sue Ellen's presenting problems in order to help them. In some situations, however, additional difficulties or underlying problems may need to be addressed in order to improve the client's situation, as the following two examples illustrate.

Ms. Georgette, a recent 35-year-old female emigré, sought help in finding employment. The worker discovered that in addition to lacking information about how to locate jobs, the client could not travel on public transportation because of her inability to read English, she had a poor work history due to conflicts with employers, and she was unrealistic about the types of jobs for which she was qualified. Based on his assessment, the worker determined that the provision of information about occupational resources would not be sufficient to help this client. He concluded that it would be necessary to help the client with her other problems, that is, her unrealistic expectations, inability to read English, and underlying difficulties with employers, in order for her to be able to obtain and keep a job.

The worker tactfully explained why he thought Ms. Georgette was having difficulties securing a job and expressed his interest in helping her with each of the issues. When he asked her what she first wanted to focus on, she said she did not know. The worker said that it seemed that the client had a lot to deal with but that her inability to read English seemed crucial in her difficulties. When the client agreed, the worker suggested that it might be helpful for them to explore where she might learn to read English and talk more about her qualifications for work and the kinds of problems that she had experienced in keeping her jobs previously.

Ms. Moore, a 55-year-old diabetic woman who had lost her vision steadily in recent years and was now legally blind, was referred repeat-

edly by her physician for help in developing skills in improving the quality of her life. Initially she did not follow through with this suggestion, and when she finally did call for an appointment, she failed to keep it. As her situation became more urgent, she again contacted the agency. Although she saw the intake worker, she showed considerable hesitancy in committing herself to attending the classes that would help her learn braille and ways of getting around, and provide information about activities and resources for the blind.

In carrying out the assessment, the worker realized that Ms. Moore had not accepted the reality of being blind nor had she dealt with the powerful meaning of her vision loss. The worker recognized that the client was not emotionally ready to undertake any of the setting's programs and that it was necessary to offer her the opportunity to talk about her hesitancy and her feelings about her condition.

COMPONENT 5: CONTRACTING

Planning and implementing intervention is not a one-sided process but involves the active collaboration of both worker and client. One way of ensuring that the worker and client are proceeding together is for them to make an explicit agreement about the problem to be addressed and the goals, focus, and structure of intervention. This action, called contracting, optimally solidifies the engagement process and is not meant to be legalistic or mechanical. Its intent is to provide a common basis from which to proceed. Its exact nature varies according to the client and the agency, can be general or highly specific and detailed, or can be verbal or formalized in writing.

Generally a full contract might include (1) the problem area; (2) the goals of intervention; (3) the means for working on the problems; (4) the duration of contact, length and frequency of meetings, and cancellation policies; (5) the worker's responsibilities with respect to activity, consistency, availability, and confidentiality; and (6) the client's responsibilities for attendance, payment, and participation.

In some situations, the client, despite exhibiting numerous problems that seem to need attention, may show ambivalence, hesitancy, wariness, or resentment about obtaining help. In these instances, agreeing explicitly to further exploration of the client's feelings about being involved in interventive efforts needs to take precedence over contracting around specific problem areas. Although contracting around this issue may seem unnecessary, it demonstrates respect for and understanding of the client, draws the client into decision making, and fosters mutuality.

The contract needs to be kept in the forefront of the interventive process because it helps to maintain direction. Either worker or client may call attention to the contract at times when the work becomes unfocused, vague, or tangential or if either participant is not adhering to the agreed-on structure, for example, by missing appointments or not calling to cancel. In these situations, it may be necessary to explore and understand the meaning of such behaviors, as will be discussed in Chapter 5. Nevertheless, the contract should be flexible as new needs and concerns arise and may require renegotiation over time.

SUMMARY

This chapter has considered different aspects of the engagement process, including the importance of establishing a facilitating environment; being where the client is; and mobilizing, releasing, and building the client's motivation. It discussed planning intervention, which includes partializing and selecting goals and focus, and contracting.

Chapter 5

The Middle Phase: Part I

B ecause ISTT draws on a range of methods and interventive techniques, both worker and client engage in many different types of
activity during the middle phase, a period in which the bulk of the
work is accomplished. Thus, it reflects considerable variability from
client to client, and its specific form stems from the individualized
goals and focus established in each case.

There are five components of the middle phase of ISTT: (1) implementing the interventive plan, (2) maintaining the focus, (3) monitoring progress, (4) dealing with obstacles to change, and (5)
managing the client-worker relationship. This chapter discusses and illustrates the first three of these components.

COMPONENT 6: IMPLEMENTING THE INTERVENTIVE PLAN

ISTT draws on techniques that are used in other forms of treatment,
including those that are open-ended or long term, and employs them
in a more active and focused manner.

Interventive Techniques

The following list of interventions and their definitions is not meant
to be exhaustive. Instead, it is a compilation of techniques that have
been identified frequently in work with individual clients. Some of

these are more general techniques, and others are more specialized and circumscribed.

GENERAL TECHNIQUES. Included in this grouping are those person and environmental interventions that comprise a common core of interventions used with most clients:

Ventilation, which involves providing clients with an opportunity to express their feelings about themselves, their life situation and experiences, and their reactions to the interventive process and the worker.

Sustainment, which involves the worker's attempts to empathize with the client by showing that he or she understands what the client is experiencing and to offer acknowledgment, validation, encouragement, and reassurance when appropriate. Sustainment can be achieved verbally and behaviorally through attentive listening, eye contact, and body language.

Exploration, which involves the worker's efforts to learn about clients' problems, thoughts, feelings, and behavior; current life situation and background; capacities, strengths, and external supports; and expectations and reactions to the interventive process and the worker.

Clarification, which involves the worker's attempts to clear up areas of vagueness, confusion, and contradiction in what clients say and to determine their understanding of the implications of their communications.

Rational discussion, in which the worker discusses various courses of action or options and their pros and cons with the client.

Reflection, in which the worker asks clients to consider and think about their thoughts, feelings, and behavior; the implications, consequences, and possible motivations and factors contributing to their difficulties; the consequences of various courses of action on themselves and others; and the motivations, feelings, and behavior of others.

Partialization, in which the worker helps clients to break down their difficulties into smaller and more manageable parts.

Education, in which the worker provides information to the client that is essential to his or her participation in the interventive process, functioning in various roles, accessing needed resources or services, and negotiating external systems.

Advice and guidance, in which the worker suggests possible ways of thinking, feeling, and behaving to the client. Advice and guidance should be used sparingly because of the importance of engaging the client's thinking about options and showing respect for the client's self-determination, strengths, and capacities.

Use of the positive relationship, in which the worker provides a safe, empathic, accepting, and encouraging presence so that clients can more easily share their thoughts and feelings; feel less alone; engage in a dialogue about their difficulties; try out new ways of thinking, feeling, and behaving; and get support in times of disappointment, setbacks, and success.

Recognizing and acknowledging strengths and accomplishments, in which the worker helps clients to identify adaptive capacities, positive traits, efforts to help themselves, small gains, and major achievements.

Use of adjunctive resources, in which the worker and client make use of additional resources or services that can be of benefit to the client in ameliorating or resolving his or her difficulties.

Collaboration, in which the worker engages with others who are significant in the client's life, involved in assisting the client, or necessary to the helping process in order to assist the client.

Advocacy, in which the worker communicates the client's needs and interests to others or intervenes to secure services on behalf of the client.

Linkage, in which the worker helps to connect the client to needed resources or services.

Mediation, in which the worker helps to negotiate between the client and others so that the client's needs can be met.

SPECIALIZED TECHNIQUES. Included in this grouping are more circumscribed techniques that are used selectively in dealing with certain types of problems and achieving certain goals:

Facilitating verbalization, in which the worker helps clients to put their thoughts and feelings into words. This is an important intervention in work with those who are not accustomed to or lack the ability to express their feelings to another person, have a tendency toward action rather than verbalization, or do not always know what they are feeling.

Reaching out, in which the worker demonstrates his or her interest in helping clients by such efforts as contacting them if they have missed appointments, offering additional appointments or telephone communication if they are undergoing increased stress or are ill, or making home visits when indicated.

Recognizing the impact of broader sociopolitical realities, in which the worker helps clients to consider the impact of such influences as racism, sexism, homophobia, ageism, cultural bias, poverty, violence, changing values and norms, immigration, and other societal and environmental factors on their lives and problems.

Providing a real object experience, in which the worker selectively meets the client's needs for a more real and genuine relationship. This may involve accompanying a client to an activity or agency; answering some personal questions or sharing some personal experiences; meeting certain unmet needs, for example, for attention, validation, applause, or dependence; and participating in shared activities such as writing resumés, looking through want ads, doing homework, and filling out job applications.

Lending ego, in which the worker uses his or her own abilities and presence to augment or substitute for the client's capacities, which may be inadequate or temporarily impaired. This may involve making telephone calls, filling out forms, or speaking to family, employers, or teachers; protecting the client or others; arranging for medical care and performing other types of concrete assistance; and urging the client to take certain actions in his or her best interest.

Mirroring, in which the worker responds in keeping with the client's needs for recognition, validation, applause, admiration, and pride.

Structuring, in which the worker helps the client to establish routines, recreation, schedules, budgets, work habits, and other activities of daily life.

Setting limits, in which the worker establishes guidelines, collabora-
tively if possible, for the client's behavior so that the worker and
client can work together.

Confrontation, in which the worker nonjudgmentally points out discrepancies, contradictions, negative consequences, maladaptive
defenses, resistances, and problematic traits and patterns.

Interpretation, in which the worker offers possible reasons for the
client's perceptions, attitudes, feelings, patterns of relating, characteristic or unusual behavior, defenses, resistance, conflicts, and
problems. Sometimes these reasons link early past events and experiences in the client's life to his or her current functioning and
difficulties.

Clarification of patterns of thinking, feeling, and perceiving, in which
the worker uncovers or amplifies clients' often hidden irrational
ideas or distortions and provides feedback about what clients are
thinking and telling themselves and how they are behaving.

Offering new ways of thinking, feeling, and perceiving, in which the
worker explores distortions and misconceptions that the client
shows and challenges these, offering new ways of thinking, feeling, perceiving, and behaving.

Rehearsal, in which the worker helps clients to anticipate and prepare for certain interactions or scenarios by practicing what they
might say and do.

Role modeling, in which the worker exhibits certain attitudes, traits,
and behaviors that clients can take on and use for themselves.

Role playing, in which the worker and client enact certain types of
interactions or roles in order to help the client practice new behaviors or gain understanding of how others think and feel.

Homework and task assignment, in which the worker and client agree
on steps or actions that the client can take outside their meetings
as part of the helping process.

Worker-Client Activity

The process of the middle phase is driven by the individualized goals
for each client. Each of the following examples, which contain ex-

cerpts from the middle phase of work with three clients, illustrates a different clustering of techniques.

THE CASE OF CLAIRE

Claire, a 16-year-old African American high school student, came to a neighborhood family service agency in a lower-socioeconomic area of New York City a month after she had been physically harassed and verbally taunted on her way home from school by a group of eight white girls. Although she was not hurt, Claire was terrified and refused to go back to school. Believing that Claire would get over the incident in time, her mother accepted her staying home, but Claire never did return to classes. Instead she performed chores and cooked dinner for her and her mother. She also cried frequently. A month later, she finally agreed to get some counseling at her mother's urging.

Claire told the worker that since the harassment incident, she had been fearful that something might happen to her again if she went to school. Because Claire seemed depressed, the worker wondered if there might be other factors underlying Claire's difficulties. Based on interviews with Claire and her mother, exploration indicated that Claire had a history of generally adequate ego functioning and was a good student, but she appeared shy and lacking in confidence, socialized infrequently, had no close friends, and exhibited a strong empathic attachment to her mother, a single parent with whom she spent most of her free time. The worker speculated that Claire's difficulty returning to school seemed to be based only in part on her feelings of lack of safety and vulnerability. It seemed likely that both separation and socialization issues also were connected to her difficulties.

The agency offered 12 sessions of treatment, including the assessment and contracting, which took two meetings. During the initial visits, Claire was hesitant and cautious but agreed to meet with the worker in order to facilitate Claire's return to school. In order to accomplish this, the worker thought it was important to help Claire to (1) express her fears, (2) find ways of increasing her sense of safety, (3) discuss her relationship with her mother in order to help her to separate from her, and (4) help her to socialize with others.

In the third meeting, the worker asked Claire to describe the harassment incident in greater detail and attempted to reach for Claire's feelings about what had occurred. When Claire became visibly agitated, the worker commented on her obvious distress, empathized with how upsetting the attack had been, and encouraged her to talk more about how it had made her feel. As Claire began to describe her anger at the "white bitches" who had attacked her, she stopped abruptly and seemed reticent to continue despite the worker's efforts. The worker then asked Claire if she was frightened of speaking about her anger to the worker because she, like the harassers, was also White. Stunned by the worker's question, Claire nevertheless nodded. The worker acknowledged that Claire's talking about her feelings might feel unsafe but added that she wanted to hear what Claire had to say and was not going to be offended, angry, or blaming. In response, Claire became more communicative.

The next few sessions centered on Claire's fears about her safety if she were to return to school and on her daily activities. In describing the chores that she did at home, she looked pleased and somewhat proud of herself. The worker wondered aloud if Claire was happy about being able to help her mother. Claire then spoke at length about how much her mother had sacrificed for her and how it made her feel good when her mom seemed relieved and in a good mood when she came home from work to a clean house with dinner on the table. The worker noted that it was a real strength that Claire was so helpful and thoughtful in spite of how upset she felt. Claire seemed pleased but then became sad. When the worker attempted to understand Claire's mixed response, she revealed that she missed school but worried about leaving her mother. When asked what she missed about school, she said she liked her classes and teachers but sometimes wished she had more friends. This opening led to a more in-depth discussion of her difficulties in reaching out to and relating to peers. The worker said, "There are a number of things we can do right now. We can try to help you feel safer about going to school, talk about ways you might make some new friends, and discuss your feelings about helping your mom. What do you want to do first?" Claire said she wanted to feel safer and wanted to know how the worker could help her make new friends.

In the sixth session, when Claire could not think of what might help *her to feel safer and make new friends, the worker made suggestions, and they discussed various options. Claire agreed to call an acquaintance to accompany her to school and to think about some social activities that she might like to pursue.*

Claire did not appear for the next meeting. When the worker called her at home to inquire about her absence, Claire blurted out that she had not gone to school and was fearful that the worker would be disappointed in her. The worker said that she understood that it was hard for Claire, and they made another appointment. When they met again, Claire said that she had called a girl who agreed to accompany her to school but Claire had not been able to follow through. The worker said that it was a positive sign that Claire had called her friend and wondered if Claire thought that there was more involved in her staying home than her concerns about her safety. Claire responded that she was worried and nervous that her mother would be upset when she came home and dinner was not ready. She had not talked to her mother about her worries because she did not want to burden her. After discussing her concerns further, the worker asked if it would help for all three of them to talk together. Claire readily agreed, and an appointment was arranged.

At this meeting, the mother acknowledged that Claire had been making life easier for her but was able to convey with some feeling that it would help rather than upset her if Claire returned to school. The mother discussed her reliance on Claire emotionally and indicated that Claire was "all she had." Because the mother appeared lonely herself, seemed to have few social outlets, and was inadvertently communicating her need for Claire to her daughter, the worker suggested that it might be helpful for the two of them to talk further about her situation in order to help her reach out to others. The mother readily agreed, and Claire seemed relieved.

The work with Claire and her mother that continued for several sessions focused on Claire's eventual return to school, her efforts to make friends, and the mother's efforts to locate a single parents' group.

Discussion

The worker's attempts to help Claire return to school led to her employing a variety of techniques. In addition to exploring Claire's diffi-

culties in more detail, she encouraged ventilation and offered sustainment. At times she clarified the meaning of Claire's communications, partialized the problem areas, engaged in rational discussion, offered advice about possible courses of action, and suggested tasks for Claire. The worker reached out to Claire by telephone when she missed her appointment, used reflection to see if she could consider the reasons for her not following through on her assignment, and involved the mother in a collaborative effort. At several points, the worker acknowledged Claire's strengths and small accomplishments. All of this work was done in the context of a positive worker-client relationship.

THE LOPEZ CASE

Mr. Lopez, a 19-year-old Hispanic high school dropout, who resided with his mother in a crime-ridden area of the city, appeared at a neighborhood family service agency accompanied by his mother. Although he came at his mother's insistence, he was cooperative with the intake worker. Both his mother and Mr. Lopez agreed that he had multiple difficulties: dropping out of school, quitting jobs, substance abuse, and some minor brushes with the police. Mr. Lopez said that he had tried to do better, but something always interfered with his staying on course. Although he was enrolled in a vocational training program, his attendance was irregular, he was smoking marijuana and drinking more frequently, and he was associating with others who were frequently in trouble with the law.

Mr. Lopez had a history of becoming easily discouraged at having to work hard with few immediate financial rewards. His peers demeaned his efforts and tried to lure him into making easy money by dealing drugs and stealing cars. When Mr. Lopez felt upset or frustrated, he had little ability to manage his feelings, control his impulses, or use good judgment, tending to avoid his obligations and escaping into alcohol and drugs.

The assessment suggested that Mr. Lopez had several strengths. He was motivated to work on his problems, intelligent, somewhat self-reflective, had family supports, enjoyed good relationships with his mother and members of his extended family, was ambitious and hard working, and showed many efforts to try to get his life together. Nevertheless, he faced environmental pressures that impeded his efforts to improve his situation, and his neighborhood and peer network provided few examples of those who had finished school, remained drug free, obtained well-paying and satisfying jobs, and enjoyed the respect of others in the community. In terms of personality issues, Mr. Lopez also showed problems with affect regulation, impulse control, judgment, and self-esteem. The worker also wondered to what degree Mr. Lopez's difficulties stemmed in part from his feeling that as a Hispanic male in an oppressive dominant culture, he would not have the opportunities available to nonminorities.

The agency offered 20 sessions. The main goal of intervention was to help Mr. Lopez to remain in the vocational training program. In order to accomplish this, the worker thought it would be necessary to address both personal and environmental factors by improving Mr. Lopez's capacity to identify the triggers for his missing class, helping him to learn to manage his feelings in more adaptive ways, linking him to activities that would present him with the opportunity to make new friends, and helping him to control his substance use.

The first two meetings with a male Hispanic worker explored the circumstances surrounding the client's missing class, seeking out friends, substance use, and getting into difficulty with the police. In response to Mr. Lopez's blaming himself for being weak, the worker acknowledged his feelings but said that it would be more helpful for the two of them together to try to understand the reasons for his actions and to find ways of helping him to stay on track than to continue to accuse himself. Although Mr. Lopez was involved in these meetings, he missed the next scheduled session.

When the client and worker met again, Mr. Lopez said that he had forgotten they had an appointment because he was out drinking with his friends. The worker asked how the client had felt about their meetings. The client responded that everything was okay. The worker commented that sometimes talking about problems can be difficult because one does not always know how to deal with the feelings that come up, and it is easy to fall back on familiar ways of handling or avoiding feelings. Mr. Lopez said, "I almost didn't come today, but my mom made me." The worker said that it was good that Mr. Lopez came despite how he felt, but asked Mr. Lopez if he resented his mother's intervention and was just coming "to get her off his back." Mr. Lopez said he knew she wanted what was best for him, and he wanted help too. The worker commented that what was occurring between them was repeating what was happening in other situations: Mr. Lopez's difficulties following through even though he wanted to. The client seemed surprised but acknowledged that he guessed that was true but did not know how to stop himself. The worker responded that this was what they needed to discuss but that in order to do this it was necessary for the client to be present. He then asked Mr. Lopez what might help him keep the appointments. The client spontaneously said that it might help if the worker called to remind him, and the worker readily agreed.

The rest of the session focused on what had led Mr. Lopez to seek out his friends. He was able to recall that just prior to meeting with his friends, he had had a conversation with his mother in which she expressed disappointment in his irregular attendance at the vocational training program, immediately after which he ran out of the apartment, hoping to meet up with his friends. When the worker asked what Mr. Lopez felt during the talk with his mother, he said he did not know. When the worker pressed him to think more about his feelings, the client said that maybe he was angry but also added that he felt upset that his mother was disappointed in him. The worker responded that when the client had upsetting feelings, he must want to get rid of them and that it was possible that one way was to go drinking with his friends. Mr. Lopez said, "What else am I supposed to do? Nobody cares about us. There's no jobs, nothing to do. Getting high is all there is."

The worker asked Mr. Lopez if he thought being poor and a Hispanic male were strikes against him. After Mr. Lopez expressed his bitter feelings about this subject, the worker acknowledged some of the harsh realities of his situation and said, "It's understandable if you feel mad and hopeless at times. I know it's not easy out there." Mr. Lopez responded that sometimes he did not know why he was even trying because the deck was stacked against him. The worker empathized with the client's feelings, adding, "There are no simple answers, but there are things that we can do together to make your life a little better."

In the fourth session, Mr. Lopez reported that he had missed only one day of school, to be with his friends and do some smoking. The worker explored what might have led to his day off, and with some prodding, Mr. Lopez was able to recall a negative comment by his teacher that left him feeling discouraged. The worker connected this experience to the client's not going to school the next day and his need to try to make himself feel better. Mr. Lopez commented, "I felt good when I was high, but I felt down on myself later because I let myself down again." The worker brought up the client's remark from the previous session that there was nothing for him to do other than hang out with his friends. He suggested that in addition to it being important for Mr. Lopez to recognize that his upsetting feelings led him to do things that he felt regretful about, it also might help if they could identify some interesting activities that the client could pursue. A discussion of Mr. Lopez's interests revealed that the two activities that he really enjoyed were soccer and working out, but he had not done these recently. When the worker asked Mr. Lopez if he wanted him to look into where there might be soccer teams nearby, the client said that would be fine. The worker asked the client if, in the meantime, he might try working out when he felt like getting high. The client said he would try but could not promise anything.

In the fifth session, Mr. Lopez reported that he had tried working out a couple of times and liked it. When his friends saw him running, however, they made fun of him and cajoled him into coming with them. After acknowledging Mr. Lopez's efforts and empathizing with his having been in a tough spot, the worker asked why he thought his friends were discouraging his efforts to change. Mr. Lopez responded, "They want me to be like them." Realizing that it was too early in their work to expect Mr. Lopez to give up his friends or to attend Alcoholics Anonymous (AA), the worker suggested that Mr. Lopez might think of a new route for his running. Later in the session, Mr. Lopez asked the worker if he had found a soccer team, and the worker suggested a few possibilities located in nearby communities. Although Mr. Lopez seemed eager to learn about the teams, he voiced misgivings about leaving his neighborhood; he had never gone to a strange area on his own. When the worker asked if it would help if he accompanied Mr.

Lopez, he looked surprised but pleased, and they arranged a time to visit the teams.

When the worker called Mr. Lopez to confirm their meeting, the mother told him that her son had left a message that he was not going to go with him but would see him at their regular appointment time. He came late for his session and was uncommunicative. With some urging, the client shared that he had missed several days of school, felt discouraged, and was thinking of dropping out of the vocational program. The worker commented that he was glad Mr. Lopez had come to their appointment and that usually when he missed school, something had occurred to trigger his reactions. Although he did not spontaneously recall anything that had upset him, he did remember a disturbing incident when the worker asked him to describe the events of the last day he had attended school. One of the teachers became angry when several members of the class were disruptive. He told the class that they were losers and would never get decent jobs. When asked how this insult was connected to his not going to school, the client responded that the teacher was unfair, and this made him angry. The worker replied, "So why would your teacher's being a jerk make you not go to school and cancel our visit to the soccer teams? You just wind up hurting yourself, not the teacher." The client said he did not know but just felt angry at everything. The worker commented that the client's anger was understandable but that his way of dealing with his anger was problematic and they needed to continue to work on this.

Discussion

In order to help the client remain in the vocational training program, the worker employed general exploratory, reflective, and sustaining techniques and specialized interventions aimed at improving Mr. Lopez's ego functioning in selected areas. The worker helped the client to identify and verbalize his feelings, reflect on the connection between his feelings and the events that triggered them, and discuss ways in which the client could better manage his feelings. In addition, the worker encouraged ventilation of his bitterness about the impact of racism and discrimination and connected his feelings about this subject to his sense of hopelessness. He offered advice and guidance, reached *out to the client, used the positive relationship and was a real object to the client, recognized the client's strengths and accomplishments, linked the client to activities that would serve as an outlet for his feelings and provide him with new means of coping with them, and used some confrontation and interpretation of the client's self-defeating behaviors and pattern of avoidance.*

THE BRISCO CASE

Mr. Brisco, a 45-year-old computer programmer and project manager, sought help at his wife's urging because he was becoming increasingly withdrawn at home and irritable with her and their children. In the first and later meetings, the worker was struck by the contrast between Mr. Brisco's intelligent and articulate verbal presentation and his disheveled physical appearance. When asked to talk about what was making him unhappy, he spoke of his uncertainty about whether to stay in his present job and spontaneously admitted that he was bringing his work problems home.

The exploration of Mr. Brisco's current employment revealed that he had developed a computer program application that he thought would be financially lucrative for his company and for him personally. Although the program was moderately successful, Mr. Brisco thought his employer was inept at marketing it and ignored his advice. Consequently, he felt angry and powerless and feared that his chance "to make it big" was disappearing. He also reported that the company was in a financially tenuous position, and he worried that it might fold. He wanted to leave the job but could not mobilize himself to look for work.

Significant in the client's work history was his having had a series of frustrating jobs, each lasting several years and ending because of the client's feelings of disappointment and anger at his employer. Mr. Brisco began each job thinking that his accomplishments would bring him great recognition and financial rewards. When these did not materialize, he became dissatisfied and disgruntled. He vacillated between aspiring to great success and believing that he should have followed a more secure but mundane career.

Personal and family history yielded the fact that Mr. Brisco had al-

ways wanted to be different from his father, who had worked in the same civil service position for thirty-five years despite his chronic unhappiness. Mr. Brisco was a loner who spent much of his early years fantasizing about inventing things. He was a mediocre student but worked hard. He wanted to be a musician. Although he pursued this for a time, he was not successful and turned to computer work. He had a stable but unhappy marriage.

Because further exploration revealed Mr. Brisco's long-standing personality traits of pessimism and negativity, the worker initially felt unsure if Mr. Brisco's work situation was as bad as he described. In addition, Mr. Brisco's attitudes about himself and others, his physical appearance, his reported interactions at work, and his irritability at home showed selected areas of problematic ego functioning, including episodically poor judgment, grandiose ambitions alternating with a sense of low self-esteem, somewhat impaired reality testing at times, poor object relations, and problems with affect regulation. The worker speculated that Mr. Brisco was having difficulty valuing what he had been able to achieve professionally at this point in his life, impatient because of the lack of recognition he desired, and also did not know how to collaborate effectively and get what he needed from his boss. Despite these difficulties, Mr. Brisco had numerous strengths. He was motivated to work on his problems and had a reliable support system. He was physically healthy, intelligent, capable of self-reflection, hard working, honest, and competent occupationally.

Mr. Brisco's insurance coverage allowed for the possibility of 20 sessions. The goal was to help him clarify the issues that were leading to his ambivalence about his work situation and either to help him accommodate to his work situation or embark on a successful job search.

In the second through fourth sessions, Mr. Brisco described the project he had worked on and its potential for being financially lucrative and gaining industry recognition. He vented his anger at his employer for not engaging in a far-reaching public relations and marketing strategy. He also discussed his anxiety about the future of the business and portrayed the business as in a state of near bankruptcy. When the worker explored further, she learned that the employer always seemed able to get new investors who would rescue the business at the last *minute. The worker asked Mr. Brisco if he might be unduly worried about the viability of the company, to which he responded that he always took the boss seriously when he complained about money but was beginning to wonder if his boss exaggerated the extent of the financial problems for his own purposes. Thus far, the boss had always been able to meet his financial obligations, and the company had increased its gross sales over time. This led to a discussion of the various alternatives that the client had considered—for example, staying on the job for a time-limited period to see if the business would survive, developing a marketing strategy of his own and discussing it with his employer, or looking for other jobs. Mr. Brisco felt that his boss was unreachable yet still hoped that he would come through.*

The worker empathized with Mr. Brisco's desire for success and frustration with his employer. This led to an outpouring of feelings of disappointment about his career and his previous jobs. He described each of his job situations in more detail. Although he felt that the previous employers had been difficult, he also acknowledged that he was impatient and would get angry rather than "play the game." He liked to do his work and recognized that he was not good at conducting his interpersonal relationships on the job. The worker asked Mr. Brisco if he set extremely high standards and expectations for himself and others, was impatient when he did not receive the recognition that he felt he deserved and when others did not perform as he thought they should, and was not able to accept more modest achievements on the job. Mr. Brisco said that this was probably true but he always thought he would be further along at age 45 and went on to discuss his feelings of failure.

In the fifth session, Mr. Brisco mentioned that he had spoken to his father, who urged him not to leave the job and lectured him on the value of civil service positions. This response angered the client. After discussing the father-son relationship, the worker asked if it were possible that Mr. Brisco's need "to make it big," his feelings of failure, and his growing frustration when he did not receive the recognition he deserved was related to his need to prove to his father that his way was right. These questions struck a chord. Mr. Brisco went on to discuss how important it was to him to be more success-

ful than his father had been and to show his father that he was right
not to take his advice to take a civil service job. The worker asked
Mr. Brisco if some of his frustration with his employer for not helping him might be connected in some way to his disappointment in
and anger at his father. The client said thoughtfully that he had
never considered that idea but acknowledged that he had a lot of resentment toward his father.

In the sixth meeting, the client unexpectedly reported that he had
gone on two job interviews but had received no job offer. This distressed him because he felt he had so much to offer, and he wondered
what had gone wrong. The worker acknowledged his disappointment
but questioned the client's view that he should have landed the first jobs
he applied for. Mr. Brisco responded that he guessed that he was not
being too realistic but did feel that he should not have to prove himself
because he had so much experience. This opening led to further exploration of why it was so important for him to prove himself and how this
need led him to put a lot of pressure on himself and resulted in his frequent frustration with his job situations.

In the seventh session, Mr. Brisco again reported on some job interviews that he had pursued that had not gone well. His description of
these meetings and how he had presented himself both physically and
verbally made the worker ask the client if he thought it was possible he
was contributing to his lack of interview success in some way. Mr.
Brisco recognized that he had not felt as excited or invested in these interviews, may have seemed indifferent, and had not attempted to dress
appropriately for the occasion. He reported becoming somewhat argumentative with a much younger male interviewer who tested his knowledge of the computer field. He realized that he had sabotaged himself in
the interview.

When the worker acknowledged how difficult it must have been to
have to deal with this man, the client expressed dismay that the work
environment was quite different than it was previously and said he felt
inadequate to compete. The worker empathized with his feelings of inadequacy and anger when his experience and competence were chal-
lenged. The client brought up spontaneously that this reminded him of
times when he was a child, and other kids bullied him. After exploring

some of these early experiences, the worker noted that Mr. Brisco had come a long way from his childhood, had considerable expertise, and could compete in the work environment. She asked Mr. Brisco to consider whether seeking a new job truly was in his best interests at this time or whether it represented a repetition of his pattern of being frustrated at what he felt like a lack of sufficient recognition, leaving his job, finding another in which he had to start over, and then becoming disappointed again. Mr. Brisco said that he did see a pattern in his job changes and really wanted to stay at his company if he thought he had a future there and could get along better with his boss. The worker said that they could talk more about this.

In the eighth session, Mr. Brisco began talking about the increased sales at the job and the potential market if only it could be tapped. He said he had been feeling better about staying on the job for a time to give it a chance and reported that his employer seemed to have an endless supply of potential investors who were impressed with the business. This led to a discussion of how Mr. Brisco might enlist the help of some other co-workers with respect to getting his employer to try some new marketing strategies. He was not sure how to go about doing this, and he and the worker discussed several strategies for the remainder of the session.

Discussion

The worker used the general techniques of exploration, sustainment, ventilation, clarification, rational discussion, reflection, recognition of strengths and accomplishments, and use of the positive relationship. This work with Mr. Brisco required greater reliance on reflection and interpretation centering on the client's work patterns, conflicting needs and wishes, compensatory grandiosity, and self-defeating behavior. In addition, the worker offered to help the client find new ways of dealing with his employer and with co-workers.

COMPONENT 7: MAINTAINING OR ALTERING THE FOCUS

In ISTT, each session should bear some relationship to the achievement of the established goals. It is the worker's responsibility to maintain the focus of intervention. Nevertheless, there are times when the initial focus must be altered or expanded to accommodate changes in the client's situation or new problem areas.

Redirecting the Client

Sometimes maintaining the focus requires that the worker redirect the client's communication. This structuring should be flexible, however, because it is important that the client be able to speak freely. The worker needs to listen attentively to what the client presents in each meeting. If the client raises new issues of concern, the worker should determine if this material is related to the problems that are being addressed, if it is necessary to work on these additional issues in order to bring about some improvement or change, or whether there is an immediate and pressing problem that requires attention.

Mr. Brisco had long-standing problems with his wife and children that periodically erupted. In one session, Mr. Brisco began by talking about an argument he had with his wife the preceding evening that centered on his discipline of their daughter. He reported his annoyance with his wife for interfering with his attempts to control his daughter's defiant behavior. Although the worker thought that Mr. Brisco was rather rigid in his approach to the daughter and would have liked to have pursued this area, she recognized that this interchange between the couple was typical of their relationship, that his family problems were not his main concern nor were they related to his work issues, and there was no indication that his interaction with his daughter was destructive or abusive. After listening to Mr. Brisco ventilate initially and asking him a few questions about the argument and how it was resolved, the worker said, "I can see that this argument disturbed you. I'd be glad to talk more about this with you, but I am mindful that your work problems are pressing." Mr. Brisco said that things would settle down at home as usual and that it did seem more important to get back to discussing his work situation.

In responding to this type of intervention, Mr. Brisco might have indicated that he wanted to continue discussing the problem with his wife. If this were to have occurred, it would have been advisable for the worker to have responded to the client's agenda even though it meant veering from the desired focus. A client whose need is not accepted will have difficulty moving forward. It is possible, however, that some clients will bring up seemingly important issues as a means of avoiding dealing with their major difficulties. How to recognize and manage this type of circumstance is discussed later in the chapter.

The Worker's Need to Refocus

A common occurrence in short-term intervention is the worker's tendencies to allow the process to drift into other areas and to pursue certain subjects that may not be pertinent to addressing the problem at hand. For example, in the case of Claire, who lived with her mother, a single parent, the worker was interested in Claire's feelings about not having a father involved in her life. In one of their meetings, when Claire expressed her worries about her mother, the worker found herself asking Claire if she ever wished her father were present so that he could help her and continued to explore more about her father and her feelings about his lack of interest in her. At one point Claire asked why they were talking about her father. The worker realized that she had gone astray and needed to refocus herself on the client's immediate concerns.

Broadening the Process

Sometimes it is necessary to focus on new concerns that the client presents and to establish new goals as a result of additional information. What is involved in achieving the initial goals may turn out to be different or more complicated than was originally thought, or new problem areas may emerge that are necessary to address to help the client.

The worker recognized midway through the process that Claire's concerns about her mother were reality based and related to Claire's not attending school. The worker's suggestion to the mother that she talk to the worker after the family session was based on her view that helping the mother to establish some social contacts might relieve some of the pressure on Claire. Thus, the worker expanded the focus of the intervention to include work with Claire's mother.

Changing the Focus

There are situations when the client undergoes a crisis or some other type of event occurs in the midst of the interventive process that necessitates changing the focus. A client may experience a loss, illness, unemployment, trauma such as rape or other type of violent assault, or pregnancy that has an immediate and significant impact on the client. Or it is revealed that the client has a different and more serious problem than was initially thought. Some difficulties take precedence over others, and the worker and client must prioritize what needs to be addressed first.

COMPONENT 8: MONITORING PROGRESS

In addition to keeping the interventive goals in the forefront with respect to maintaining the focus of treatment, it is important for the worker to take responsibility for monitoring the progress, or lack of progress, that the client exhibits in reaching the treatment goals. The worker needs to balance the task of monitoring whether the process is leading in some positive direction with the need for letting the client proceed at his or her own pace. A common pitfall in the middle phase of intervention is for the worker either to allow too much time to elapse before noting the absence of progress or to expect too much of the client too quickly.

Indicators of Improvement

Evaluating progress requires that the worker start out with some definite ideas about what constitutes positive movement for a particular client on the way to achieving the interventive goals. Thus, there are early benchmarks that tell the worker that the client is moving in the right direction. The worker uses indicators such as the client's involvement in the interventive process, interaction with the worker, steps that the client takes on his or her own behalf, and changes in thinking, feeling, behavior, and interpersonal relationships. For example, when a suspicious or reticent client who has difficulty talking about his problems begins to speak more spontaneously and candidly, this may signal that the client is feeling safer with the worker and more engaged in the interventive process. Or when a client who has blamed others for his or her problems begins to acknowledge that he or she may have contributed to the difficulties in some way, this would suggest that the client is developing some capacity for self-reflection. Likewise, a client who drinks heavily and has been resistant to attending AA manages to attend a meeting, this would indicate that the client is beginning to accept the idea that he or she is an alcoholic.

In the cases of Claire, Mr. Lopez, and Mr. Brisco, although the clients had not reached the established goals at the points at which the vignettes left off, there was ample evidence that each of the clients was moving in a positive direction. Claire attended sessions regularly, was open in discussing her concerns with the worker, seemed less depressed, attempted to implement the tasks that she and the worker had agreed on, was willing to involve her mother in the treatment, and seemed well on the way to returning to school. Although Mr. Lopez was still having difficulties with his attendance at the vocational training program and in managing his upsetting feeling states, nevertheless he was clearly engaged with the worker in addressing his problems, was continuing in school, was trying to take steps to cope with his feelings more effectively, and was able to begin to reflect on and tolerate some confrontations of his self-defeating behavior. Finally, Mr. Brisco was able to clarify some of the underlying reasons for his ambivalence about leaving his job, was able to begin to temper his grandiose strivings and frustration at not receiving the immediate recognition and financial rewards he sought, was able to reflect on the connection between his current feelings and his past relationship with his father, could reflect on his self-defeating behavior, and was moving toward a discussion of how to deal with his job situation better.

Addressing the Amount and Nature of Progress

When the worker observes that the client has made small gains, taken positive steps, accomplished major changes, or improved in other ways, he or she should acknowledge these developments. This feedback gives clients a sense of hope and confidence that they can achieve more. Sometimes clients are not fully aware of their own progress, so the worker's observations are especially important.

When there is a seeming absence of improvement, the worker may defer addressing this issue until more work is undertaken or comment on and explore the reasons for such insufficient progress. In some situations, it may be necessary for the worker to reexamine his or her assessment and expectations or even to renegotiate interventive goals.

SUMMARY

This chapter has described the first three components of the middle phase of intervention. It defined the techniques most frequently used in ISTT and gave case examples that illustrated how these techniques cluster and are used in implementing intervention. The chapter then discussed how to maintain or alter the focus of intervention and monitor progress.

Chapter 6

The Middle Phase: Part II

I n order to move the work of the interventive process forward, the worker needs to identify and address any obstacles that arise to achieving the interventive goals and to recognize the impact of and manage the worker-client relationship. This chapter considers both of these aspects of the work as they emerge in the middle phase of intervention.

COMPONENT 9: DEALING WITH OBSTACLES TO CHANGE

The worker's attitudes toward the nature of short-term treatment (Chapter 2), ability to assess and engage the client (Chapters 3 and 4), and skill in establishing realistic goals, selecting and using appropriate interventions, and focusing and monitoring the interventive process (Chapter 5) contribute to successful outcome. But even when workers hold positive attitudes toward short-term intervention and are highly attuned, experienced, knowledgeable, and skillful, the middle phase rarely proceeds smoothly and steadily forward. Lack of progress or oscillations between forward steps and lack of movement arise in the normal course of the work.

Reasons for Obstacles to Progress

During the interventive process, the worker must be attuned to signs that something is interfering with or obstructing progress or that the client is feeling frustrated or discouraged. Sometimes clients will say directly that they are unhappy with their lack of accomplishment or with some aspect of the treatment. In many instances, however, clients may reveal their negative feelings through excessive silence; having little to say, giving short answers, or being vague; changing or avoiding subjects; talking incessantly or bringing up new problems or issues; missing appointments; and lateness (Greenson, 1967; Strean, 1978). The presence of any of these signs does not necessarily mean that an obstacle to the treatment exists. Often it is preferable for the worker to remain attentive to the client's communications for a time before concluding that some block is present and must be addressed.

Change is difficult for a variety of reasons: (1) clients are fearful of what is new and unfamiliar; (2) they have difficulties altering established and sometimes ingrained ways of perceiving, thinking, feeling, and behaving because they are so habitual and have served important functions; (3) certain modifications take a long time; (4) change may be associated with both positive and negative consequences; (5) clients may become discouraged at what seems to be little or slow movement; (6) they may have inner obstacles that interfere with progress; (7) the environment may be nonsupportive or overtly destructive to client change; and (8) the environment may not contain sufficient resources, or resources that do exist may be difficult to access. Additionally, obstacles to the interventive process occur because of issues arising within the worker-client relationship. Because of its importance in ISTT, its general features and associated potential difficulties will be discussed separately later in the chapter.

FEAR OF CHANGE. It is not unusual for people to fear what is unfamiliar. Consequently, even when clients want to try out new behaviors, they are apprehensive about the consequences of change. For example, a woman who is angry and hostile toward co-workers and supervisors on her job yet wants to get along with others may worry that she will be taken advantage of and victimized if she becomes pleasant and cooperative. Likewise, a man who has difficulty investing in his studies but is ambitious and wants to be successful may fear that others will begin to expect too much of him should he begin to do better. Similarly, a woman who wants to be more assertive with and respected by a verbally abusive husband may be concerned that if she speaks up for herself, he will leave her. Or a male client who has low self-esteem and wants to make new friends may be scared at the prospect of people getting to know him and seeing what he is really like. Finally, a woman who sees herself as inadequate and dependent may become quite uncomfortable at the prospect of giving up these aspects of her identity.

DIFFICULTIES ALTERING WHAT IS HABITUAL. Certain ways of perceiving, thinking, feeling, and behaving are established at an early age and become ingrained. Although they may have once served an adaptive function, they also have had negative consequences or are now outdated and self-defeating. For example, a child of alcoholic parents who learned to be self-sufficient may feel alone and unsupported by others as an adult and wish to become more intimate but is accustomed to his patterns of doing things on his own and not needing or reaching out to others. A high school dropout who was severely criticized as a youngster and views himself as stupid and a poor student may persist in this belief even though there is objective evidence that he is intelligent and capable.

Additionally, there are clients whose lives are chronically chaotic and who live from crisis to crisis as a result of both environmental and personality factors. When they come for help, they often seek immediate relief and resolution of their difficulties and are easily frustrated if the helping process does not immediately help them. Such clients tend to bring in new and pressing problems that repeatedly interfere with established focus and goals.

TIME REQUIRED FOR CHANGE. Even when clients begin to take positive steps, it takes time and practice for certain changes to occur and take hold, and there may be temporary setbacks. Thus, a woman client who has severe problems with impulse control and loses her temper with others when she is even mildly frustrated may begin to experiment with new ways of channeling her frustration and responding to situations but resorts to tantrums when she experiences more stress. When she falls back on her previous dysfunctional behavior, she may show frustration with herself or treatment and want to end the interventive process.

POSITIVE AND NEGATIVE CONSEQUENCES OF CHANGE. Many of the options that clients face have mixed consequences, making it difficult for them to choose a course of action. For example, a woman with few occupational skills who contemplates leaving an abusive relationship with a man who has nevertheless financially provided for her and her children adequately is faced with the prospect of having to struggle financially and be the sole provider for herself and her children were she to separate from her spouse. A substance abuser who wants to stop using drugs may have to cut himself off from his friends and endure feelings of loss and loneliness in order to maintain abstinence.

DISCOURAGEMENT ABOUT LACK OF PROGRESS. Because progress often is slow or occurs in small increments, clients may become discouraged. This is true particularly with clients who have inordinately high expectations of themselves, exhibit low frustration tolerance, are enduring multiple and continuing stressors, have unrealistic goals, or face ongoing frustrations and environmental obstacles. Sometimes such discouragement leads clients to blame themselves or the worker and even to withdraw from treatment. For example, when a man who is trying successfully to overcome his tendency to yell and scream at his children after a bad day at work experiences a return of his temper outbursts when severely stressed, he may berate himself and the worker for his seeming lack of progress. Similarly, a woman who wants to overcome her anxiety about driving alone for long distances may minimize the small gain of being able to drive a few miles in her area and begins to question what this small step has to do with her long-range goal. Finally, a woman who is motivated to have her children returned to her after having been placed in foster care is overwhelmed by the numerous demands on her to visit her children, enroll in a parenting class, find adequate housing, locate a job training program, and attend individual counseling. As a result of her increased sense of stress, she begins to doubt that she will reach her goal.

INNER OBSTACLES TO CHANGE. When clients are unable to implement the changes they desire, the reasons may lie in inner impediments, or what has been termed resistance. When a client seems to be having difficulty making progress or staying focused, or has an apparent set-back, it is important first to consider the issues discussed above rather than immediately assume that the client is being "resistant." When inner blocks are operating, they may originate from many sources; conflicts originating in early childhood about competition, dependency, pleasure, autonomy, sexual intimacy, assertion, or appropriate anger may generate guilt or severe anxiety that impedes the client's ability to achieve his or her goals. In other instances, interactions that make the client unhappy and that he or she wishes to change are caused by the client's long-standing need to repeat earlier experiences with significant others. Such childhood interactions sometimes result in negative internalizations of the self and others and distorted patterns of thinking and perceiving from which clients have difficulty freeing themselves. Additionally, resistance may stem from the fact that clients exhibit personality traits that they view as parts of themselves and do not wish to change, even though such characteristics may be maladaptive, problematic to others, and responsible for the client's difficulties.

ENVIRONMENTAL OBSTACLES TO CHANGE. There are occasions when the conditions of the client's interpersonal or environmental milieu actively work against the client's involvement in treatment and efforts to make changes. Such reactions may impede progress, exert pressure on clients to remain as they are, or cause them to withdraw from treatment. For example, when a woman who seeks treatment because of her unhappiness with her domineering husband begins to be more assertive and noncompliant, her husband may become even more controlling, blame the therapist for destroying their relationship, and demand she end the treatment. This state of affairs may induce intense conflict in the client. An adolescent who is struggling to become more autonomous may encounter escalating parental strictness or punitive actions that thwart the teen's attempts at independence. Finally, when an African American woman, whose children are in foster care, mobilizes herself with the help of the worker to find new housing in a safer neighborhood, she meets with repeated refusals on the part of white landlords to rent to her even though these apartments have been advertised.

Because helping clients obtain certain types of resources may be an indispensable or major part of the interventive process, their lack of availability may stand in the way of achieving treatment goals. Often workers and clients experience considerable frustration in their attempts to locate and access such services as substance abuse programs, vocational training programs, after-school programs, shelters for battered women, inpatient psychiatric treatment, and supervised living situations. Moreover, helping clients to secure entitlements and other types of concrete services may meet with continued delays and impediments.

Overcoming Obstacles to Change

Sometimes the client will state spontaneously that the treatment is not going well. In these situations, the worker needs to acknowledge and explore the client's reactions and explore the reasons for them. When the worker observes behavior that causes him or her to wonder if an obstacle to the work may exist or that the client seems to be feeling frustrated or discouraged, it is important for the worker to share this observation with the client in a nonjudgmental, empathic manner. If the client agrees with the worker, further exploration can proceed. If the client does not agree, it may be useful for the worker to wait until it becomes more apparent whether his or her observations are justified before raising the issue again with the client.

Empathizing with the client's feelings and discussing the reasons that the client gives for his or her reactions and behavior may be sufficient to move the process forward or can serve as a basis for generating new strategies for working on the client's problems. Sometimes it is helpful to educate the client about the change process and the common feelings it engenders. For example, after five meetings with the worker, a young adult female survivor of childhood sexual abuse, who sought treatment to help her deal with intrusive thoughts that were interfering with her ability to be physically intimate with her husband, began to express her discouragement about ever overcoming her problems. In sensitively exploring the client's feelings, the worker learned that the client felt that she should be able to get over her difficulties quickly, that talking about her feelings would not help, and that it was wrong for her to expect outside help. The worker explained that it was not unusual for clients who had similar experiences to find it hard to talk about disturbing feelings and early experiences because they had to block out their feelings in order to survive their abuse. She added that children who are abused often feel they are not supposed to or will be blamed if they talk about their experiences and consequently feel quite alone and expect a lot of themselves. The client nodded silently; becoming tearful, she said it was hard to acknowledge what had happened to her, but she did feel that she wanted to try to deal with her problems.

Just as frequently, however, the worker many need to offer possible explanations or interpretations to the client about what may be impeding progress based on an understanding of the client's unique personality, internal dynamics, patterns of relating, or life situation. This may occur particularly when the obstacles result from internal rather than external factors. There may be a tendency for workers using a short-term approach to offer such explanations quickly, forcefully, and repetitively even though the client may not be ready. Because such interpretations may be difficult for the client to assimilate or may lead the client to feel blamed, it is important for the worker to be tentative, tactful, and sensitive. Discussion of the client's responses to the explanations given and of ways the worker can help the client to overcome his or her difficulties in making progress can help get the work back on track. For example, in working with a male client who sought help for relationship problems to which his alcoholic behavior was contributing, the worker noted that the client was coming up with repeated reasons for not attending AA and was continuing his drinking despite his stated intent to stop. When the worker commented on the difficulty the client was having getting to AA meetings and said that it must be hard for the client to face living without alcohol, he agreed that he found it hard to accept that he could not drink and was avoiding meetings and also was trying to control his drinking on his own. The worker explored the client's fears about what it would be like not to drink and acknowledged his efforts to try to stop by himself. She added that it seemed very important to him to try to maintain his sense of autonomy, that this was likely related to how much he had been controlled by others in his early life, but that his efforts were not working and that he needed to try something else. The client reluctantly agreed that he had not been able to curb his alcohol intake for more than a day. The worker then began to focus on what would help the client attend AA meetings and how to develop other means of coping with the disturbing feelings that led him to drink excessively.

A more complex situation occurs with clients who, despite their wish to feel better or change their situation, do not recognize those aspects of themselves that are contributing to and maintaining their problems. Because certain obstacles to progress result from deeply entrenched internal blocks or from rigid perceptions of the self and others, they pose problems in all forms of treatment but are particularly challenging in time-limited approaches. Sometimes workers use confrontation with such clients and point out the self-defeating, destructive, or maladaptive aspects of their attitudes or behavior in the hope that employing this technique will disrupt clients' views of themselves and others enough and make them more open and available to new ways of thinking and acting. The indiscriminate use of this strategy, however, can result in the client's feeling assaulted by the worker, the rigidification of the client's problematic stance, angry and provocative outbursts, or withdrawal from treatment.

Rather than use confrontation, generally it is preferable for workers to acknowledge that they understand the important function to the client of what may appear to be a dysfunctional attitude or behavior and try to engage the client in exploring its meaning and purpose. For example, a woman who takes pride in her ability to stand up for herself at work when her employer is critical or demanding and is suspended frequently for insubordination may not see her behavior as problematic. Instead of confronting the self-defeating nature of this behavior in the work situation, a worker might acknowledge how important it must be for the client to appear and feel strong when she thinks that others are trying to take advantage of her. This recognition might lead the worker and client to explore how the client used her anger and combativeness to fight her way out of inner-city poverty and an abusive family and how she fears appearing vulnerable. The worker also might use this information to help the client see that what was once a strength may now be a liability in certain situations.

Another means of addressing the type of difficulty described is through the use of cognitive techniques that attempt to help the client to recognize the presence of certain ways of thinking, feeling, and behaving, to understand that these ways of responding are distorted, irrational, one-sided, or limited, and to develop new and more adaptive alternatives.

COMPONENT 10: MANAGING THE WORKER-CLIENT RELATIONSHIP

In ISTT the worker-client relationship is a pivotal element in the interventive process. Chapter 4 discussed the importance of this aspect of treatment in engaging the client during the initial phase of the work. Certain features of the worker-client relationship, however, acquire more significance during the middle phase of intervention.

Five elements of the worker-client relationship need to be taken into consideration: (1) the working alliance, (2) the real relationship, (3) transference, (4) countertransference, and (5) worker attitudes, expectations, beliefs, values, and biases.

The Working Alliance

The working alliance involves the client's willingness and ability to work jointly with the worker on the problems for which the client seeks help. It requires that the client perceive the worker realistically as a reasonable helping person and continue to cooperate in achieving the goals they have identified. The working alliance is necessary for the work to proceed and enables the client to continue to struggle with his or her problems even when more intense feelings and potentially problematic reactions to the worker or to the process may occur. For example, the client's ability to recognize the worker's desire to be helpful may propel the client to stay with the process despite his or her discouragement or fears.

The monitoring and maintenance of the working alliance can be accomplished in part by the worker's asking the client at times how he or she feels the work is progressing. This query affords the client the opportunity to share both positive and negative reactions to the interventive process, permits adjustments to be made that may contribute to the work, and helps to remind both worker and client of the goals and focus of the treatment.

If the worker recognizes that the client is not participating as fully as possible or does not seem to use the worker as a collaborative partner, it is advisable for the worker to explore the client's expectations of their mutual responsibilities in the helping process and identify ways in which greater mutuality can be attained. Sometimes it is useful for the worker to reiterate that they are working together, to point out small gains that have been made, and to show confidence in the client's ability to get the help or make the changes that he or she desires in the time allotted.

The Real Relationship

The client and the worker are "real" people, each displaying and bringing to the helping process distinctive personality traits and particular styles of relating. This can either enhance or detract from the work. On the positive side, the client and the worker may connect on the basis of certain shared or valued characteristics. On the negative side, clients may respect the worker's credentials, capacities, and willingness to be of help but may react negatively to their realistic perceptions of certain aspects of the worker's personality, surroundings, or behavior. It is important for workers to accept and explore clients' feelings nondefensively, to alleviate clients' concerns if possible, or to reassure them that the worker is able to be of help to the client despite the presence of certain characteristics. Sometimes the very act of talking about the client's perceptions and concerns can reduce them sufficiently for the worker to proceed. For example, a mother who is overburdened by her children may feel that a young, single, inexperienced worker will not be able to understand her difficulties or offer the needed advice or guidance. If the worker is able to elicit and show empathy for the client's feelings, the client may feel more understood and connected to the worker and better able to trust the worker to be of help.

The worker may have a sincere desire to help the client but also may find certain client traits, behaviors, or attitudes annoying, threatening, or offensive. Although the worker's reactions may be understandable given the client's presentation, it is necessary for workers to convey acceptance and respect for the client, try to understand the meaning of the client's behavior, and strive to find something in the client that they can value (Noonan, 1998).

Because many clients have been deprived of authentic and attuned relationships or appropriate role models, there are times when it is useful, if not necessary, for workers to be more genuine and real with the client, allowing their personalities to show in the treatment. They can be humorous, show appropriate affect, or share selective information about themselves to the client when it is indicated diagnostically (Goldstein, 1995a, 1997).

"Being real" does not mean revealing personal information indiscriminately or acting spontaneously at all times. It is not uncommon for inexperienced workers to feel that they have to divulge personal information in response to clients' questions. Although telling a client that it is not one's policy to answer personal questions can be quite off-putting in many instances, it is important for workers to feel that it is all right to tell the client that they are not comfortable with answering certain questions until they understand more about what the client wants to know. Often clients ask for personal information because they are trying to determine if the worker can understand or help them, and they do not really want or need to know the actual answers to their questions. It may be more meaningful to the client if the worker understands and addresses the client's latent communication.

When clients begin to depend on or feel attached to the worker, they sometimes become concerned about the time-limited nature of the worker-client relationship. It is vital for the worker to explore clients' anxieties and fears, empathize with their anticipated feelings of loss or uncertainty, and support their strengths. Even if the client does not bring the subject of termination up spontaneously, it is necessary for the worker to discuss with the client the ending date of the interventive process. This allows both worker and client to keep the end point in sight, talk about the progress that has been made and the remaining work that needs to be accomplished, and address any feelings the client is experiencing about ending.

Transference

Because clients bring their past experiences, patterns of relating, unmet needs and wishes, and internal conflicts to the treatment process, some of their reactions to the worker do not result solely from the impact of the worker's real personality. *Transference* is a term used to describe those attitudes, feelings, and behaviors that the client experiences toward the worker that stem from the client's own personality. These responses can be positive or negative, foster or obstruct the work, or be important indicators of the client's personality and patterns of relating to others. For example, a client's idealization of the worker may be based more on the client's past experience with or need for a perfect mother than on the worker's admirable characteristics. This attitude may contribute to the client's feeling that help is possible—or lead the client to feel disappointed in the worker if progress is not forthcoming immediately. This transference reaction may reflect a more specific response that the client shows to the worker as a representative of authority, or it may represent the client's usual manner of relating to others, that is, looking up to them and then becoming depressed when they do not live up to the client's expectations. Or a client's insistence that the worker's questions are really criticisms may stem from the client's having had a highly critical caretaker. The client's sensitivity to seemingly neutral interventions may make it difficult for the worker to explore meaningful areas of the client's functioning. As in the example above, the client's transference may be specific to the treatment situation or reflect his or her expectation that others will be critical.

Short-term approaches generally tend to minimize transference because they are highly structured, time limited, here and now focused, and reality oriented, and emphasize a high level of worker activity. Consequently, they do not stimulate intense responses as frequently as does a more unstructured and open-ended approach. To the degree that mild forms of positive transference may arise in brief treatment, they can be an asset to the therapeutic alliance and do not need to be explored or diluted. In contrast, even mildly negative reactions that begin to emerge need to be addressed so that they do not interfere with the therapeutic alliance. For example, with a client who begins to experience the worker as a controlling authority figure because of the client's past experiences or tendency to distrust the intentions of others, it may be important for the worker to foster the client's reality testing, reaffirm the mutuality of the process, and restate his or her desire to help the client.

Some clients do develop intense transference reactions despite the treatment structure or the worker's best efforts to minimize such responses. In fact, in some cases in which clients have experienced traumatic losses, neglect and abuse, abandonment, separation, or rejection, the time-limited nature of brief treatment can reawaken unmet and frustrated needs. There are times when deeply felt positive connections can serve as a corrective experience for the client if these are understood by the worker and managed in ways beneficial to the client. The potential pitfalls of such reactions, however, result from the stimulation of intense unmet needs or from the time-limited nature of brief treatment that necessitates the client's being able to separate from the worker who has become significant to the client. Consequently, it is necessary for workers to be cautious, sensitive, and skillful in handling this aspect of the interventive process.

Intense positive or negative transference reactions may disrupt the working alliance; clients feel convinced of the reality of their distortions, are overwhelmed by their intense feelings and needs, or become demanding of gratification and angry when frustrated. In many instances, the worker may be able to diffuse these responses by remaining steadfast and empathic, engaging the client's observing ego in an effort to restore the therapeutic alliance, and helping clients to understand the origins and significance of their behavior. If the worker is unable to reduce the intensity of the client's reactions, treatment may become stormy, or clients may leave prematurely. The propensity for these more extreme responses exists particularly with clients who show more problems in overall personality functioning or have been victims of childhood abuse.

When the client's transference goes beyond being specific to the worker-client relationship and reflects the client's major internal conflicts, characteristic patterns of relating to others, unmet needs and longings, self-vulnerabilities and deficits, and internalized object relations, it may be useful for the worker to help the client recognize the similarity between the client's responses in the treatment situation to his or her daily life and problems. Then the worker and client can explore the client's propensity to think, feel, and behave in certain ways that are detrimental to him or her and help the client to develop a more adaptive repertoire of responses. For example, a client whose presenting problems revolved around her attitude toward her teachers and classmates at a vocational training program was dismissive, curt, and snippy when the worker tried to be helpful. During the course of their work together, the worker was able to use her observations of the client's behavior to help the client understand how people at the program might experience her as problematic and to identify and practice more appropriate ways of interacting with others. When the client did experiment with new behaviors, she found that people responded to her better.

This worker elected to assist the client in modifying her behavior directly rather than investigating the developmental roots of her defensive and antagonistic stance. Sometimes, even in a short-term approach, the worker may focus on helping clients to understand the origins of selected aspects of their problematic current functioning as part of the change process.

Not all of the client's intense reactions to the worker are the result of transference. Sometimes the worker's attitudes, behavior, or comments may be such that the client's responses are appropriate. Although the worker's demeanor, tone of voice, or interventions may be well intended, they may reflect a lack of attunement, inexperience, or a lack of self-awareness or self-discipline on the part of the worker. It is important for workers to be self-scrutinizing and open to the possibility that they may be responsible in some way for clients' strong reactions, even when clients may seem highly reactive and oversensitive. For example, in responding to an adolescent girl's account of an incident in which another student made threatening comments to her, the school social worker commented that the client must feel humiliated. Becoming quite angry, the adolescent replied, "I'm angry, not humiliated. Why would you say something as stupid as that? Why don't you just ask me what I'm feeling instead of telling me?" The worker retorted, "If you don't like the way things are here, you can find yourself another school." The student stormed out of the office. Although the worker thought that the student was hostile and belligerent, the supervisor pointed out that the worker's initial comment not only was based on a mistaken assumption but also was insensitive given the fact that adolescents generally do not want to be told what they are feeling, particularly by parental figures. She acknowledged that the student might have overreacted but also expressed her concern that the worker had compounded the problem by threatening her.

Countertransference

Workers, like clients, bring their experiences, patterns of relating, unmet needs and wishes, and internal conflicts to the treatment process. Thus, some of their reactions to the client do not result solely from the impact of the client's real personality. In the example above, the worker's use of the term *humiliation* to describe how her adolescent client might have felt may have reflected how she had felt in certain situations when she was an adolescent. Additionally, her rejecting and punitive reaction to the client's angry outburst might have stemmed from her own difficulties in handling anger and noncompliance.

   Countertransference is the term used to describe the attitudes, feelings, and behaviors that the worker experiences toward the client that stem from the worker's own personality. Like the client's transference, the worker's countertransference can be positive or negative and can foster or obstruct the work. For example, a worker with unmet dependency needs as a result of nonnurturing parenting may find herself quite fond of and interested in helping a warm and outgoing but needy recently widowed older woman. The worker's positive feelings may enhance her empathy with and investment in the client. But they also may interfere in the worker's encouraging the client to become more involved in other relationships and activities and to do more for herself. Or a worker's somewhat angry and judgmental response to a domineering middle-aged man may reflect the worker's own early experience with her controlling father and cause her to be unable to be sensitive to what he might be experiencing.

The worker's capacity for self-awareness is a crucial aspect of all intervention. Because they are human beings, workers need to accept that they will have a host of feelings and reactions to clients and their behaviors that are not inherently good or bad, right or wrong. What is important is that workers try to identify, understand, and discipline their reactions so that they are not conveyed to clients in ways that are detrimental to the treatment. The more that workers can acknowledge and understand their countertransference, the less likely it is that they will act on their reactions. Such self-scrutiny and restraint may be difficult at times, and there may be occasions when workers have blind spots or act impulsively. Honesty and openness in communicating that one has made an error or been insensitive often can be helpful in ameliorating the effects of the worker's mistakes or lack of attunement and conveys the worker's humanity. The use of supervision and consultation can assist the worker in identifying and managing potentially disruptive countertransference reactions. If the worker begins to recognize that he or she experiences certain types of reactions repeatedly to different clients—for example, angry reactions to a client's dependency or whining behavior—it might be useful for such a worker to look into the reasons for these responses rather than accept them unquestioningly.

Some clients themselves may entice the worker into re-creating dysfunctional interpersonal interactions by means of their behavior in the treatment. Thus, the client unwittingly may provoke or induce the worker into experiencing certain feelings or playing certain roles. Although it is not always easy to recognize when this process is occurring, the worker should be alert to his or her own strong, urgent, and unusual feeling states or to boredom, apathy, hunger, preoccupation, or sleepiness. As with other types of countertransference, the worker should strive to identify and understand the reasons for his or her reactions, which in these cases may arise from feelings that the client has difficulty experiencing or owning or from the need to have the worker feel about or act toward the client in a similar fashion to significant others in the client's life.

Worker Attitudes, Expectations, Beliefs, Values, and Biases

The worker's reactions to the client also may be influenced by his or her attitudes, expectations, beliefs, values, and biases. This can lead the worker to be too identified with clients who are very much like him or her—or distant, unrelated, or judgmental with those who are very different. Thus, a worker who herself has been a survivor of domestic violence may expect a female client who is experiencing a similar situation to implement the same course of action and in the same time frame as did the worker and may become frustrated when the client is unable to do so. A married, heterosexual female worker who views homosexuality as acceptable but not desirable may have difficulty empowering a lesbian client who is struggling with coming out to her family to do so.

The importance of the worker's awareness that his or her attitudes, expectations, beliefs, values, and biases have an impact on how he or she perceives and relates to the client cannot be underestimated. Although there may be a tendency on the part of social workers to see themselves as accepting and respectful of everyone because this is an important professional value, they are not immune from having preconceived attitudes about clients with particular diagnoses or problems, people of color, or those reflecting certain ethnicities, social class, religion, gender, sexual orientation, and other types of diversity. While striving to be accepting of differences, it is preferable for workers to be aware of their stereotypical and negative attitudes than to deny their existence. Such recognition can enable workers to be more attuned to clients and free them to address such differences and explore their impact with clients.

Finally, workers have certain expectations about how clients are supposed to behave during the course of the interventive process. Workers often value clients who are verbal, insightful, motivated, intelligent, able to relate easily, and cooperative. When clients do not conform to the worker's ideas, they may view the client as "difficult," may interpret the client's behavior as "resistant," may intentionally or unintentionally provoke the client to leave treatment, or may find a reason for referring the client to another worker or setting. Rather than blame the client, it is important for workers to alter their expectations and relate to the uniqueness of each client (Noonan, 1998).

SUMMARY

This chapter began with a discussion of many of the common obstacles to the change process that arise in the middle phase of intervention and suggested strategies for dealing with them. It moved to a consideration of various aspects of the worker-client relationship that can foster or interfere with the treatment and ways to manage these responses.

Chapter 7

The Ending Phase

The ending or termination phase of the interventive process is as complicated and significant as earlier phases and contains multiple tasks. How the worker handles the termination often enables clients to consolidate the gains that have been made, continue to work on their own, or arrive at a plan for further intervention or referral to other resources. It also sets the stage for their seeking help in the future should this be necessary. This chapter discusses the four components of the ending phase of ISTT: (1) addressing termination and its implications, (2) reviewing progress and identifying unresolved issues, (3) resolving the worker-client relationship, and (4) referral and follow-up.

COMPONENT 11: ADDRESSING TERMINATION AND ITS IMPLICATIONS

The approximate termination date of ISTT generally is established by worker and client at the outset of the interventive process and is kept in sight during the middle phase. Because of increasingly rigid policies regarding the time-limited nature of treatment and the type of client problems that are being addressed in short-term intervention, the ending phase does not coincide necessarily with successful achievement of the client's goals. It is initiated when the worker helps the client to focus on the amount of time and contacts remaining in order to bring intervention to a close. The worker should introduce the subject of ending at a point that leaves sufficient time for the worker and client to address the relevant issues. The exact amount of time necessary for the termination phase will vary based on the overall number of sessions or time allocated for the treatment and can range anywhere from two to four meetings.

In contrast to some authors who minimize the extent of clients' reactions to ending and give little attention to this phase (Epstein, 1992; Beck, Emory, & Greenberg, 1985), in ISTT it is important for the worker to elicit clients' thinking and feelings about termination. Although clients have agreed to an ending point in the initial phase, they may show surprise when reminded that the date is approaching or may manifest a variety of common reactions, including anxiety, positive anticipation, fear, disappointment, sadness, distress, anger, indifference, or lack of interest in the issue.

The worker generally should empathize with a client's stated feelings and explore them. If clients do not show any obvious reaction or do not seem to want to talk about ending, the worker might comment on the client's lack of response and ask the client if he or she might have some feelings that are difficult to discuss. Sometimes it is useful for workers to give clients permission to have feelings about ending by indicating that others in this situation often show a range of emotions. Obviously the degree and nature of the client's reactions will influence how the worker proceeds.

COMPONENT 12: REVIEWING PROGRESS AND IDENTIFYING UNRESOLVED ISSUES

In many instances, the client's reaction to the subject of termination will fall within a manageable range that affords the worker an opportunity to review and reinforce the progress that the client has made, support his or her other strengths and capacities, and express confidence in the client's ability to go forward on his or her own.

A necessary part of the termination process and an important means of helping clients to cope with their possible anxieties and fears about ending treatment is through discussing their progress, identifying unresolved issues, determining additional work to be done in the time remaining, and identifying steps that the client can take or activities or resources that he or she can pursue that may be beneficial to the client after the work is completed.

Along with exploring the client's perceptions of his or her progress, the worker also should share his or her observations regarding the client's accomplishments. This is important particularly with clients who may not be able to articulate their progress or recognize small gains that they have made. For example, Mr. Hoffman, a 52-year-old resident of an adult home for chronically mentally ill individuals (see Chapter 3), initially spent his disability check within days of receiving it. Over the course of treatment, he became able to control his spending for a more extended period of time despite some infrequent inappropriate purchases. Nevertheless, at the point of ending, he focused on what he had not been able to accomplish rather than on his improved impulse control and judgment. When the worker observed this tendency, she stated that she felt the client was minimizing his efforts and noted the benefits to the client of his attempts to control his spending.

In reviewing progress, the worker should help the client to recognize the ways in which he or she has improved and identify the reasons for the changes that have been made. With this understanding, the client may be better able to sustain his or her gains and extend new ways of thinking, feeling, and behaving to other areas. It also may be useful to anticipate that because a client's changes are new, some temporary setbacks may occur but that the client possesses the ability to resume his or her improved functioning.

In reviewing the course of treatment, worker and client need to identify any unresolved issues or problem areas and discuss what can be done so that the client can make further progress. Although some additional gains or consolidation of change can be expected in the remaining sessions, it may be necessary for the worker and client to discuss further options that may be necessary or desirable, among them (1) the worker's renegotiation of the contract with the client to continue for an additional period of time if there is indication that this would be beneficial to the client and it is feasible in terms of agency policy, worker availability, and economic and practical considerations; (2) the worker's spacing of the remaining sessions with the client at greater intervals in order to give the client more time to reach his or her goals while still having the worker available; (3) the worker's location of supportive services or other types of community resources that might be helpful to the client; and (4) the worker's encouragement of the client to return to the agency or the worker at a future time.

There are times when, for a variety of reasons, clients have not made inroads in dealing with their problems despite the best efforts of both worker and client. There may be clients who are unable to get the adequate housing they need or locate a drug treatment program that has vacancies; cannot resolve their relationship problems with an abusive partner or an acting-out adolescent son or daughter; cannot free themselves from the stress of their ongoing caretaking responsibilities for a physically disabled parent; cannot abstain from alcohol or drugs; cannot separate from a destructive marriage; or are noncompliant with medication. Situations of this type are difficult for both parties.

If the client's problems have not improved because of a lack of necessary resources or his or her life situation is chronically stressful or intractable, the worker needs to empathize with and validate the client's reality and identify avenues of support of which the client can avail himself or herself, with the worker's assistance. Alternatively, if the client's difficulties seem to represent inner obstacles to change or more entrenched personality characteristics and patterns of relating, the worker should help the client accept that something is getting in the way of progress, understand the reasons for it, and focus on what, if anything, the client is motivated to do to address the problems. The worker needs to be cautious about concluding too readily that a client is unmotivated or unwilling to change because there are other possible explanations for a lack of progress, including insufficient worker expertise, a poor fit between worker and client, or insufficient time.

COMPONENT 13: RESOLVING THE WORKER-CLIENT RELATIONSHIP

Because the worker-client relationship is an important element of ISTT, there may be times when a client reacts quite strongly to the idea of having to end, making it necessary for the worker to stay with and address the client's feelings in more depth than would be indicated with clients whose reactions are more modulated.

Endings may engender an acute sense of loss, particularly in clients who have rarely, if ever, experienced a caring, accepting, and respectful relationship or in those who have come for help at a time of significant loss and for whom the relationship with the worker has played a crucial role in working through their grief. In both instances, having to terminate may be painful. Endings also frequently engender upsetting feelings about previous losses that clients have experienced that intensify their reactions to separation from the worker. Moreover, some clients interpret the ending of the interventive process as a form of rejection and abandonment that makes them feel that they have failed and are unimportant to or not valued by the worker. These reactions may be accompanied by feelings of powerlessness, emotional and economic deprivation, unmet dependency needs, helplessness, or aloneness.

The worker's ability to accept and empathize with the client's strong feelings may help the client to feel understood. Sometimes the worker may be able to contribute to reducing the intensity of the client's feelings by helping the client to see the connection between his or her current reactions and earlier painful experiences and by offering the client the opportunity to talk about and rework these past losses and injuries.

There are clients who show other types of responses that the worker also may find difficult to manage: those who tend to fall back on previous and less constructive ways of handling their problems when they realize that the interventive process is coming to a close in the hope that treatment will continue; those who present with new and sometimes urgent problems that require immediate attention in order to make the worker feel that his or her presence is necessary; and those who leave precipitously because they cannot bear to be left or to talk about their feelings.

Once clients manifest any of the reactions mentioned, the worker must be empathic and try to educate them about the connection between their responses and the impending termination. Even the most sensitive and skillful worker, however, may not be able to prevent or help clients work through their reactions because they are unable to withstand the stress of ending in any other way. Although these responses may be dismaying and demoralizing and lead to a lack of positive closure, it is important for the worker to understand that such behavior does not necessarily mean that the client has not been helped.

Because clients tend to exhibit their usual ways of coping with endings or stressful situations when they are faced with terminating the worker-client relationship, it is useful for workers to be prepared for clients' reactions. This preparation can enable the worker to prevent some unfortunate developments by anticipating these with the client in some instances and helping the client to manage potential responses in more constructive ways.

In contrast to clients who show strong feelings about ending, some clients exhibit little or no reaction. Although this may be defensive in some instances, there are times when the worker needs to accept clients' statements at face value. This may be difficult for a worker who feels particularly connected to a client or who has extended himself or herself in an effort to be helpful. The client's ease in terminating, indifference to the separation, or lack of acknowledgment of the worker's efforts may result in the worker's feeling that he or she is unimportant. It is important for workers to refrain from personalizing clients' feelings or their absence in such instances and to understand that a client's businesslike or matter-of-fact way of dealing with termination may be characteristic of his or her way of relating to others or may enable the person to leave.

Workers too have a variety of reactions to the process of ending that stem from both the current relationship with the client and past experiences with others. Some of the more common responses are feelings of attachment to a particular client that result in the worker's becoming sad or sorry to see the client go, disappointed at not knowing how clients are faring after they leave, and frustrated that the process and goals of intervention are limited along with the belief that more could be accomplished if treatment were to continue.

To the degree that workers are aware of the nature and reasons for their feelings about ending, they usually will be more able to manage these constructively than if they are not aware of them. Workers who are not in touch with what they are experiencing may act in ways that are not beneficial to the process. For example, they may detach themselves from the client; show insensitivity to or minimize clients' feelings or their significance to clients; miss sessions; fail to recognize and validate clients' accomplishments; point out additional problem areas or unresolved issues in an effort to influence the client to remain in treatment; or refrain from dealing with the ending altogether.

There are positive aspects to the termination process for clients that stem from attainment of goals, positive experiences with the worker, and the benefits that result from their enhanced sense of mastery or dealing with earlier unresolved issues. "Because experiences of success and mastery accrue to the ego's overall sense of competence, the ability to move forward in the present can lead to an enhanced sense of self-esteem and competence" (Goldstein, 1995a, p. 225). Successful endings can result in a worker's satisfaction at having participated in relieving a person's stress and emotional pain, helping a client to achieve some improvement in functioning in a relatively short time frame, and sharing in a client's personal struggle and growth process.

COMPONENT 14: REFERRAL AND FOLLOW-UP

Although adjunctive services should be integrated into the interventive process from the outset if necessary, it may be indicated for the worker to locate additional resources during the termination phase. Such activity may be essential to helping the client achieve his or her goals, sustain the gains that have been made, or address new or additional problem areas. The worker might consider the use of other mental health and social agencies; self-help or support groups; mentoring, educational, or vocational training programs; transitional or residential facilities; preventive service programs; or religious, social, occupational, and community organizations. If the client has had a positive experience with the worker, he or she might be more willing to become involved with other sources of help than was true at the beginning of the interventive process.

Because of their attachment to the worker, some clients may have difficulty pursuing a new resource or feeling positive about it. Thus, it is useful for clients to have contact with such services or resources before the worker and client actually end their work so that the worker can help the client make the necessary contact and provide the client an opportunity to discuss his or her reactions to the referral.

In contrast to those who believe that termination should be absolute (Davanloo, 1978; Mann, 1973; Sifneos, 1972, 1979), in ISTT it is important for the worker to leave the door open and convey that it is not a failure or weakness if the client needs to return in the future. Communicating acceptance of the client's possible need for future help is particularly important in the current scene given the constraints of health care and the severity and multiplicity of the problems that clients present. The worker and client should establish a time for and means of follow-up, usually within a month of ending. Such contact helps the client to feel that the worker is still available, although in a circumscribed way, that the worker has an ongoing interest in the client's progress, and that there will be an opportunity to discuss with the worker how he or she has been doing at some point in the future.

Many of the issues described in this chapter are illustrated in excerpts from the ending phase of the Lopez case, presented in Chapter 5.

THE LOPEZ CASE: ENDING PHASE

Mr. Lopez, a 19-year-old Hispanic man, presented with multiple difficulties, consisting of dropping out of school, quitting jobs, substance abuse, and some minor brushes with the police. He made significant progress in attending his vocational training program more regularly, managing his angry impulses more constructively, spending less time with friends who tended to use alcohol and drugs heavily and engage in antisocial activities, and becoming more focused in achieving his career goals than he was prior to intervention. Mr. Lopez appeared to have established a strong bond with his male Hispanic worker, who also enjoyed working with the client and identified with his struggles.

Because the contract for their work together involved 20 meetings, the worker noted in the middle of the sixteenth session that although they had talked about the time-limited nature of treatment, it was now time to consider how they were going to bring their work together to a close. He added that they had four remaining meetings. Mr. Lopez looked surprised and said, "That's not much time." He then became silent.

Worker: *You seem quieter than usual. What are your thoughts about our having to end?*

Mr. Lopez: *It's no big deal. I'm used to people coming and going.*

Worker: *What do you mean?*

Mr. Lopez: *What difference does it make? What do you care?*

Worker: *I do care about what happens to you, and I can understand that you might be angry that we have to end our work.*

Mr. Lopez: *I'm not angry or upset! I have other things to talk about!*

Worker: *I know you have other important things on your mind that we need to discuss, but we also need to talk more about the progress you have made and what else we are going to do in the time we have left.*

Mr. Lopez: *Maybe we should just stop now.*

Worker: *You are saying that you are not angry, but your tone and words tell me that you do have strong feelings about our having to end.*

Mr. Lopez: *What if I do?*

Worker: *We have been working together for many months, and we both know that one of your difficulties was that when you became upset and angry, you would try to avoid the feelings and situations that caused your distress and then engage in activities that were self-defeating. Although you're doing a lot better, I'm concerned that feelings about me and our ending might lead you to act in a way that goes against your best interests.*

Mr. Lopez: *What do you mean?*

Worker: *There have been times when you missed school, sessions with me, and soccer practice and drank a lot with your friends when you were upset and angry.*

Mr. Lopez: *You're right, but I really have other things I want to talk about now.*

Mr. Lopez missed the next scheduled meeting but agreed to another appointment when the worker called him.

In the next session, Mr. Lopez began by talking about his week. When the worker inquired about why he has missed his session, Mr. Lopez replied that he realized afterward that he was upset about having to end and that he was going to go drinking with his old friends, but he remembered what the worker had said and stopped himself. He even had thought of not showing up today but knew that was not a good thing to do.

Worker: *It's really good that you stopped yourself from your old behavior and that you came today.*

Mr. Lopez: *I don't know what to think. Sometimes I feel like you're the only person I can talk to and who believes in me. Then I think you're just doing this because it's your job.*

Worker: *You mean if I really cared about you, I'd find a way that we could keep working together?*

Mr. Lopez: *Why do we have to stop?*

Worker: *I also have feelings about the rules, and I wish I could change them so that we could continue, but I can't. We can talk about the progress that you have made and help you think about future plans.*

In reviewing his progress, Mr. Lopez acknowledged that he was doing a lot better but could not readily pinpoint what he was doing differently and why. The worker pointed out that Mr. Lopez seemed more able to identify the triggers for his frustration that led him to miss class and had learned new means of tolerating and discharging his anger and discouragement. Mr. Lopez agreed and added that he really enjoyed the activities in which he had become involved and was making new friends.

In response to the worker's question about what he thought had helped him to achieve these gains, Mr. Lopez replied that he thought the worker really cared about him even when he screwed up. The worker asked what he thought might help him when the worker was not around. Mr. Lopez said he was not sure, because he had drifted back to his old ways before. The worker asked if there was anything different this time. The client responded that he had learned that there were ways of feeling better without having to mess himself up, that he liked the fact that he was doing better in his training program, and that he did feel stronger. The worker also said that it was important that Mr. Lopez had continued to try despite setbacks and disappointments and that this success was important for him to remember in the future. He also commented on the client's many strengths that he had shown during the interventive process.

In the eighteenth session, Mr. Lopez came in and flung himself in the chair, saying he had really messed up during the week by getting into an argument with one of his male teachers at the vocational training program, who threatened to suspend him. Fortunately, the director of the program intervened. Because of the improvement Mr. Lopez had shown, the director told him he would give him another chance if he apologized. Mr. Lopez was relieved and did what the director asked.

> Worker: Do you think there is any connection between our ending and your outburst at your teacher? Sometimes when we're angry at one person, we express our feelings at someone else.
>
> Mr. Lopez: I just feel lousy and lost. I don't know why.
>
> Worker: Can you say a little more about what you're feeling?
>
> Mr. Lopez: I feel like no one gives a damn. All I have is my mother. I never knew my father. He left just after I was born. My mom's brother was good to me. We used to do a lot together, but he ended up in jail when I was 10.
>
> Worker: What was that like for you?
>
> Mr. Lopez: I don't remember. I just know he was here one day and gone the next.
>
> Worker: Like me?
>
> Mr. Lopez: Are we just going to say good-bye and that's it? How come I don't have any say in this?

Worker: You mean you didn't have any say about your father, your uncle, and now me?

Mr. Lopez: That's right! My father didn't care enough to come and see me, and I don't know whether my uncle is dead or alive.

Worker: It was hard for you not to have any control over what happened or to be able to express your feelings. It's true that we have to end, and neither of us can change that, but at least we can talk about how you feel. Having to end doesn't mean I will stop being interested in hearing about how you are doing. One thing we can do is schedule a follow-up meeting in about a month after our last session.

Mr. Lopez: You've done all right by me. I just hope that I can stay on track.

Worker: Let's talk about ways that you can do that.

In the next-to-last session, worker and client reviewed the course of their work together and focused on how Mr. Lopez could maintain his progress. They discussed the client's options were he to become stressed or overwhelmed. But the choices seemed limited; there were few resources in the community. Nevertheless, the worker suggested the possibility of Mr. Lopez's talking with his soccer coach or the director of the vocational training program in the event that he had some type of problem, because these two individuals had shown some interest in him. The worker also assured Mr. Lopez that he could call him if he felt in need and asked Mr. Lopez when he wanted to schedule the follow-up appointment.

In the twentieth and final meeting, Mr. Lopez came in quite talkative and described in detail the somewhat positive events of the preceding week. At one point he pulled a small package out of his jacket pocket, put it on the desk, and pushed it toward the worker.

Mr. Lopez: This is for you.

Worker: That's really nice. Shall I open it now?

Mr. Lopez: Sure.

Worker: A mug. I'll use it with my morning coffee. What a great gift! I have something for you too. Here.

Mr. Lopez: I didn't think you would give me something. Can I open it?

Worker: Sure.

Mr. Lopez: This is a great poster! He's one of my favorite players.

Worker: You have a lot to offer, and I've really liked working with you. It hasn't been easy, but you have stayed with it. You may hit some rough spots because the behaviors that you have learned are new. I have confidence in you. I'll be seeing you in a month, and we can talk about how things have been going for you.

Discussion

The worker initiated the termination phase when there were four remaining sessions so that there would be time to discuss the ending. The client reacted with surprise and denied that the ending mattered to him. The worker attempted to explore what he might be feeling, and when Mr. Lopez continued to say he didn't care while concurrently acting as if he did, the worker pointed out this discrepancy. Knowing how Mr. Lopez usually handled disturbing feelings, the worker tried to prevent the client's avoidance and acting out by discussing his characteristic means of coping.

Although Mr. Lopez did miss his next session with the worker, he did not act in a self-defeating manner. He was able to begin to talk about his feelings about ending, particularly his feeling that the worker did not really care about him. The worker tried to help the client recognize that he would remain interested despite having to end, began to review the client's progress with him, and attempted to help the client identify the specific nature of and reasons for his progress.

The client began to show some regression in that he resorted to acting out his angry feelings at school. Nevertheless, he was able to salvage the argument with his teacher and continue the termination process. He began to think about the previous losses of his father and uncle, and the worker helped him to express feelings about these events that he had not spoken of before. The worker was able to empathize with the feelings of powerlessness that the client had experienced in the past and was experiencing again. He also helped him see that he could talk about his feelings with the worker, who also would remain available to him, albeit in circumscribed ways.

Worker and client were able to review the course of treatment and identify possible, though limited, sources of future assistance. In their final meeting, the client showed some working through of his feelings about ending as evidenced by his giving the worker a small gift that expressed his feelings of gratitude. Not only did the worker choose to accept this gift, but he also gave the client a small present that reflected the worker's interest in what was important to the client.

SUMMARY

This chapter has discussed the major tasks of the termination phase of ISTT. It emphasized its role in helping clients to review and consolidate their progress and identify further work to be done, in resolving relationship issues, and in setting the stage for further work if necessary.

SPECIAL PROBLEMS AND POPULATIONS

Chapter 8

Crisis-Oriented ISTT

Although crisis intervention is a variant of short-term treatment, not all short-term work is crisis oriented (Parad & Parad, 1990, p. 9). This chapter discusses the special nature and different types of crises and describes and illustrates the use of crisis-oriented ISTT in a range of client situations.

THE NATURE OF CRISIS

Everyone who comes for help experiences some stress or discomfort, but not all trying circumstances fit the definition of crisis. Many authors (Caplan, 1964; Flegenheimer, 1982; Parad & Parad, 1990a; Rapoport, 1962) have defined crisis situations as characterized by (1) an upset in a person's equilibrium in which his or her customary means of coping and problem solving are overwhelmed or insufficient to meet the demands of the task at hand and (2) subjective feelings of distress, including bewilderment, danger, confusion, impasse, desperation, apathy, helplessness, urgency, and discomfort (Parad & Parad, 1990a, p. 8).

The crisis situation usually consists of four interrelated factors: (1) the precipitating event, (2) the perception of it as threatening and meaningful, (3) the disorganization resulting from the stressful event, and (4) the coping tasks that are necessary to resolving the crisis and that may be adaptive or maladaptive (Parad & Parad, 1990a, p. 5).

Although it is thought that the state of crisis is time limited (Parad

& Parad, 1990a, p. 7), intervention is necessary for a variety of reasons. The resolution of crisis situations is not always optimal. An individual's functioning after the crisis is resolved may be the same, better, or worse than it was before the crisis. Moreover, because the client's usual coping mechanisms are overtaxed or have become ineffective and the client is in a state of disequilibrium during a crisis, he or she may be more open to influence by another and amenable to change than under normal circumstances.

There are certain common life events such as the death of a loved one, serious illness, or acts of violence that likely would trigger crises for most individuals who experience them. The specific impact of even this type of event, however, generally is dependent on the subjective meaning it has to the person. In certain instances, rather than being the average predictable response that most people would have under similar circumstances, the crisis state results from the fact that a current event has reawakened past traumatic experiences or unresolved issues (Jacobson, Strickler, & Morley, 1968). In addition, there is considerable debate about whether some individuals may be more vulnerable than others to the impact of certain events (Parad & Parad, 1990; McFarlane, 1991).

Although the state of acute upset usually is time limited, so that the crisis itself may last only about six to eight weeks, the situation that triggers the crisis state may be ongoing, as exemplified by a recent widow who must go on living without her husband or by a daughter who must become and continue to serve as the caretaker for an elderly father who has suffered a stroke. Some clients may seek help after the immediate crisis has subsided but at a time when they still are struggling with the aftermath and the continuing consequences of the crisis with which they require assistance. There are other situations in which a client is unaware that his or her presenting problems are related to a previous crisis that has not been resolved effectively, as might be the case with a recently divorced mother who is depressed and having difficulty managing her children but does not recognize that all family members are reacting to the loss of the father. Working with these types of problems requires that the worker understand that the client's difficulties are related to the impact of a crisis, the coping strategies that the client has used, and the ongoing new demands of the client's life situation.

TYPES OF CRISIS

Many, but not all, crises occur as a result of a traumatic event, such as rape, domestic or other acts of violence, illness, injury, death, divorce, or unemployment (Abarbanel & Richman, 1991; Brekke, 1991; Burgess & Holmstrom, 1974; DeRoche, 1995; Lindemann, 1944; Sokol, 1983). Some less dramatic and potentially pleasurable and challenging life events such as geographic relocation, job changes, or promotion also may have a powerful impact (Holmes & Rahe, 1967).

There are other types of disequilibrium that sometimes are referred to as normal crises because they occur as a result of the usual course of the human growth and developmental process. For example, individuals enter new life cycle stages such as adolescence, young adulthood, or mid- or later life that throw them off balance and require new coping strategies (Tabachnick, 1991). Role transitions, such as going to college, going from being a student to becoming a worker, being single to being part of a couple, becoming a parent, being promoted to a supervisory level, becoming a caretaker of an elderly parent, or retiring from the job market may create crises (Le Masters, 1957; Pruett, 1990).

At the other end of the spectrum of situations that may produce crises are disasters that affect large numbers of people, such as fires, transportation crashes, floods, hurricanes, and terrorist attacks (Grossman, 1973; Lindemann, 1944; Mor-Barak, 1991). Finally, posttraumatic stress disorder (PTSD) is a special type of crisis situation that encompasses events that usually are outside normal life experience for most people (McFarlane, 1991, p. 69). Traumas may include violent or terrifying situations or disasters or wartime experiences that threaten life or physical safety, destroy homes or property, or confront people with terrifying acts (Gaston, 1995; Graziano, 1997; Grinker & Spiegel, 1945; Marmar, 1991; McFarlane, 1991; McNew & Abell, 1995; Patten, Gatz, Jones, & Thomas, 1989). Such experiences engender horror, helplessness, and intense fear. This type of crisis can manifest itself immediately following the traumatic event or can show its effects repetitively and even many years later, as is the case with many veterans of the Vietnam War and with adult survivors of childhood sexual abuse.

PTSD is differentiated from other types of crises by certain features: recurrent and intrusive recollections or images, thoughts, perceptions, or dreams of the events; intense psychological and physiological distress to cues associated with the traumatic events; avoidance of stimuli associated with the traumatic events; psychic numbing that includes detachment from feelings and others, a restricted range of affect, poor memory of certain aspects of the trauma, or inability to contemplate one's place in the future; and symptoms such as difficulty sleeping, irritability or outbursts of anger, problems concentrating, hypervigilance, and exaggerated startle responses (APA, 1994, pp. 209–210). When traumatic events, such as sexual abuse, rape, battering, or performing duties that are violent or destructive of others as in wartime or certain occupations, are associated with some type of stigma, excessive shame, guilt, or responsibility often accompanies the experience.

Because of the defenses and coping mechanisms that individuals draw on to help them deal with extreme trauma, clients with PTSD often are unable or do not wish to discuss the elements of the trauma. They may alternate between using avoidance and denial and becoming flooded and overwhelmed by their earlier experiences. The defense of dissociation is common in which the individual totally represses the memories of disturbing events or the painful and overwhelming affects associated with them. He or she may not remember the events, may recall them without the affects, or may begin to reexperience them when they are triggered by certain stimuli. Alcohol and drug abuse, risk-taking behavior, gambling, compulsive eating, excessive spending, and sexual promiscuity are common among trauma survivors because such behaviors serve the purpose of helping the client ease or numb the psychic pain (Marmar, 1991). The personality traits, defenses, and symptoms that develop to deal with the trauma often result in misdiagnosis and inappropriate treatment.

Frequently, the events that result in the client's state of disequilibrium are associated with more than one type of crisis. For example, an individual who is entering a new life stage may also suffer the loss of a parent. There may be multiple stressors that impinge on a particular individual, as might be the case with a male client who is diagnosed with HIV, who must leave his job because of his illness, and whose spouse leaves him. Clients who present in this manner should be differentiated from those who manifest a chronic state of crisis—for example, a client who goes from one destructive relationship to another, mismanages money, and has a history of repeated job loss. Although crisis-oriented ISTT might alleviate some of the client's problems temporarily, it is likely that the client soon will undergo another crisis. It would be preferable for such a client to use treatment to improve his or her overall level of coping rather than to manage one crisis after another.

SPECIAL EMPHASES

Crisis-oriented intervention generally is focused on helping clients to gain some relief from their acute distress and master certain affective, cognitive, and behavioral tasks that are necessary to resolve the crisis effectively. The goals are to help clients to resume their precrisis level of functioning (Golan, 1978), improve their coping capacities, and rework past unresolved issues (Jacobson, Strickler, & Morley, 1968).

ISTT is an active and relatively circumscribed approach whatever the circumstances of the client. The difference between the application of ISTT to clients in crisis and those who are not in crisis is one of emphasis. The worker who is dealing with clients in crisis:

1. Initially encourages considerable ventilation, offers sustainment, and accepts the client's need to go over the disturbing events and their impact at various points in the treatment in order to gain a sense of relief, control, and mastery.
2. Recognizes that a formal assessment must be timed flexibly and when the client is ready to participate.
3. Focuses on obtaining an understanding of what has precipitated the crisis, including what it means to the client and what underlying problems or issues it may have triggered from the client's past, as well as on the client's precrisis level of functioning.
4. Understands that the client's reactions are valid even if the pre-

cipitating event does not seem particularly upsetting to the worker.

5. Enables the client to feel safe, secure, and hopeful that the worker is an expert or benign authority who can help the client.
6. Is accessible to the client, flexible in scheduling appointments, and willing to reach out.
7. Provides validation for and education about clients' reactions; elicits their concerns; partializes and problem-solves about immediate courses of action; mobilizes strengths; involves support systems and locates external resources; offers advice, guidance, and information; assigns or assumes specific tasks; and makes appropriate interpretations expeditiously in order to stabilize the client and improve clients' coping capacities.
8. Encourages the client to try out new ways of thinking and behaving.
9. Anticipates with the client what needs, demands, and recurring feelings may arise in the future.
10. Recognizes the significance of the worker-client relationship to the client as a source of support and strength during the ending phase.

With clients who have PTSD, intervention should be based on an individualized assessment of clients' ego functioning and their ability to tolerate the exploration of their overwhelming earlier experiences. An assessment of the current support systems that clients have in their lives also is important because the recovery work can become quite intense and anxiety producing, sometimes necessitating emergency interventions (Goldstein, 1995a, p. 284). The goal of intervention is to help the person to begin the work of recovery that will need to continue over time with the supports of significant others. Talking about the details of the trauma, their implications, and the affects associated with it are crucial, as is the person's ability to restructure his or her view of himself or herself and the world.

Acceptance, consistency, empathy, genuineness, safety, and validation are important ingredients of a therapeutic holding environment in the beginning stages of working with those who have PTSD. When clients are reluctant to disclose or discuss the traumatic situation or when they lack memory of it, the worker must proceed with caution. Timing is important in pursuing details. All too often inexperienced and zealous workers push for the specifics too quickly or try to recover traumatic memories before the client feels safe or has experienced some lessening of defenses and feelings of fear, badness, shame, and guilt. These must be dealt with sensitively and empathically before more intensive exploration can occur (Gaston, 1995; Graziano, 1997). When the client is better able to tolerate such exploration, it should be done in tolerable doses (Marmar, 1991, p. 408). The worker always should give the client the option to take a break from discussing intense experiences and feeling states.

THE INTERVENTIVE PROCESS

Although the emphases described are applicable to all crisis situations, there may be a different constellation of strategies based on the nature and type of crisis that the client presents and the client's needs and level of functioning. In the Channing case, which follows, the client, who underwent a crisis as a result of a sudden hospitalization and subsequent nursing home placement, was seen by the social worker for 14 sessions over a six-week period.

THE CHANNING CASE

Mrs. Channing, a 73-year-old divorcée, was admitted to a nursing home following an extended hospitalization after a fall. The accident was related to increasing numbness in her legs due to Parkinson's disease and weakness due to poor nutrition. Mrs. Channing was confused and unable to return to her home because of her deteriorated physical condition, inability to care for herself, need for extensive physical therapy, inadequate housing, and lack of social support. She had one sister but was not on speaking terms with her, and her two children lived out of state. She had no friends and no involvement with local social service agencies. She received Medicare and Social Security.

The attending physician requested that a social worker see Mrs.

Channing immediately because she was agitated, refused to eat, and cried continually, saying she wanted to go home. When the worker entered her room, Mrs. Channing was lying uncovered, staring at the ceiling. The worker introduced herself and began to explain her function and role. Mrs. Channing interrupted her, saying, "I'm not old and sick like all these people. I don't know why I'm here. I just want to go home to my own house." The worker noted that she seemed very overwhelmed and commented that it was understandable that Mrs. Channing would be so upset because she was in a new place with unfamiliar people and had just been through a month-long hospitalization.

Mrs. Channing began to recount to the worker the ordeal of the hospitalization and her move to the nursing home. The worker listened attentively and encouraged the client to talk about what had happened to her. While telling her story, Mrs. Channing was quite emotional, tense, and tangential. She ended her presentation by saying she was scared about what was happening to her and she did not want to die in a nursing home. The worker empathized with how fearful Mrs. Channing seemed to be and told her that the first few days of such a placement were difficult and frightening for most people, that she had helped many people like Mrs. Channing, who were in similar circumstances, that she would be available to talk to the client, and that she would do everything she could to help her. The worker added that the placement was not necessarily permanent and they could meet the next day to talk further. She then asked if there were anything she could do to help Mrs. Channing feel more comfortable. The client said she wanted to be left alone. The worker wrote down her name and telephone extension and gave it to the client.

At their meeting the following day, Mrs. Channing told the worker tearfully that she had not slept all night. "I can't believe that I've ended up here and don't know how to get out." The worker listened to the client's complaints and then encouraged the client to talk about what had led to the hospitalization. After a few minutes, the worker asked what her life had been like prior to the hospitalization. Mrs. Channing shared that she and her father had lived together until his fatal heart attack two years earlier. Subsequently, she lived alone in the apartment, did not go out much, and spent her days and evenings watching TV.

She and her sister had never been very close, and their relationship had deteriorated after the father died. Her sister was angry because Mrs. Channing had not kept up the apartment, was not taking care of herself, refused to go to the doctor, and would not socialize.

In response to the worker's invitation to talk more about her father, Mrs. Channing readily shared that they had lived together for about twenty years. She had moved in with him when her children had grown and left home. She had divorced her husband many years earlier. She loved her father, thought he would always be there, and was unprepared for his death. She added, "I know that I don't have many years left. I have a lot of regrets, but do I have to die here?" The worker told Mrs. Channing that based on her discussions with the patient's doctor and the team, it seemed quite possible for Mrs. Channing to return to the community if she followed the doctor's orders, worked consistently with the physical therapist, built up her strength, and agreed to having a part-time aide when she returned home. The client seemed visibly relieved. The worker asked if Mrs. Channing might want her to call the client's sister to let her know how she was doing or whether she wanted to do this herself. The client seemed pleased at the worker's offer and said she would like her to make the call if it was not too much trouble.

The next day, the worker told Mrs. Channing that her sister wanted to talk to her and visit and had asked that she call. Because the client seemed calmer, the worker asked about the status of Mrs. Channing's apartment. It still was available but required a thorough cleaning and considerable repair work. "My father used to take care of everything. It's so overwhelming. I don't know where to start." The worker asked if her sister might be of some help and suggested that the three of them meet together. The worker also took this opportunity to learn more about Mrs. Channing's background and functioning.

In the following session, worker and client talked about Mrs. Channing's feelings of isolation since her father died. After considerable discussion of her relationship with her father and her sense of loss, the worker shared with the client what she thought they could do together and her thinking that Mrs. Channing's depression before entering the hospital was related to her not having adjusted well to the death of her father. Mrs. Channing replied that she had been depressed since her father died and just assumed that this was the way it would always be. The worker said it was important for her to try to make a life for herself. Mrs. Channing agreed. The worker said that a first step was for her to join a support group that the worker facilitated so that she could meet other residents and begin to socialize. Mrs. Channing was hesitant but agreed when the worker urged her to try it one time; if she didn't like it, she did not have to continue.

Over the next three weeks, the worker and client met six times. They talked a great deal about the client's father's death, the earlier loss of her mother, the estrangement from her sister, the divorce from her husband, and the fact that her children lived so far away and seemed unconcerned or at least unavailable to help her. They also discussed the client's health, including her fears about the progression of the Parkinson's disease. Mrs. Channing acknowledged that her way of dealing with her health was self-destructive and asked if the worker would help her find out more about the condition. They prepared a list of questions for her to ask the doctor.

The worker tried to enlist the sister's help in preparing for Mrs. Channing's eventual discharge. When her sister saw how motivated and realistic she appeared, she agreed to get the apartment cleaned and repaired. The worker also submitted a home care application and obtained an approval of four hours per day. Finally, the worker mobilized the team's interest in Mrs. Channing, whom they monitored carefully and supported actively. She made substantial progress. She was walking with a walker, and her overall physical health, mood, and emotional attitude had improved.

As part of the termination process, which occurred over a two-week period, worker and client talked about what it would be like when Mrs. Channing returned to her apartment. Concerned that the client might fall back on her old patterns, the worker suggested that Mrs. Channing attend a local senior center. Fortunately, one of the nursing home residents whom Mrs. Channing had come to know also was planning to attend this center and the client did call to arrange a visit for herself and the worker.

In discussing her feelings about ending with the worker and leaving the nursing home, Mrs. Channing expressed fear of being without the worker's support. She laughingly suggested that she volunteer at the nursing home. "That way I can still see you once in awhile." The worker responded that she had enjoyed meeting with Mrs. Channing and was happy that she was able to go home. She acknowledged the efforts that the client had made and expressed her confidence that she could continue to do well. She supported the client's desire to volunteer and keep active.

When the actual discharge date was set, Mrs. Channing became angry, saying it was too soon and that she wasn't yet ready to leave. Worker and client discussed the client's feelings about yet another loss. They also agreed that the worker would do a home visit in three weeks and that the worker would be available by telephone. At that time, the client appeared to be managing reasonably well with the help of the home health aide. Although she had not followed through on the volunteer work, she was attending the senior center, keeping her medical appointments, and spending more time with her sister.

Discussion

Mrs. Channing's current crisis resulted from the traumatic impact of her sudden hospitalization and subsequent transfer to the nursing home. She had undergone a previous crisis at the time of her father's death, with which she had coped maladaptively and which had lingering effects. In addition, Mrs. Channing was struggling with the developmental issues of aging, declining health, and fear of the future. She used avoidance, denial, regression, and turning against the self in dealing with her situation. Her coping capacities, particularly in the areas of her object relations, self-esteem, judgment, and sense of mastery, were limited even prior to her father's death. The client's strengths were her intelligence, self-reflective capacity, sense of humor, perseverance, and capacity to relate to others. The immediate crisis made Mrs. Channing more open to intervention, more accepting of the seriousness of her situation, and more motivated to help herself.

The worker attempted to help Mrs. Channing cooperate in her medical rehabilitation, help her return home, and enable her to function more effectively at home. The emphases in the work included the use of ventilation, listening, sustainment, and validation; education, *advice, and guidance; use of the relationship; being accessible and reaching out; partialization, task assignment, problem solving, and some interpretation; collaboration with the client's sister and the team; encouragement of new ways of behaving; use of adjunctive services; anticipation of the client's future needs; and help in bringing closure to the worker-client relationship. The interventive process afforded Mrs. Channing the opportunity to resolve not only the current crisis but also to improve her adaptation to the earlier loss of her father and to her increasing age and health problems.*

The following example shows a client who experienced a different type of crisis.

THE RICHARDS CASE

Mr. Richards was doing rather well in life. At age 39, he occupied a management position in a good company, lived in an apartment in New York City with his male partner of eight years, and recently had purchased a house in the country. He and his partner had an active social life with a small circle of intimate friends. Mr. Richards had always prided himself on his resilience in dealing with life's vicissitudes. He maintained a tense but close relationship with his mother, toward whom he felt responsible, and somewhat distant but cordial relationships with his siblings, who looked to him for advice and support.

Suddenly two events occurred that devastated him and threw him into a state of crisis. The first was being informed that he and his partner would have to move from their sublet apartment because the owner planned to reclaim it. When he received the news, Mr. Richards became furious; could not sleep or concentrate; felt panicky, confused, and helpless; and had trouble working. After a month, he mobilized himself with the help of his partner, and they found a somewhat smaller but nevertheless fine apartment by New York standards. Although his acute distress subsided, he remained depressed after the move. He had trouble getting accustomed to his new surroundings and spent hours every day ruminating about the move and wondering if there might have been some way to avoid it. It never occurred to him to seek help.

The second event occurred soon after the move: his company was going to be sold, and his future there was uncertain. Mr. Richards's panic intensified. Although it soon became clear that it would take at least a year for the company to finalize the sale and that he would be offered a good severance package were his job to be eliminated, Mr. Richards felt that his entire career was about to deteriorate. His earlier symptoms following the news about his apartment returned. After many weeks of sleeplessness, rumination, and agitation, he attempted to find another job and made a lateral move at the same salary in order to avoid "waiting for the axe to fall." He ruminated about both the apartment and the old job, going over whether he had done the right thing by moving in both situations. He was moody in his personal life, did not want to socialize with friends, was argumentative, and picked fights with his partner, who was telling him to "get over it already and get on with your life." He could not stand his new job, which he considered to be chaotic and disorganized despite the company's excellent reputation. He feared that he would never find another position like the one he had previously, worried that his career was going downhill, and blamed himself for being a failure. He soothed himself by drinking and eating more than usual. He finally sought help at the urging of friends who were concerned about him because he remained severely depressed and agitated.

Significant in the client's history was the fact that his family had lived a financially secure lifestyle until his father lost all of his money, became ill, and died of a heart attack during Mr. Richards's adolescence. Prior to this, Mr. Richards had greatly admired his father, whom he wanted to emulate. Nevertheless, he did not overtly mourn his father's death; there was no time, and the family did not encourage expression of feelings. Soon after his father's death, Mr. Richards was shocked to learn of his father's poor management of his business and money. He felt very responsible for the family and also felt deprived of the material things he had taken for granted previously. An excellent student, Mr. Richards never felt that he was the smartest, and this left him with feelings of inadequacy. Nevertheless, he was able to attend college and obtain interesting and well-paying jobs after graduation. However, he always had a sense of foreboding that he would lose everything. He was hypervigilant for any sign of potential threat to his well-being and was quite perfectionistic in everything he did so as to ensure that he did not fail. His expectations of himself and others were unrealistic; and he often experienced a loss of self-esteem if anyone criticized him and considerable disappointment if anyone failed him.

By the time Mr. Richards came for help, he recognized that there was something "screwy" about the intensity of his reactions, although he could not stop ruminating and make himself feel better. He indicated that he had been having suicidal thoughts that frightened him and said, "No one commits suicide over losing an apartment and having to change jobs." His only explanation for his reactions was that he did not tolerate change very well, especially when it was thrust on him.

The experienced worker recognized rather quickly that Mr. Richards's adaptation to life indeed was based on having to maintain a sense of control and perfection that likely stemmed from his underlying feelings of inadequacy, insecurity, and sense of failure. It also appeared that the client both identified with and feared being like his father, who had been forced to declare bankruptcy and whose death left the family in dire straits. Consequently, the worker believed that the loss of the apartment and news about his company's takeover not only undermined his usual coping mechanisms but also stimulated his worst anxieties and fears.

Because Mr. Richards was aware that his crisis was more complicated than it seemed on the surface, it was possible for the worker to share her thinking with him about what seemed to be underlying his current state. In addition to encouraging Mr. Richards to talk about what the apartment loss and job change meant to him, the worker was able to engage him in exploring elements of his past prior to and after his father's death and to help him make connections between these events and his view of himself, sense of responsibility, need for material success and security, perfectionism, fears of failure, worry that his world would fall apart, and need for control. Another emphasis in the work was helping Mr. Richards to realize that his career was not in jeopardy. Midway through the 12-session treatment, the client reported feeling much better and that a weight had been lifted that he had carried for many years. The work began to focus on supporting Mr.

*Richards in his search for a new position that would offer him more sat-
isfaction, helping him to ease some of his need for control and perfectionism, and assisting him in finding sources of relaxation other than
excessive drinking. The client found a new job quite quickly and felt
optimistic about his future.*

*Because the crisis that brought Mr. Richards to treatment was re-
solved, termination of the treatment seemed indicated. As part of reviewing their work together, the worker did express to the client her
concern about several issues that she felt might cause him to have problems in the future: his high expectations of himself and others, his loss
of self-esteem when criticized, the degree to which he tended to over-
work, and his keen sense of responsibility for others that resulted in his
taking on the problems of his family members. Although Mr. Richards
acknowledged that he might want to work on these issues in the future,
he felt good about his progress and wanted to see how he did on his
own. He indicated that he had learned it was important to be able to
seek help and did not think he would avoid doing so in the future should
the need arise.*

*At their follow-up meeting one month later, Mr. Richards said he
was doing well. But approximately one year later, Mr. Richards called
to resume treatment because he felt he found himself extremely worried
and depressed about his relationship with the person to whom he reported at work. After ruminating about this for a week, he recognized
that it might be useful to talk over the situation before it escalated. He
also had come to the decision that he wanted to address some of the
other issues that he had been trying to ignore.*

Discussion

*The events that caused Mr. Richards's crisis—the loss of the apartment
and his company's takeover—not only were assaults in themselves but
also triggered his worst underlying anxieties: that he would be homeless, on the one hand, and turn out to be like his irresponsible father,
on the other. Although he mobilized himself to deal with the current
events, he was not able to resolve the underlying issues that they stimulated. In the treatment of his crisis, it was necessary to identify and address the past events that were reawakened to help the client connect*

his present reactions to his experiences, and to support the client's problem-solving and coping capacities in dealing with his situation. Intervention appeared to help him work through a traumatic event in his adolescence that contributed to shaping his self-concept and adaptation to life.

This case example, however, also shows a client whose basic self-concept and ways of dealing with himself and others made him vulnerable to stress. The crisis-oriented treatment did not attempt to modify these basic characteristics. The positive experience that the client had with the worker and the interventive process, however, enabled him to identify a potentially dysfunctional pattern that reemerged somewhat later and to seek help before a new crisis developed.

In contrast to the previous two examples, the following case illustrates a client whose crisis was triggered by the more normal life event of going away to college.

THE CHAN CASE

Ms. Chan, an American-born 18-year-old college student of Chinese background, sought help from the school's counseling center. A very successful student academically in high school, she had received a full tuition scholarship for her college studies at a prestigious urban university that was far from her home and family. As her first-semester final exams approached, she felt stressed and feared that she would fail. Although she had graduated in the top 10 percent of her high school class, she worried that the college competition was too much for her and that she would lose her scholarship. She could not concentrate, felt panic stricken when she thought about writing papers or studying for her exams, and was unable to sleep. She thought about taking a leave of absence in order to return home but did not want to disappoint her parents.

The client reported that she had been feeling alone and isolated since coming to school in the early fall. She was overwhelmed by the sprawling campus, the large number of students in her classes, and the highly competitive nature of her classmates. She had little contact with her professors, who seemed remote, uninterested, and unavailable. Unfa-

miliar with the city, she felt frightened traveling on buses or subways. The client spent most of her time studying at the library. Although she liked her roommate, she did not feel that she had much in common with her. She had been feeling somewhat anxious and depressed during the semester, and the pressure mounted as her examinations approached.

The worker gleaned that Ms. Chan was the first member of her family to attend college and that she and her parents had high expectations for her. She had attended a small, private high school in a suburban community, where the teachers and students interacted frequently and she had been active in extracurricular activities. She went to a college away from home because she wanted to be more independent of her family, who were loving but very protective. She did not think much about what it would be like for her to be away because she took it for granted that she would continue to do as well academically and socially as she had done previously.

In exploring the client's background, the worker learned that Ms. Chan came from a closely knit family where tradition and culture were highly valued. She spoke fondly and lovingly of her parents, siblings, and extended family, who lived nearby. She enjoyed family gatherings and wished she could be part of them. She missed her high school, where she had played basketball and been on the school newspaper, and her friends, particularly her boyfriend, whom she had not seen since the Thanksgiving break.

The worker determined that Ms. Chan was experiencing a developmental crisis related to the separation from her family and the stress of being in a new and challenging environment but that she had many strengths. The client had been successful, competent, and popular in high school but had been uprooted from the virtual safety and security of her family and friends into an unfamiliar, unwelcoming, complex, and competitive environment. Placing high expectations on herself, she questioned her capabilities and felt disconnected from other students and faculty. She believed she could do the work but could not get control over her anxiety and fears.

The worker shared his thinking about the nature of Ms. Chan's crisis to her and explained that her reactions were understandable and common among entering students who were away from their families *for the first time rather than a reflection of her weakness. He and the client agreed to meet for 10 sessions, the amount of time allotted by the counseling center. Because of the client's anxiety about her finals and her lack of a campus support system, the worker suggested that they meet twice weekly for three weeks and then weekly for the remaining four sessions. The worker hoped that if Ms. Chan could successfully complete her finals, they could address the issue of widening her social network and connection to others.*

The main focus of the first six sessions was to provide the client with a support system, lessen the pressures that she was placing on herself, and help her prepare for her finals. The worker elicited the client's fears about disappointing herself and her parents, her expectations that she attain straight A's, and her feelings of loneliness. Because she had not talked to anyone about what she was experiencing, the client felt very relieved to have someone to listen to her who was accepting and understanding. The worker and client discussed the realistic demands of college, the dramatic differences between the environment to which she was accustomed and her new surroundings, and the client's lack of anticipation and preparation for her undertaking. The worker was able to help the client recognize that she might be overly concerned about her parents' reactions. The worker encouraged her to speak to her parents about how she was feeling. When she contacted them, they told her that they knew the adjustment to college might be hard, she should not worry about them or pressure herself so much, should try to do her best, and they had confidence in her.

The worker also helped Ms. Chan to look realistically at her abilities, and they talked about concrete ways in which she could organize herself to write her papers and study for exams. The client did much better than she expected on her finals, and after visiting her family during the semester break, she resumed seeing the worker for the remaining four sessions. The focus of their work turned to helping the client begin to make new friends. Much of the client's previous social life had revolved around school activities or family gatherings. The worker and client discussed possible activities in which Ms. Chan could involve herself. He drew on her interests in writing and music and suggested that she look into joining the campus newspaper and try out for the chorus. Ms. Chan agreed to look into these possibilities. In their final meeting, the client reported having followed through on her task and was quite excited about the prospect of these new activities and making new friends.

Discussion

In this case, in which the disequilibrium stems from a more normal maturational and role transition process, the need for ventilation in the beginning usually is not as great as when the client experiences a more traumatic set of circumstances. Often clients feel relief when they are helped to recognize that their reactions are common to the stage of life or role transition with which they are struggling and to identify some of the factors in the current situation that are contributing to their stress. Once the worker assessed that Ms. Chan was experiencing what appeared to be an uncomplicated developmental crisis, he was able to normalize her anxieties and fears and help her to cope more effectively.

The next example illustrates the work with a Vietnam veteran who suffered from PTSD long after the war and who had not been treated previously.

THE HARRINGTON CASE

Mr. Harrington, a 50-year-old Vietnam veteran, was referred to the social worker at the methadone maintenance clinic after he complained to the psychiatric nurse about his anxiety and depression. The worker learned that Mr. Harrington had been attending the program for three months but was fearful of returning to drugs. He missed his wife, who was in a long-term rehabilitation program, and their son, who was temporarily placed in foster care. He feared losing his apartment because he earned only $125 per week and received $120 a month for a leg wound he had suffered during the war. In discussing his financial situation, he complained bitterly about the government, feeling that no one cared about the veterans: "We're the ones who fought their fight, and now they act like they're doing us some kind of favor. It's bullshit." When the worker commented that he certainly did seem angry at the *government*, Mr. Harrington responded, "It doesn't really matter now. All that counts is keeping my apartment and getting my wife and child back." Sensing the client's urgency, the worker suggested that they meet the following day. Mr. Harrington agreed, saying that he would have something to look forward to. The worker also gave Mr. Harrington the 24-hour emergency number.

At their second meeting, Mr. Harrington seemed more relaxed, and when the worker commented on this Mr. Harrington said he was glad he had the appointment. The worker learned that Mr. Harrington had grown up in a lower-middle-class family in New York City. He was not close to his family, did not have many friends, and spent much of his time alone. He had worked from an early age to earn spending money. An adequate although not good student, he left school in the eleventh grade to be on his own and eventually joined the military. After basic training, he was sent to Vietnam, where he started taking drugs to "get control of my fear." Wounded during an ambush, he was discharged from the service after three months in the hospital. When he returned to the States, he reluctantly went to live with his family and worked as a machine operator. He did not socialize because he felt he did not have much in common with other people his age. At this point in the session, Mr. Harrington looked at the worker, and the following interchange took place.

Mr. Harrington: You look old enough to remember Vietnam. Are you a vet?

Worker: Yes, I am, but I never saw the fighting.

Mr. Harrington: Well, at least you know what it's like to be in the service and remember the way we were treated when we came home. People called us "baby killers" and shunned us.

Mr. Harrington then spoke of his extensive drug use, which he stopped when he returned home but then resumed. He discussed meeting his wife and how they would get high together. They married when she became pregnant. They both struggled with intermittent drug use.

Mr. Harrington: Drugs make me calm for a while, and I sleep better.

Worker: What's the trouble with your sleeping?

Mr. Harrington: I don't want to talk about this anymore. What am I going to do about my rent? I don't want to lose my apartment.

Worker: I know that we need to talk about your money issues, but you seemed to get upset when I asked about your sleep problems. Can you tell me why the question bothered you?

Mr. Harrington: I don't want to talk about the nightmares. I just wanted to talk about getting my wife and son back and what to do about my finances.

Worker: We don't have to talk about your nightmares now if you don't want to, but it seems important to talk about them soon since they're so disturbing to you.

The worker and client spent the remainder of the session going over Mr. Harrington's finances and exploring various options, including his obtaining additional part-time work, vocational training, and learning to budget. The worker also agreed to try to find out if Mr. Harrington might be eligible for additional GI benefits. They set up an appointment for the following week.

Mr. Harrington called two days later; he really needed to talk to the worker, he said. They met later that day. When Mr. Harrington came in, he was visibly upset about a nightmare that he had had. He related that he had not had nightmares for three months, since he had stopped using heroin. He thought the drugs had caused them and that they were gone.

Mr. Harrington: Last night I woke up screaming, shaking, and crying, and couldn't even try to go back to sleep.

Worker: Tell me about the nightmare.

Mr. Harrington: No! I don't want to talk about it. It all will be too real. I just want to forget about it.

Worker: I can see how frightened you are, but not talking about it doesn't seem to help. We can go slowly, and if it feels like too much, we can stop.

Mr. Harrington: They're always about the war and involve horrible scenes of torture, shouting, shooting, and people screaming. Sometimes I see my buddies being killed, or I see villagers, women and *children. I feel like I'm back there in the jungle. I've tried not to talk about it to anyone or even to think about it for years. No one would want to listen anyway. Even if they did, there are some things I couldn't tell anybody. People would think I'm a monster.*

Worker: I've worked with many vets from Korea, Vietnam, Grenada, and the Gulf War. They have been through a lot, and I don't feel that any of them are monsters.

Mr. Harrington: I feel comfortable with you. I can talk to you because you're a vet and you've heard this stuff before. Even when I'm awake, I see and hear things that happened while I was in Vietnam.

Worker: Can you talk about it?

Mr. Harrington: I heard a loud noise on the street and thought I saw people covered with blood running in all different directions. I tried to hide but knew the enemy would get me. I called out until I heard someone yell, "Hey man, are you crazy or something?" Then I came to my senses. This has happened to me before. The flashbacks last only a minute or two, but when they're over, I'm all sweaty and shaking.

Worker: That's a very disturbing experience. Are there other bad things that happen?

Mr. Harrington: I'm afraid of loud noises and am on guard even in my apartment. I can't get away from my own thoughts except when I take drugs.

The worker explained to Mr. Harrington that his sensitivity to noise, being on guard all the time, and unwanted thoughts were common among people who had gone through experiences such as his. He assured Mr. Harrington that his reactions were by no means crazy. When the worker asked how Mr. Harrington felt about talking, he said he felt relieved. The worker said that it can be relieving to have someone to talk to, and he was glad that Mr. Harrington felt a little better. The session ended with a discussion of the status of his benefits.

In the next session, the following interchange occurred:

Mr. Harrington: I didn't really want to come today. I don't want to talk about my war experiences any more. I just want to get on with my life.

Worker: You have been trying to do just that for many years, but the past just keeps coming back.

Mr. Harrington: How is going over it all going to help?

Worker: Talking about traumatic experiences, although upsetting temporarily, can lessen their power and help you feel better in the long run. I've seen this happen before. There is a connection between your wartime experiences and your problems sleeping, drug use, depression, and anxiety.

Mr. Harrington: I do want to feel better. It's just so hard to remember.

Worker: I know it is, but you are not alone. I should mention that I received your medical records, which indicated that you were diagnosed with PTSD a long time ago and might be eligible for another 50 percent disability.

Mr. Harrington: I do know about that, but I don't want to apply. I let everyone down as a soldier with the drugs and all.

Worker: You are blaming yourself for things that happened as part of your job.

Mr. Harrington: You don't know the things I did in the war.

Worker: No, I don't, but I can see that you have been suffering for many years, have tried your best to put the war behind you, and now need to try another way.

Mr. Harrington: Maybe you'll think I'm a monster.

Worker: I think it's you who feels this way.

Mr. Harrington: I've witnessed and taken part in many killings.

Worker: That's must have been pretty awful for you.

Mr. Harrington: After a while you get used to all the killing. The first time I killed someone, I cried like a baby. Then after a while I could kill at the drop of a hat. A buddy told me it would be easier if I took some heroin. I tried, and he was right. It got so that I'd go on missions just for the fun of it.

Mr. Harrington than started to sob uncontrollably. The worker put his hand on Mr. Harrington's shoulder and sat quietly. When Mr. Harrington stopped crying, he looked at the worker and began to speak again:

Mr. Harrington: How can you stand to be with me? What kind of person am I?

Worker: You had to do your job and survive. All of your buddies and everyone in the war were in the same boat.

Mr. Harrington: Not everyone has messed up.

Worker: A lot of vets have had a very hard time and have not had enough help.

Mr. Harrington: I haven't cried like this in years. I've been afraid that if I started, I would never stop.

Worker: I can see that is an upsetting idea, but such fears are not unusual when a person has been through so much. We'll take it slowly, one step at a time.

Mr. Harrington: I've had enough for today. I'm tired.

Worker: I understand.

The worker asked how Mr. Harrington thought he would be after the session and what his plans were for the next few days. He said he did not know how he would feel but that he had some odd jobs lined up and was hoping to visit his wife. They continued to talk about the impending visit. Before ending, the worker cautioned Mr. Harrington that sometimes when people start to talk about very upsetting events, more memories and thoughts come back, and this is normal. They talked about what Mr. Harrington could do to comfort himself, and Mr. Harrington said that sometimes praying helped, and he might return to church. The worker and client set up another appointment in four days, and the worker encouraged Mr. Harrington to call if he felt the need.

At the beginning of the fifth session, the worker asked how Mr. Harrington had been doing since their last meeting. He responded that he was having more thoughts about the war and was glad that the worker had warned him that this might happen. He was also thinking *again about drugs. The worker commented that using drugs or alcohol was a means that many people use to try to get some relief from the feelings related to painful experiences but that the relief was short-lived. The worker then asked if Mr. Harrington could talk about the thoughts he was having. The client said the thoughts and memories were all jumbled, and he was not even sure if they were real memories or just things he imagined had happened. The worker again assured the client that this was normal and explained, "The best way for us to do this is for you to try to tell me from the beginning of the war step by step what you can remember. We'll go slowly—just a little bit at a time."*

The client began at the beginning telling the worker what Vietnam looked like, about his unit, and the first time he went into combat. The worker asked the names of his buddies, what they were like, and the details of his first combat experience, including what he was feeling. When Mr. Harrington seemed overwhelmed by what he was saying, the worker told him to take a deep breath and rest a minute. He informed the client when there was about 10 minutes left in the session and asked how he was feeling. He said he was drained and that maybe he needed a few minutes to pull himself together. The worker agreed and asked if he would like a glass of water. He accepted the offer. The worker and client then talked a few minutes about his visit to his wife and his having gone to church.

In the sixth session, Mr. Harrington began by asking the worker what he should talk about and seemed reluctant to resume talking about his war memories, even with the worker's encouragement. After letting the client chat about other subjects for a time, the worker commented that it seemed hard for Mr. Harrington to return to what they had been discussing previously and wondered if there were a way that he could make it easier. Mr. Harrington replied that he had felt somewhat better and was afraid that he would get worse again but knew that he needed to stick with it. The worker suggested that they could begin where Mr. Harrington had left off in their last meeting, and the client resumed the work.

Over the next six weekly meetings, Mr. Harrington continued to describe his experiences in the war, his feelings about having killed innocent people as well as enemy soldiers, his guilt about being glad that he survived when so many of his friends had died, and his anger at the way people viewed soldiers who had fought in Vietnam. In addition to encouraging ventilation and offering sustainment, the worker focused on helping Mr. Harrington to think about his role in the war and the performance of his duties in different and more positive ways; to experiment with new means of coping with his upsetting feelings; to get more involved with his church and join a support group for other men with PTSD; and to continue visiting his wife. By the time the interventive process came to an end after 16 sessions, Mr. Harrington continued to be drug free, had applied for additional disability benefits, and was sleeping and feeling better than he had in many years.

Discussion

Mr. Harrington's difficulties were indicative of PTSD that was triggered by his experiences during the Vietnam War and had never been treated. His disorder resulted in his extensive substance abuse, chronic sleep problems, and marginal functioning over a considerable period of time. His functioning prior to the Vietnam War reflected self-reliant attitudes and that he was somewhat of a loner but did not show any serious type of emotional disorder. In addition to having intrusive thoughts and memories, flashbacks, nightmares, hypervigilance, some dissociative states, severe anxiety, and feelings of shame and self-blame, Mr. Harrington used avoidance, denial, turning against the self, and substance use to cope with the effects of his wartime trauma. The forced separation from his wife and son and his efforts to be drug free intensified his feelings of anxiety and depression and resulted in his referral to the social worker at the clinic.

Mr. Harrington's PTSD emerged only gradually after he felt safe with the worker, who was supportive, empathic, and himself a veteran. The worker recognized the symptoms of PTSD and saw the opportunity to help the client deal with his impairment. The worker attempted to help Mr. Harrington to recognize the need for and benefit of addressing his wartime experiences and their impact on his functioning. Although the client was fearful of and reluctant to share the details of his earlier trauma, he was motivated to do so because of the intensification of his emotional distress and the worker's reassuring approach.

The worker's sensitivity and acceptance were instrumental in helping Mr. Harrington to trust the worker, engage in the process of discussing and working through his traumatic experiences, and restructure his self-concept and view of others. The emphases in the work included the use of ventilation, listening, sustainment, and validation; education, advice, and guidance; use of the relationship; being accessible and reaching out; partialization, problem-solving, and cognitive restructuring; encouragement of new ways of behaving; and use of adjunctive services.

SUMMARY

After discussing the nature of crisis and its different types, this chapter described 10 major emphases in crisis-oriented ISTT. The four case examples that were presented reflected crises resulting from traumatic events, including those that led to posttraumatic stress disorder, and from developmental stages and role transitions. They also showed the techniques and interventive strategies employed to help the clients resolve their crises.

Chapter 9

Clients with Emotional Disorders

S ometimes the problems for which clients seek help are symptomatic of an emotional disorder. When this is the case, ISTT may
be used to alleviate the client's underlying condition or improve the
client's functioning within the confines of the disorder. In either case,
workers must be able to recognize the presence of certain syndromes,
and their interventive plan must embody specific foci. In discussing
four major types of emotional disorder, this chapter considers the specific foci of ISTT and illustrates the interventive process with clients
who present with these disorders.

DEPRESSION

A depressive disorder needs to be differentiated from depressed feelings
that most people experience at points in the normal course of life or as
part of another problem such as bereavement.

Definition

Depression is classified as a mood disorder. It is painful to the individual and usually causes impairment in social, occupational, or other important areas of functioning. There are different types of mood
disorders that involve depression, such as dysthymia, major depressive
disorder, and manic-depressive illness, in which there is a cycling of al-
ternately depressive and manic episodes. The common characteristics

that lead to the diagnosis of depressive disorder are depressed mood most of the time; lack of interest or ability to get pleasure; feelings of worthlessness; recurrent thoughts of death or suicide; and symptoms such as weight loss, insomnia, fatigue or loss of energy, psychomotor retardation or agitation, and problems concentrating or making decisions (APA, 1994, pp. 162–163).

Although there is disagreement about whether the main causes of depression are predominantly biological, psychodynamic, cognitive, interpersonal, or environmental (Austrian, 1995; Beck, Rush, Shaw, & Emery, 1979; Karasu, 1990; Scott & Stradling, 1991; Wright & Borden, 1991), most clinicians agree that depressed individuals share common feelings and thoughts: helplessness and hopelessness, vulnerability to disappointment and loss, states of anger turned inward, vulnerability of self-esteem, suicidal ideation and intention, a pessimistic explanatory style, acceptance of depressed state as normal, inability to identify triggers, and an inclination to expect negative responses from others (Luborsky et al., 1995, pp. 15–17).

Many studies have shown that a variety of psychotropic medications may be effective in relieving depressive symptoms but that psychosocial treatment alone or in combination with drugs also is successful in alleviating depression and improving a person's overall functioning (Elkin, 1994, pp. 114–139). Moreover, psychotropic medications are not necessarily effective for everyone and have the potential of producing side effects that may complicate their use.

Specific Foci

The goals of ISTT with depressed individuals are to relieve their depression and improve their functioning and to help them better deal with the impact of the depression on themselves and others. Although intervention embodies all of the components of ISTT that were discussed in Part I, its specific foci may include the following components:

1. Educating clients about the fact that many of their troubling thoughts, feelings, and behavior are symptoms of depression and that it is possible for them to feel better.

2. Helping clients to feel less responsible for their depressive symptoms and to lessen any stigma that may be attached to the disorder.

3. Learning about the history of the depression and clients' attempts to cope with it.

4. Identifying the current triggers (problems, interactions, experiences, thoughts, feelings, and behaviors) or consequences of the depressive symptoms.

5. Exploring the connection between a client's present state and past experiences, vulnerabilities, or unmet needs that may be contributing to or causing the depression.

6. Determining what the main dynamic, if any, of the depression seems to be—for example, anger turned inward; loss or fear of losing a significant other or meaningful role, activity, source of satisfaction, health, physical vitality, or well-being; blows to self-esteem; failure to live up to one's expectations or ideals; feelings of powerlessness or guilt; a means of staying connected to a lost object; a way of gaining needed attention; an attempt at expressing anger at others; or a characteristic attitude toward life.

7. Helping clients to understand whatever dynamic or past issues that may be operating in their depression and to find ways of dealing with these more effectively.

8. Identifying clients' attitudes toward or ways of perceiving themselves or others that may be causing, intensifying, or perpetuating their depression.

9. Helping clients to modify their more negative and pessimistic attitudes about the self and others, become more positive and affirming, and develop more assertive and constructive patterns of relating and behaving.

10. Assisting clients in improving their problem solving about the areas of their lives that are contributing to their difficulties.

When clients show suicidal ideation or other manifestations of their suicidal intent or self-destructiveness or desires to inflict harm on others, addressing these issues must take precedence over other interventions. Protective measures should be undertaken if clients are at significant risk and cannot be relied on to control their impulses. Alternatively, workers can use contracts in which clients promise to refrain from acting out or engage them in problem solving about ways to help them alleviate their distress and desperation.

The Interventive Process

The following example of a client who was seen for 20 sessions illustrates many of the specific foci mentioned.

THE BUTLER CASE

Ms. Butler, a divorced 38-year-old African American, was referred to a community mental health center for therapy by her physician, who thought she was depressed and placed her on Prozac, an antidepressant medication. She also had cystitis that was aggravated by her consumption of over 10 cups of coffee a day, which she used to help herself get out of bed in the morning.

In inquiring about the history of the client's depression, the worker learned that Ms. Butler had been hospitalized briefly for depression three years earlier after several significant events occurred in close proximity to one another: Ms. Butler's husband of 10 years left her for another woman, she lost her job because of poor attendance, and a close friend died. After discharge, she discontinued her medication and did not follow up on outpatient psychiatric treatment. She went to live with her alcoholic father and his elderly sister, received Social Security and Medicaid, and rarely left the house or socialized. When she arrived for her first session, she appeared depressed and hopeless but denied suicidal thoughts. The worker noted that the client appeared well groomed but lacked energy. Her ability to cope, problem-solve, and regulate her self-esteem and impulses was impaired.

Exploration of her history revealed that Ms. Butler was the youngest of three children. She said she was estranged from her oldest brother (age 48) and seldom had contact with a highly successful older sister (age 45). When Ms. Butler was 15, her mother, who had a long history of depression, alcoholism, and physical problems, died of liver disease. The client stated that both parents had been emotionally abu-

sive and neglectful in providing even the basics of food, shelter, and clothing. Describing herself as shy and timid, she was an average student who attracted little attention from her teachers. She had a few friends but was not popular. After graduating from high school, she worked as a clerk-typist in a bank and married her husband in her mid-20s. She reported that he was abusive and alcoholic, but she felt dependent on him. She wanted children but had several miscarriages and never gave birth. Despite their chronic problems, the couple did socialize and spend time together.

Ms. Butler worked at a few different jobs as a typist and word processor. She had little contact with her family, had few involvements outside marriage and work, but did go to church regularly and occasionally attended Adult Children of Alcoholics (ACOA) meetings. She met a woman friend there whom she described as like a mother to her, and her illness and death were a shock. When Ms. Butler's husband left her, she felt lost and hopeless about her life. When she subsequently lost her job, she became more withdrawn.

Despite having had a family history of depression and a childhood history of neglect, inconsistency, and many losses, which undoubtedly contributed to her being somewhat depressed, dependent, and unfulfilled all of her life, Ms. Butler appeared to maintain reasonably adequate functioning and to be able to enjoy herself at times until recent losses led to her increasingly depressed state.

In the first session, the client blamed herself for her lack of energy, motivation, and ability to get on with her life. The worker supported the efforts the client had made to keep going, as well as her having sought help at this time. She also explained the role of depression in causing many of the client's symptoms, including her excessive feelings of responsibility and self-blame. Additionally she discussed how talking with the worker coupled with taking Prozac might help her. The meeting concluded with the worker and client's contracting to meet twice weekly for five weeks, and if indicated, weekly for 10 sessions, for a total of 20 sessions. The worker asked the client to keep a daily journal of her thoughts and feelings, reduce her intake of coffee, and continue to take her prescribed medication.

The second session took place three days later. Although the client had kept the journal, she thought it was a useless exercise: "All I wrote about is how alone and lost I feel and how weak I am." The worker empathized with the client and supported her efforts in keeping the journal in spite of how she felt. She then began to explore the client's feelings of aloneness. Ms. Butler said she became worse several years earlier but also reported often feeling lonely during most of her childhood and adult life.

Ms. Butler: It feels like I can't hold on to anyone or anything.

Worker: Can you say more about what you mean?

Ms. Butler: My best friend died of cancer. She was like a mother to me. She would listen to me and give me advice. We would take walks together and shop. Why did she have to die? I wish I could have helped her more.

Worker: What could you have done?

Ms. Butler: I just think I should have been able to do something, but that's just the story of my life. I don't think I've been of any help to anyone.

Worker: You are being very hard on yourself. That's part of being depressed.

Ms. Butler: Then maybe I've been depressed all of my life.

Worker: As you are talking about yourself and your life, it is hard for me to get a sense of what you are feeling.

Ms. Butler: I don't have any feelings anymore. I feel numb and lifeless. I can't even cry.

Worker: Were you able to cry after your husband left and your friend died?

Ms. Butler: I cried my eyes out, and then I got angry at everyone, but it didn't bring them back. I just don't see anything positive ahead for me. I've never been an optimistic person or liked myself very much.

Worker: You have had a hard life with a lot of losses and disappointments.

Ms. Butler: I still should be able to get out of bed in the morning.

It's so difficult. I think I would feel better if I could get myself up and moving.

The worker explored how Ms. Butler felt when she awakened. Initially it was difficult for the client to pinpoint what she felt, but with the worker's gentle prodding, she spoke of her sense of aloneness, her wish to escape from her empty life, and her feelings of responsibility for all that had happened.

Worker: It is hard to feel so powerless over your life.

Ms. Butler: Everything feels so overwhelming.

Worker: We need to take it one step at a time. Can you think of anything that might help you get started in the morning?

Ms. Butler: Coffee used to help, but I'm trying to drink less. I don't know what else might help. I used to like to watch TV and read the newspaper. The TV is in the living room, and my father doesn't bring the paper home anymore. Sometimes I don't even get dressed.

Worker: What shows do you like?

Ms. Butler: I like the Today show and some of the other talk shows.

Worker: Do you think you could try to go into the living room and turn on the TV a few times this week and watch for a while? Perhaps you also could try to get dressed and go for a walk to get the paper one morning.

Ms. Butler: Well, at least I can try.

The worker and client met six times over the next three weeks. The client continued to write in her journal, and the worker used the journal entries as the starting-off point for the sessions.

Worker: There can be different kinds of emotions that people have when they are depressed, such as sadness, anger, disappointment, longing, or feelings of aloneness. It would be helpful to be more in touch with your feelings. For example, when you think about your husband, what emotions come up?

Ms. Butler: I miss the good times, even though he drank and yelled a lot.

Worker: Tell me a little more about the good times.

Ms. Butler: He had a great sense of humor and liked to have fun.

Worker: You seem very sad.

Ms. Butler: I guess I am. I don't like to feel this way.

Worker: I can understand that, but the feelings are still there, and they come out in other ways.

Ms. Butler: I don't know what I did to make him leave me.

Worker: It seems hard for you to believe that he was the one who had the problems.

Ms. Butler: That's what my friend used to tell me. She said that I was too good for him. I wish she were still here. I used to feel better when I talked to her. Oh dear, I'm crying.

Worker: It's okay to let out your feelings.

In another session, the client brought up her feelings of responsibility, low self-esteem, and pessimism.

Worker: It's understandable that you come to think about yourself and others in these ways as a result of all you have been through.

Ms. Butler: What if I had been different as a child? What if I had been more like my sister? Maybe things would have turned out differently?

Worker: You keep telling yourself that something is wrong with you and that you are responsible for everything that has happened. Do you ever think that your parents failed you in some ways? You were the child who needed to be taken care of.

Ms. Butler: I always felt that it was my job to take care of them.

Worker: I can see that you have felt this sense of responsibility for a very long time and you carry that burden into your other relationships as well.

Ms. Butler: What other way is there?

Worker: You have needs too, and it is sad that most people in your life have been unable to be there for you since you were very young.

Ms. Butler: I've never thought of it that way.

The worker and client continued to discuss some of the difficult experiences she had had earlier in her life with her family and then later with her husband.

In another meeting, the client said she did not know how to keep herself from having negative thoughts.

Worker: It might be helpful when you are blaming yourself for a red flag to go up that signals you to stop a minute and tell yourself that you are not a bad person and do not have to keep feeling that you are.

Ms. Butler: Do you really think that might help?

Worker: There's nothing to lose by trying, and then we can talk about what happens and explore why you have these thoughts about yourself.

By the ninth session, it was apparent that Ms. Butler felt less hopeless and was showing improvement in her ability to mobilize herself. The worker began to focus on the client's isolation from others. The client said she felt fearful of being rejected because of her feeling that she had nothing to offer anyone. The worker attempted to help her correct her perception of herself by discussing how she had established other relationships with people at work and at ACOA meetings. In this session, the worker and client also discussed the fact that 11 sessions remained. At the end of the meeting, she asked the client to think about ways of increasing her contacts with others. The client thought that she might attend ACOA or her church, and the worker supported these ideas.

Ms. Butler failed to appear for the next meeting nor did she call. When the worker telephoned to see what had happened, the client said she was too depressed to come in.

Worker: Has anything happened since we met that disturbed you?

Ms. Butler: Nothing. I just think all this talk is a waste of time. I'm a hopeless case, so why bother with me?

Worker: You seem angry.

Ms. Butler: I'm not angry. I'm disgusted with myself. Nothing is ever going to change.

Worker: I can hear that you are upset, but it's important for you to come in so we can talk.

In looking at the worker's notes from the previous session and the telephone conversation with the client, the worker's supervisor suggested *that her mention of termination may have made the client feel that the worker, like everyone else, was going to abandon her. She noted the client's tendency to use avoidance and turn her anger on herself. The worker realized too that the main reason the client was improving was their relationship; ending the treatment was going to be difficult.*

In the tenth session the client initially denied having any reaction to the worker's comments in their prior meeting. The worker commented that it would be understandable if Ms. Butler was distressed about the limited time remaining in the light of the many losses that she had experienced, as well as their positive connection. The client acknowledged that thinking about ending had upset her because she could talk to the worker, felt less alone, and did not want to lose her. The worker said that ending might be hard for the client since she had lost so many people in her life but that they did have time left. She added that the fact that Ms. Butler and the worker had made a good connection was indicative of the client's ability to form new relationships with others. The client agreed to try to attend an ACOA meeting the following week and to resume going to church.

The next part of the treatment focused on the client's experiences at ACOA and church and involved the worker's suggestions about ways that Ms. Butler could reach out to others and discussion of the client's attempts to do this and her tendency to blame herself when her initial efforts seemed unsuccessful. She also helped her to develop alternative interpretations of others' reactions and new ways of relating to others. The client made progress, but the ending phase of the treatment was very difficult for both worker and client. Ms. Butler experienced a resurgence of her depressed feelings, but the worker was able to help her deal with her sense of loss. Her small successes in mobilizing herself and reaching out to others led her to feel that she might continue to make progress without the worker. Worker and client arranged for follow-up and telephone contact if necessary.

Discussion

The worker used a combination of psychodynamic, task-oriented, and cognitive-behavioral techniques in order to help the client resolve her depression and decrease her social isolation. Within the context of a

supportive relationship, the worker encouraged ventilation and explo-
ration of the client's symptoms and relevant history; offered sustain-
ment and guidance; provided education and assigned certain tasks;
engaged the client in problem solving; helped the client to identify and
label her feelings; corrected some distortions in her thinking; enabled
the client to make connections between her early losses and deprivation
and her current state of depression; addressed the client's reactions to
the subject of termination that led to some resistance to treatment; en-
couraged the client to reach out to others; and helped her to develop
new ways of interpreting others' reactions to her.

ANXIETY

Like depression, anxiety disorders should be differentiated from anxious feelings that are common to everyone or part of other syndromes
such as borderline personality or psychotic disorders.

Definition

Three of the more common types of anxiety disorders are panic attacks;
agoraphobia, social, or other types of phobias; and generalized anxiety
disorder. Panic attacks are characterized by a discreet period of intense
discomfort in which there are multiple physical symptoms and severe
emotional distress so that the person seeks to avoid those situations that
might engender such an episode. Agoraphobia, social, and other types
of phobia reflect fears of specific kinds of situations, avoidance of those
circumstances, and severe, if not disabling, anxiety and terror when facing the feared situations—for example, being outside one's home alone,
going to a party, crossing a bridge, or traveling in an airplane. Generalized anxiety disorder is associated with excessive anxiety and worry that
occur over a long period of time, difficulties controlling the anxiety and
worry, and physical symptoms, such as restlessness or being keyed up or
on edge, becoming easily fatigued, irritability, sleep disturbance, difficulty concentrating, and muscle tension. All of these disorders result in
significant distress or impairment in social, occupational, or other important areas of functioning (APA, 1994, pp. 199–218).

Although there are differences of opinion as to whether the main causes of anxiety disorders are biological, psychodynamic, or cognitive-behavioral (Austrian, 1995; Beck, Emery, & Greenberg, 1985; Crits-Christoph, Crits-Christoph, Wolf-Palacio, Fichter, & Rudick, 1995; Shear, Cloitre, & Heckelman, 1995; Wright & Borden, 1991), there is agreement that individuals with anxiety disorders commonly experience excessive worry and dread and engage in attempts to avoid anxiety-provoking stimuli or situations or difficulties controlling worrisome thoughts or feelings.

Medications can be helpful in relieving anxiety symptoms, but they often have side effects, and in the case of minor tranquilizers, they are easily abused and may become addictive.

Specific Foci

The goals of ISTT with individuals who have anxiety disorders are to relieve the anxiety or phobic symptoms and to improve their functioning and/or to help them better deal with the impact of their disorders on themselves and others. The practitioner can use all of the components of ISTT but the specific foci of intervention may include the following components:

1. Educating clients about the fact that their symptoms are related to anxiety rather than other causes such as physical illness.
2. Helping clients to see that their anxiety symptoms may be ways of dealing with unwanted, unknown, or troubling thoughts and feelings or part of their characteristic way of thinking about life.
3. Identifying and labeling the current triggers (problems, interactions, experiences, thoughts, feelings, and behaviors) or consequences of the anxiety symptoms.
4. Establishing the underlying causes of the anxiety—for example, unwanted or threatening thoughts and feelings; separation and loss; autonomy and independence; guilt; success or failure; loss of control; rejection and criticism; positive attention; fear of making mistakes, disappointing the self and others, or being exposed or found out; or illness, aging, and death.

5. Exploring the connection between the client's current state and past experiences, vulnerabilities, and unmet needs that may be contributing or causing the anxiety symptoms.
6. Identifying clients' attitudes toward or ways of perceiving themselves or others that may be causing, intensifying, or perpetuating their anxiety.
7. Enabling clients to understand whatever dynamic or past issues that may be operating in their anxiety and to find ways of dealing with these more effectively.
8. Encouraging clients to make small steps toward facing their anxiety.
9. Helping clients to find ways of talking themslves through, putting aside, limiting, or alleviating their anxious thoughts and feelings, and behaving.
10. Helping clients to improve their problem-solving abilities in situations that trigger their anxiety.

The Interventive Process

In the following case, ISTT was used in helping a client who presented with severe anxiety.

THE HAMILTON CASE

Ms. Hamilton, a 40-year-old divorcée, sought help at a mental health clinic for long-standing anxiety that included hypervigilance, a sense of dread, muscle tension, fearfulness of specific situations and sometimes heart palpitations, shortness of breath, jittery feelings, and cold sweats. Although she had suffered from these symptoms for as long as she remembered, only recently had she begun to feel that her life was unmanageable. She felt anxious much of the time, was unable to enjoy or feel excitement about anything, and was increasingly horrified at the extent to which her life was restricted. She avoided all potentially anxiety-producing situations such as driving alone, flying, going to unfamiliar places, and venturing more than short distances from home. She wanted to be more adventuresome, independent, able to travel and able to enjoy life itself. She took Ativan, a minor tranquilizer, on an as-needed basis but did not like relying on it.

Ms. Hamilton lived in an apartment above her father in a three-family house that he owned. Her older brothers, all of whom were married, lived nearby. She was employed as a teacher, was dedicated to her students, and had some close friends, whom she had known for many years. The client reported that she had been a shy, sensitive, and easily frightened child and experienced periods of increased anxiety since high school. She recalled having difficulty going to kindergarten, making the transition from elementary to high school, going to college, traveling alone to her first job, making the adjustment to marriage, vacationing with her husband, going through her divorce, and mourning her mother's death. The client had sought counseling for the first time when she was going through her divorce. Ms. Hamilton said that she had read all the self-help books she could find on anxiety and had tried most of the exercises recommended, but nothing seemed to help. A year ago she reluctantly asked her physician for medication.

The youngest of four children and the only female, Ms. Hamilton was close to her family with whom she spent considerable time and shared common interests such as handball and singing. When Ms. Hamilton was five years of age, her mother was diagnosed with bone cancer of the leg; she recovered but continued to require frequent hospitalizations and was frail and relatively housebound. The client had fond memories of her mother, who had passed away five years earlier from a heart attack. The client remembered her as having a positive attitude and never complaining. She described her father as very involved with the family and somewhat overprotective. Ms. Hamilton lived at home during college and after until she was 30, when she married a man whom she thought was kind and caring but with whom she was not in love. They were not compatible and divorced amicably six years ago.

Ms. Hamilton wanted short-term treatment that would be very structured and focused on decreasing her symptoms. Her insurance covered 15 sessions. When she asked if the worker had ever treated anyone with anxiety like she had, the worker assured the client that she had and that she thought she could be helpful to Ms. Hamilton. The worker explained that in order to help her, they would need to identify the thoughts and feelings that both triggered and were associated with her anxiety and fears, help her to find ways of managing her anxiety better so that she could do more of the things she wanted to, and explore the possible underlying reasons for her symptoms in order to alleviate them. The worker and client agreed to meet weekly, and the worker suggested that the client might try to be aware of what she was thinking about when she began to experience her anxiety symptoms.

The worker's assessment suggested that Ms. Hamilton showed reasonably intact ego functioning and many strengths. She was successful at her job, had a good support system, was intelligent, related easily, and was motivated for treatment. She also appeared very controlled and tense, worried, dependent, and unable to relax and enjoy her life. Based on Ms. Hamilton's history, it seemed likely that her symptoms had multiple determinants: separation anxiety related to her mother's illness and hospitalizations, an early challenge to her sense of safety and security, suppression of and guilt about normal thoughts and feelings that seemed dangerous or selfish in the light of her mother's frail condition, identification with the mother's restricted life, and the absence of encouragement and role models for autonomous behavior.

Ms. Hamilton began the second session by reporting an incident that had triggered her symptoms during the week. Although she had taken her medication when she started to feel jittery, she recalled that just before she got the "shakes," she had been thinking about her father's upcoming vacation:

Ms. Hamilton: I felt guilty and selfish because rather than thinking about his safety, I worried that something would happen to me while he was away.

Worker: It sounds as if you think that's a bad thought.

Ms. Hamilton: It's just not right to be so concerned about myself. He deserves a vacation. I should be happy for him.

Worker: You have needs too. It's normal to think about oneself at times. Attempting to push away such thoughts or feelings can actually bring on anxiety.

Ms. Hamilton: If I let myself think that way, I'm afraid that I will get even more anxious.

Worker: What specifically are you afraid of?

Ms. Hamilton: I'm afraid I'll get out of control or go crazy or have a heart attack. I don't even want to talk about it now.

Worker: I'm not going to let anything happen to you. Can you try to tell me what you worry about?

Ms. Hamilton: I picture myself running wildly through the streets to get someplace safe, like my apartment, or blurting out things that don't make any sense. Do you think I'm crazy?

Worker: You're very far from being crazy but are very afraid of even normal thoughts and feelings. It's important for you to tell yourself when you start to feel this way that you are not going crazy or becoming ill and that you will be all right.

Over the next three sessions, the worker maintained the focus on the client's symptoms and helped the client to identify the thoughts that preceded and triggered her anxious feelings, to be more tolerant of the thoughts that were so unacceptable to her, and to make a conscious effort to reassure herself that her thoughts were understandable and would not result in her losing control. By the fifth session, the client reported that during a conversation with a friend, she started to get nervous and quickly got off the telephone. She tried to remember what she had been thinking just before it happened, realized that she was irritated, and was amazed that the feeling of nervousness actually subsided.

In the sixth session, the client said that she had been wondering why she is so anxious:

Ms. Hamilton: I don't understand why I am this way. What is the matter with me?

Worker: Perhaps there is a connection between your anxiety and fears and the fact that your mother was sick and spent a lot of time in the hospital and was away from you when you needed her. All through your childhood, you must have worried about whether she would get sick again.

Ms. Hamilton: My mother was a brave woman. She never let on that she was in pain and was always cheerful, but we could see how hard it was for her just by looking at her face, and we always worried about her health.

Worker: You learned at a very early age that the world was not safe.

Ms. Hamilton: When I came home from school, I always worried about whether my mother would be there or what kind of day she had.

Worker: It would have been terrible if you did come home to find that she wasn't there. Maybe thinking about it all the time was a way of protecting yourself.

Ms. Hamilton: Your saying that is really strange. One day when I was in high school, I was feeling really good. I wasn't thinking about anything, and when I got to the front door my oldest brother told me that Mom had been rushed to the hospital. I couldn't believe it. I was in shock. She got better, but what I remember is that I had been having such a good day that I forgot to think about her. It was like the one day I wasn't worried, something happened.

Worker: You seemed to feel that worrying kept her safe and that having a good time led to her illness.

Ms. Hamilton: I hadn't thought about it that way. I know I felt really guilty about having a good time and not thinking about her.

In the seventh session, when the worker asked if the client had thoughts about their previous meeting, Ms. Hamilton replied that she was conscious of feeling guilty a lot of the time. The worker connected this to the client's early experiences and commented that children worry that they will burden or upset a parent who is ill if they are angry or wish things were different or want things for themselves. She added that sometimes children feel responsible for the parent or that they should not have good times if the parent cannot join in. The client sighed and said that it hurt her to see her mother so sick: "I also felt bad for my father, who spent so much time taking care of her." The worker said that it had been a hard time for everyone, especially Ms. Hamilton, who was a child who loved her mother but who also had needs of her own that had to be put aside. The worker added that it was possible that Ms. Hamilton's difficulties venturing out from her home might also be related to feeling that she should stay home and take care of her mother.

In the eighth session, the client reported that she had had a better week than she had had for a very long time. The worker thought this *might be a good time for them to discuss small steps that Ms. Hamilton might take toward overcoming some of her fears. Because walking was an activity that the client enjoyed and could do near her home, the worker focused on helping Ms. Hamilton to expand her horizons. The client was fearful of walking without a companion and of going too far. They discussed how she might experiment a little in a way that would make her feel safe. They agreed that in addition to her reminding her-self that the anxiety would not hurt her, she might keep the house in sight as she walked a short distance alone. The client agreed to try this.*

In the ninth session, the client reported with excitement that she went walking by herself twice, but when she reached the corner of her block she started to get nervous. She told herself that she was close enough to get home if she needed to and tried to walk farther. She com-mented that she was astonished that she walked another block and wasn't even that anxious.

In the remaining six sessions, the worker continued to focus on sup-porting the client's here-and-now functioning directly and on connect-ing her current anxieties to her past experiences. Ms. Hamilton continued her efforts to face anxiety-provoking situations such as walking alone and driving near her home alone. The combination of her increased understanding of the likely causes of her anxiety, her im-proved ability to identify and accept her thoughts and feelings, her abil-ity to talk herself through anxiety-provoking situations, and the success of her small, concrete steps in expanding her activities helped her gain confidence and trust in her ability to face more difficult challenges. At the time the treatment concluded, the client planned to practice her new behaviors. Although the worker suggested that it might be benefi-cial for Ms. Hamilton to obtain some additional help from participating in a support group, the client said she wanted to try it on her own until the follow-up visit.

Discussion

The main interventions that the worker used were (1) identifying some of the triggers and thoughts and feelings associated with her client's anx-iety and fears; (2) helping the client to accept that her so-called negative or unacceptable thoughts and feelings were normal and understandable and that she was not crazy or in danger of losing control or having a heart attack; (3) teaching her to talk herself through her anxiety and fears; (4) helping the client to connect her current anxiety symptoms to her early experiences related to her mother's illness and its aftermath; and (5) problem solving with and encouraging the client to make small steps toward facing her anxiety. Although she was not cured by the end of the treatment, she was making slow and steady progress.

SCHIZOPHRENIA

This disturbance involves more profound and pervasive symptoms than do depressive and anxiety disorders and tends to be associated with severe impairments in interpersonal relationships, self-care, and social, occupational, and other areas of functioning. Not all schizophrenic individuals have the same degree of disability, and many are able to achieve some independence and stability. They vary in their ego capacities, family supports, and environmental resources.

Definition

The four main subtypes of schizophrenia are paranoid, disorganized, catatonic, and undifferentiated. They are defined by the predominant symptomatology at the time a person is evaluated. The common features of these and other subtypes are delusions, hallucinations, disorganized speech and thinking, or catatonic behavior; negative symptoms such as flat, constricted, or inappropriate affect; lack of will; and social withdrawal (APA, 1994, pp. 147–159).

Although there is increasing evidence that schizophrenia has a biological basis, there also are psychodynamic, developmental, familial, and environmental factors that appear to contribute to this disorder (Austrian, 1995). Whatever the cause, individuals with schizophrenia generally exhibit impaired functioning in many areas: coping with internal and external stimuli and environmental demands; maintenance of ego boundaries; reality testing, thought processes, impulse control, judgment, object relations, perception, memory, concentration, comprehension, and ability to organize and synthesize perceptions; and problem-solving capacities, skills in daily living, and ability to cope with stress (Goldstein, 1995a, pp. 268–274).

Treatment generally is not aimed at "curing" the disorder but on helping to reduce and control symptoms, improve social functioning, and prevent further deterioration or relapse. Major tranquilizers or antipsychotic drugs seem to help many, though by no means all, schizophrenic individuals to become less symptomatic and more organized in their thinking and behavior, but they do not necessarily enable them to function more autonomously and to cope with interpersonal relationships, work, and other social roles. Additionally, noncompliance with medication is a serious problem in causing repeated psychotic episodes, and many schizophrenic individuals are at risk of developing more acute flare-ups of psychotic symptoms whether or not they take medication regularly. The use of psychotropic drugs is not without its problems since they tend to have side effects, some of them quite severe and irreversible.

Successful intervention requires a combination of interventions: medications; provision of external structure such as supervised independent apartment arrangements, halfway houses or residences, group homes, day hospitals, and sheltered workshops; case management, in which a worker oversees and coordinates the client's treatment, living arrangements, and functioning in the community and intervenes on the client's behalf (Iodice & Wodarski, 1987); individual treatment aimed at enhancing the client's capacities, communication, daily living, interpersonal, and problem-solving skills; family intervention focused on helping the family understand and support the schizophrenic member and modify dysfunctional interactions with him or her; and mobilization of and linkage to social resources (Goldstein, 1995a, pp. 268–274).

Specific Foci

The goals of ISTT with individuals who are schizophrenic are to restore or improve their functioning, help them prevent a recurrence of a more acute state, enable them to maintain themselves in the community, and assist them in dealing with the impact of their disorder. The specific foci of intervention may include the following components:

1. Provision of information regarding schizophrenia with respect to multiple factors that make the individual prone to certain thoughts, feelings, and behavior.
2. Discussion of the rationale for and implications of certain interventions, including the use of psychotropic drugs and their side effects.
3. Identifying and labeling the environmental stressors that may contribute to increasing states of disorganization.
4. Identifying and building on the client's strengths.
5. Sustaining and enhancing coping capacities and improving communication, daily living, problem solving, interpersonal, and socialization skills.
6. Using the worker-client relationship as a vehicle for anticipation and rehearsal of new ways of behaving with others and for reality testing.
7. Planning with the client, locating resources, and advocating.
8. Collaborating with and involving others on behalf of the client.
9. Monitoring the client's condition, including his or her use of and response to medication.
10. Intervening in crisis situations.

The Interventive Process

In the following example, a man with the diagnosis of chronic schizophrenia is helped to maintain employment by means of ISTT focused on improving his ego functioning and capacity to relate to others.

THE WILKES CASE

John Wilkes, a thirty-three-year-old single Caucasian, was referred to a supportive work program by his counselor at the New York State Vocational Educational Services for Individuals with Disabilities (VESID). He was diagnosed with chronic schizophrenia, paranoid type, and was taking an antipsychotic medication, Mellaril, and Cogentin for side effects. Mr. Wilkes resided with his parents and his younger sister and her two children. Although he had held numerous jobs previously, at this time he was supported financially by his parents and received Medicaid.

At his initial appointment, Mr. Wilkes appeared highly motivated for full-time work and indicated he was seeking help merely to please his parents. Although he had shown difficulties maintaining jobs in the past, he was unconcerned about his ability to succeed. He reported that his parents wanted him to get a job but were overly protective, doubting of his capacities, and fearful that the stress of a full-time job would cause a relapse. Mr. Wilkes admitted that he had held a number of jobs previously that he had quit or had to leave. When the worker asked for details, Mr. Wilkes responded with exasperation, saying he had been over all this so many times and asked the worker if she had read his records. The worker said she knew it was hard for the client to have to repeat himself but indicated that it would help her to get to know him better if he could tell her his story in his own words. Mr. Wilkes reluctantly agreed and in a rather mechanical way recounted his job history.

The worker learned that the client had worked previously as a file clerk, a messenger, and a receptionist. Four months earlier, he was on a job for eight weeks when he thought that people were talking about him. After confronting his co-workers, they denied it. He then became argumentative and was told to go home for the day. When the worker inquired about what he thought his co-workers were saying about him, the client explained that he believed they had observed him taking his medication and were talking about his being a "mental case." After this incident, he stopped taking his medication, his functioning on the job deteriorated, and he was terminated. His parents brought him to the emergency room, and he returned to his medication regimen.

The client and worker talked about his other job experiences, and the worker learned that Mr. Wilkes would function adequately for about a month and then some problem would arise. The client believed that others provoked him and were responsible for his difficulties and that he had not found the right job. He told the worker that he had been hospitalized first in his late adolescence and twice subsequently. He knew he had to take his medication, but when he felt good, he stopped taking it. He added that he had learned his lesson and would not do this again. He did not think he needed any help and just wanted to get back to work.

The worker supported the client's desire to work and indicated that her role was to help him to succeed in the job. She explained that the agency places clients in positions, and she would be available to help him with any problems that might arise, particularly problems that others might cause him. She asked if he would like his parents to join them at some point in the future. The worker explained the procedures of the program, and they contracted for 12 sessions with the explicit purpose being to help Mr. Wilkes stay employed.

In the second session, the worker informed Mr. Wilkes that she would be able to secure employment for him as a file clerk in a small law firm where he could work three days a week initially and switch to full time later. He immediately asked if his co-workers would know about his psychiatric problems and that he took medication. The worker explained that because it was a supportive work program, only the supervisor would know of his difficulties. Mr. Wilkes became angry and said he did not want anyone to know because it was none of their business if he was schizophrenic. He feared that everyone would start talking about him again. As the worker explored Mr. Wilkes's fears, it became clear that he was attributing to others his own negative feelings about his psychiatric diagnosis and the fact that he had to take medication. The worker then asked the client what he knew about schizophrenia. Although the client had some intellectual understanding of his condition, it was clear to the worker that he had not accepted it on an emotional level. The worker and client spent much of the session exploring the subjective feelings Mr. Wilkes had about his condition and its implications. The worker tried to help the client understand that he was not "weak," "stupid," or "crazy," gave him additional information about schizophrenia, and reaffirmed her desire to help him succeed at work. Mr. Wilkes agreed to try the new position, and the remainder of the session was spent discussing the particulars of the job, his fears of beginning, and how he thought his parents would react.

The third session focused on the client's initial adjustment at the job.

He enjoyed the work and found his supervisor helpful and understanding, but he remained distant from his co-workers. He said he just wanted to do his work and was fearful of getting into hassles with others. By the fourth session, Mr. Wilkes reticently reported that he had had an altercation with a co-worker who had accused him of misfiling a document. He was adamant that it was not his fault, and he yelled at the co-worker, who complained to the supervisor. The supervisor reprimanded Mr. Wilkes for yelling. In talking to the worker, Mr. Wilkes kept repeating that he had not made a mistake. The worker told Mr. Wilkes that she could understand his distress at having been falsely accused but pointed out that his supervisor likely was more concerned about his yelling. The worker asked if he could think about other ways of dealing with his co-workers in the future. Mr. Wilkes became suspicious of the worker's motivation and accused her of blaming him when he had not done anything wrong. The worker said she was not blaming him; she just wanted to help him to find a better way of managing situations at work so that he could keep his job. "That is what you want, isn't it?" Mr. Wilkes agreed and became calmer. The worker and client talked about strategies for handling such difficulties and role-played how Mr. Wilkes might have more effectively dealt with the problem.

In the fifth session, Mr. Wilkes appeared somewhat depressed and said he did not know if the job was going to work out.

Mr. Wilkes: It's happening again. The other people at work are ignoring me and talking about me.

Worker: What do you think they are saying about you?

Mr. Wilkes: They probably are saying that I am stupid or crazy. Maybe the supervisor told them I was schizophrenic, and that's why they are avoiding and making fun of me.

Worker: I suppose that is possible, but you told me that you wanted to stay by yourself, and maybe they are respecting your wishes.

Mr. Wilkes: Maybe. But that doesn't explain why they are talking about me.

Worker: What made you think the others were talking about you?

Mr. Wilkes: They were laughing.

Worker: Is it possible that the men were just joking with one another to pass the time rather than talking about you? Most people want some relief from their work and to socialize some. It's possible that because you are so sensitive about your illness, you tend to misinterpret others' reactions. It would be good if you could consider this possibility.

This led to further discussion of Mr. Wilkes's negative feelings about himself, particularly that being schizophrenic meant that he was not able to succeed. The worker pointed out the capabilities that he had demonstrated previously and suggested that just because he felt inadequate did not necessarily mean his co-workers shared his opinion or that they even knew about his condition. Mr. Wilkes said he wanted to work but was fearful that he could not take the stress. The worker suggested that it might be helpful if she set up a meeting with Mr. Wilkes, his supervisor, and herself to find out what the supervisor had told others, what she thought about his job performance, and how she might assist him on the job.

The three of them met the following morning, and the supervisor, who was accustomed to working with disabled clients, was supportive of Mr. Wilkes and praised him for being conscientious, punctual, and competent. She assured Mr. Wilkes that she had not shared any information with his co-workers and she had not heard anything negative about him. She did share that Mr. Wilkes seemed uncomfortable around the other men and women and that she thought they left him alone because that was the way he wanted it. When the worker asked the supervisor how she thought the workers would respond if Mr. Wilkes were to reach out to them, she indicated that she thought they would be accepting.

In the sixth session, Mr. Wilkes said he felt a little better at the job but still uncomfortable with his co-workers. In addition, his parents continued to be worried about the job stress and wanted to talk to the worker. A collateral session was scheduled. The worker and client then focused on Mr. Wilkes's interactions with his co-workers:

Mr. Wilkes: I just don't think that people like me, and I don't know how to talk to people. The only people I speak to are my family.

Worker: I'm a person, and you seem to be able to talk to me pretty well, and you also get along with your supervisor.

Mr. Wilkes: You're different.

Worker: Maybe we can practice here how you might talk to your co-workers.

Mr. Wilkes brought his parents to the seventh session. The worker listened to their fears, noted their caring and concern, and indicated that she understood that they wanted only what was best for their son. Mr. Wilkes explained to his parents how much it meant to him to be successful at work, and the worker added that with their support, she thought that he could succeed. She explained that the client felt confused by their concern and interpreted it as a lack of confidence in his abilities. They assured their son that they knew he was capable but that they worried about him. The worker suggested that it might be helpful for them to attend an organization that was founded and run by families who had a member diagnosed with schizophrenia. The parents took the information and said they would attend a meeting.

In the eighth meeting, Mr. Wilkes reported proudly that although he had a problem with his supervisor over a work assignment, he had taken the worker's advice about how to approach a disagreement and said it had helped to have practiced with the worker. The worker congratulated him for the way he had handled himself and reminded the client that they had four remaining sessions. Mr. Wilkes responded with disappointment and some fear. The worker empathized and wondered if it might help if they spaced the sessions out to every other week and spoke on the telephone during the alternate weeks. That would give them two more months of working together. The client was visibly relieved, and they discussed how to use their remaining time together. The worker also took the opportunity to suggest that the client might want to think about joining the group that she had referred his parents to.

Over the next two months, the worker and client continued to focus on his adjustment at work. His reality testing, impulse control, judgment, and self-esteem improved, and he was able to use strategies that they had discussed and role-played to avoid or resolve conflicts. Al-

though he interacted with his co-workers minimally, he was less suspicious and uncomfortable. He attended some group meetings with his parents, and these helped him to become more accepting of his condition. At their follow-up six weeks after the termination, Mr. Wilkes was continuing to function well on his job and was planning to attend more group meetings.

Discussion

The worker focused on (1) helping the client to gain more understanding of his condition, lessening the stigma that he attached to it, and pointing out how he attributed his negative feelings about himself to others; (2) identifying and building on his motivation and capacity for work; (3) developing the client's understanding of what was interfering with his success on the job and helping him to develop new ways of coping with his supervisor and co-workers; (4) using the worker-client relationship for practicing new interactions with others; and (5) collaborating with the client's work supervisor and parents on behalf of the client and referring the parents and the client to a resource that would help them cope with the client's condition.

PERSONALITY DISORDERS

Because of their entrenched nature, personality disorders constitute a particularly vexing group of disturbances for brief treatment. Although psychodynamically oriented and cognitive-behavioral short-term models have been used with clients who show this type of disturbance, not all clients display the motivation and capacities that make such approaches possible.

Definition

Individuals with a personality disorder usually show enduring dysfunctional traits and patterns of perceiving the self and relating to others and the world, problems in affectivity, and difficulties with impulse control. Such characteristics, however adaptive they may have been at one time, are inflexible and pervasive across a broad range of personal and social situations, lead to significant distress or impairment in many areas of functioning, and tend to deviate markedly from the expectations of the individual's culture. There are 10 specific types of personality disorders: paranoid, schizoid, schizotypal, antisocial, borderline, histrionic, narcissistic, avoidant, dependent, and obsessive-compulsive (APA, 1994, pp. 275–286).

Individuals with a personality disorder tend to view all of their behavior as a natural part of who they are, even though it may be readily apparent to others that their traits and patterns are problematic. For example, a man who has a highly suspicious bent would not view this trait as a liability but as a necessary and justifiable reaction to life even though others experience his mistrustful attitudes and behavior as distancing. Such persons generally do not know they have a personality disorder, nor do they want help for their disturbance per se. Instead they want relief from the problems or suffering that result from their usual ways of functioning in the world without seeing that it is their characteristic behavior that gets them into trouble. They often blame others for their difficulties.

Specific Foci

When clients do show the motivation and capacities described in Chapter 1, ISTT can encompass efforts to treat the client's personality disorder itself through a combination of psychodynamic and cognitive-behavioral methods. Because individuals who present with a personality disorder usually seek help to relieve their situation or suffering but not to change anything about themselves, ISTT generally attempts to help the client to see how selected aspects of his or her usual functioning are connected to the problem at hand and to assist the client in modifying these and acquiring more adaptive coping strategies. This may require that the worker and client understand the function that the problematic characteristic serves in the client's overall adaptation to life, that they address the consequences to the client of relinquishing it even in part, and that they work on helping the client to consider and adopt alternative ways of dealing with life. Clients may wish to continue the patterns that are hurtful to them because they also provide some benefit; for example, excessive drinking may be harmful but also serves to alleviate depression. Consequently, in order to engage clients in making very specific and concrete changes, it may be necessary to appeal to their better interests, that is, to help them recognize the benefits of altering or giving up behavior that they do not think is problematic and that they enjoy.

Although personality disorders may be associated with core conflicts and defenses, it often is the case, particularly with clients who have more severe personality problems, that the client shows certain ego, object relations, and self-deficits. Helping clients may require that the worker educate them about what aspects of their functioning are interfering with their lives and to help them in establishing new skills. For example, a client who lacks object constancy, that is, the ability to hold on to a positive sense of a significant person when separated from or frustrated by that person, may characteristically seek out others to soothe them without regard for whether or not such individuals are decent, caring, safe, and appropriate. It is unlikely that brief treatment will help such a client to establish the object constancy that is lacking. It can enable clients, however, to begin to understand their experience around separations or, when frustrated, to track their patterns of behavior, find ways of managing their needs differently, and learn how to exercise better judgment about and set limits on others.

The Interventive Process

The following case illustrates the use of ISTT with a young woman who presented with a borderline personality disorder that reflected serious impairments in her ego functioning, self-regulation and self-esteem, and object relations.

THE LEIGH CASE

Ms. Leigh, a 25-year-old struggling actress who supported herself by being a waitress at a trendy New York restaurant, sought help at the insistence of her father, who lived in a distant city. She had confided in him that she was very upset after an ill-fated romance and had resorted to staying out all night at clubs and drinking excessively in order to cope with her aloneness. She consulted a psychiatrist, who prescribed Paxil, an antidepressant, and urged her to attend AA. Ms. Leigh described him as depressed and tense and more in need of help than she was. She was grateful that he wanted to see her only intermittently.

After going to an AA meeting, she decided that this form of assistance definitely was not for her and that she could stop drinking on her own. When walking home, she saw a mental health clinic and entered, asking if she could talk to someone. After several sessions with a woman therapist who told her repeatedly that she was self-destructive in her choice of men and her lifestyle and needed long-term treatment, she left. Her insurance company gave her the names of several social workers who worked privately, and she called one for an appointment. By this time she had used 5 of the 20 therapy sessions that her insurance allowed and had 15 remaining.

When Ms. Leigh entered the office, the worker saw an attractive, meticulously made-up, blond, polite, and seemingly poised young woman who spoke in a dramatic and humorous manner about herself and her life. She soon became tearful and emotional after she brought the new worker up to date on what had recently transpired. She spoke of her sense of aloneness and desperation and her concern that her depression was getting in the way of her pursuing her acting career. Although the worker tried to get a picture of the client's life and background and why the previous worker thought Ms. Leigh was self-destructive, it was difficult to do so because Ms. Leigh tended to jump from topic to topic in a somewhat disjointed manner. She said she had stopped going out to clubs because she didn't want to drink or meet men who only wanted to have sex with her but now was isolating herself and eating too much, which was making her gain weight and hate herself. She said she couldn't stand her job but needed the money; she was in debt because she didn't budget and overspent on taxis everywhere and buying expensive shoes. She also described being angry at her roommate for rarely being at home and at her other friends for being superficial and self-involved, in contrast to Ms. Leigh, who was more intellectual and concerned about others. In talking about her parents, Ms. Leigh described her mother as a beautiful and talented woman who had spent her life sleeping until noon and taking drugs the rest of the day, and her father as a handsome, hard-working, devoted, and successful businessman who had rescued her mother from poverty but had abandoned her for his career early in the marriage. The client said she did not know what she would do without him, yet she also said he lived in another orbit from earth and rarely descended: "I expect every man I meet to be as kind as my father, and instead they're just as crazy but never as nice. I've never met a man I didn't think was a major disappointment. Don't you agree?"

The worker's internal response to all this was to feel overwhelmed and confused. She tried her best to stay attuned to the feelings underlying the client's comments, particularly her feelings of not having anyone she could count on, not knowing where to turn, and her enormous sense of disappointment in others. Her empathic comments did seem to resonate with the client, who said she wanted to return.

In their second session, the client appeared without makeup and looked tired and somewhat disheveled. She explained that she had been up all night at a club because a friend of hers had come in from out of town and wanted to party. Ms. Leigh said, "Don't worry, I didn't have anything to drink other than club soda. I'm not an alcoholic. I only drink when I decide I want to, and I don't want to now." Ms. Leigh then described having met another man who was really good looking but "had empty spaces where his brains belonged." She went to his apartment and became enraged when he pushed her to have sex. She left hurriedly despite his promise that he would not bother her. When she got home, she called him, and they arranged to meet later in the week. When the worker asked what made Ms. Leigh agree to see him again, she replied that she knew he wasn't good for her but she didn't want to be alone. She explained that things like this always seem to happen to her, and she had been in some pretty scary situations, which she began to describe. The worker then understood why her predecessor had confronted Ms. Leigh with her self-destructiveness but restrained herself from making the same mistake.

Worker: How do you feel about what happens when you meet a man who seems to be interested in you and whom you find attractive?

Ms. Leigh: I know it's never going to work out.

Worker: How do you know?

Ms. Leigh: I know that something always goes wrong. I meet the wrong guys.

Worker: If you think that way, what makes you go out with them?

Ms. Leigh: Well, I don't really mean I know it's not going to work out. I hope I'm going to meet Mr. Right instead of Mr. Wrong, but it just doesn't happen. I don't know why. Sometimes I think I've found someone good, and then I feel so abandoned and I crash. I hate that. That's why I give them a hard time.

Worker: It seems difficult for you not to go out with a guy once he seems to show some interest in you. Do you ever find yourself thinking that it might be better not to go out?

Ms. Leigh: I want to have fun.

Worker: It seems that you often wind up feeling disappointed or really upset. Is the fun worth it?

Ms. Leigh: It's better than being by myself.

Worker: Tell me more about what that is like for you.

Ms. Leigh: I feel cut off. I have always been this way. I can't concentrate or sit still. Sometimes I can't even watch TV, although I always keep it on when I'm alone. I get down on myself and feel like something is wrong with me or that I'm not as attractive as I think I am. Sometimes I get panicky, and I try to call someone on the telephone. That's why I run up huge bills. Now I'm eating all the time. I used to smoke but I stopped. I never drink by myself.

Worker: Well that's good. I'd like to try to help you with your feelings of aloneness, because I think you would feel more in control of your own life if you could handle being by yourself and you might be better able to focus on your career. You say you want to have fun, but you also seem to pay quite a price as a result of some of the relationships you have had.

Ms. Leigh: You're so serious. What's your sign? I need to know your astrological sign. Please tell me.

Worker: I'm an Aries. What does that tell you?

Ms. Leigh: My father is an Aries. I knew there was a reason I can talk to you. That's a good sign.

Worker: What do you think about our meeting for the next few months to try to help you with your being able to be by yourself more, exercise more choice, and get back to your acting?

Ms. Leigh: See you next week.

Although the worker realized that there was a great deal about Ms. Leigh that she did not know, she liked her lively, albeit somewhat flamboyant, presentation. She seemed quite intelligent and verbal, but she did exhibit many of the characteristics reflective of borderline personality disorder (APA, 1994, pp. 280–281). She appeared to have a fluctuating sense of identity; problems being alone; and issues with abandonment, impulsiveness and self-destructive behavior; maladaptive patterns of relating to others and unstable relationships; and emotional instability, including angry outbursts. Moreover, she seemed to have problems in object constancy and self-soothing, saw others in black-and-white terms, showed difficulty maintaining a good inner core, and had difficulty regulating her self-esteem. The worker knew it would not be possible to help Ms. Leigh with all of these issues in 15 sessions but felt she might be able to help Ms. Leigh develop better ways of dealing with some of her urgent needs that propelled her into self-destructive situations.

In their third meeting, Ms. Leigh bounded into the office, flopped into the chair, and kicked off her shoes. She immediately launched into an account of her most recent adventure in the singles' scene. At a wedding in Connecticut, the photographer, whom she later learned was a doctor, had come on to her. She described him as gorgeous and a great dancer. They spent the night together just lying next to one another because she told him that she did not want to have sex. In the morning, he approached her sexually, and despite her lack of interest, she went along. He said he couldn't believe how they had clicked and that he would call her the next evening. She waited by the telephone, but he never called. She became furious and called him. When he acted as if he hardly knew her, she started yelling at him, and he responded that she was a "nut case" and if he had had any interest in seeing her again, he didn't any longer. She told him he was a creep. Ms. Leigh said she had decided to take a vacation from men but now felt totally alone and was feeling desperate. She complained that she did not know what to do with herself.

Worker: Well, you certainly have been through a lot this week. If we can go back to the beginning, I wonder what you were thinking you wanted to have happen when you met him.

Ms. Leigh: I wanted him to like me, and I thought he did.

Worker: It seems as if you felt that you had to become involved very quickly with him in order to get him to like you.

Ms. Leigh: I told him I didn't want to have sex.

Worker: What made you change your mind?

Ms. Leigh: It didn't really matter that much to me, and I could see it did to him. I wanted him to like me.

Worker: Aren't there other things about you to like?

Ms. Leigh: I think there are, but why can't I meet someone like my father. My mother was so lucky! I don't know what her life would have been like if he hadn't come along.

Worker: It sounds like you feel that your life can't amount to much unless you find someone like your father. I wonder why that is?

Ms. Leigh said she knew she had put her father on a pedestal but she felt that he had been there when her mother took to her bed. An only child, she described her role as taking care of her mother and making her laugh. Ms. Leigh was left to fend for herself. Even as a child, she spent a lot of time playing characters she saw on TV or in the movies, visiting museums, and taking art lessons. Her father worked long hours, and she would wait to have dinner when he came home. He always was supportive but ignored his wife's neglect of her. Ms. Leigh was an excellent student but was not very popular in school. Born with a genetic deformity, she had large, visible welts on her body, which were corrected as she got older. She began to have friends and date when she entered college. She was in love with a young man whom she met there, and they had a stormy on-and-off relationship for two years until they graduated. He used to see other women, and that would make her jealous and lead to their not seeing one another for a while. She said she still thought about him; he was the only one she ever really liked and whom she felt liked her for herself.

The worker was struck by this history, which explained some of the basis for Ms. Leigh's low self-esteem, feelings of aloneness, craving for male attention, inability to care for and soothe herself, and identity confusion. It also suggested that she was a very bright, curious, and unusual child who cultivated her intellect and artistic talent from an early age. In fact, it seemed that she had done rather well under difficult circumstances.

Because Ms. Leigh's difficulties coping with her feelings of aloneness and her pattern of premature involvements with inappropriate men were so central, these two issues became the major foci of the work. In sessions 4 through 12, the bulk of the work consisted of helping her to value who she was; understand the difficulties she had in holding on to positive experiences with others or good feelings about herself; find and engage in soothing and comforting thoughts and activities; tolerate her sense of aloneness; exercise better judgment, set more limits, and be more honest in her relationships with men; and undertake small steps toward achieving her career goals.

In exploring her feelings of aloneness, the worker helped Ms. Leigh to connect her current state to her past experiences as a child when she was forced to spend so much time by herself and care for her mother without any recognition or nurturing of her needs. The worker also addressed what it must have been like for Ms. Leigh given her physical deformity and the impact of this condition on her self-esteem, feelings of attractiveness, sense of worth, and relationships with others. In addition to being empathic with these early experiences, the worker helped Ms. Leigh to problem-solve about ways she could talk herself through her feelings of aloneness by substituting more affirmative and reassuring thoughts and about new behaviors that she could institute to ease her anxiety.

With respect to her interactions with men, the worker helped Ms. Leigh to examine her belief that men would like her if she immediately became physically involved with them. She also connected this view to the client's long-standing low self-esteem. They discussed the importance of Ms. Leigh's getting to know men before she trusted them and of differentiating her expectations of relative strangers from her feelings about her father. The worker supported Ms. Leigh's efforts to control her impulses and be firm in saying no when she meant no.

Toward the end of this period, Ms. Leigh seemed to be less chaotic and more grounded. She even looked better. She complained of being lonely but had not resorted to drinking, excessive binging, or picking up strange men. As she began to have more energy, the remaining three sessions focused on helping her to make and implement a plan to study with a well-known acting teacher and attend some auditions. The worker and client reviewed her progress and the areas of vulnerability. The client wanted to continue seeing the worker and said she was going to ask her father to help her financially. The worker was willing to reduce her fee so that the client could continue. Ms. Leigh seemed pleased at this idea but never came to the final session. She left a message saying that she had decided to go home to visit her family and would call the worker when she returned to New York.

Discussion

The Leigh case showed long-standing, multiple, and serious personality difficulties. Although a longer-term treatment seemed indicated, the constraints of insurance necessitated a partialized approach. The major aspects of the client's problems that seemed accessible to intervention were issues around her aloneness, self-esteem, and relationships with men. The worker educated Ms. Leigh about how her reactions to her aloneness were getting her into difficult situations and helped her to see that it was in her better interest to alter her behavior, even though she was drawn to it. The worker helped the client to connect her current state to her past life experiences and helped her to problem-solve and establish new ways of thinking and behaving.

SUMMARY

This chapter discussed and illustrated the use of ISTT with clients who present with the characteristics of four major types of emotional disorder: depression, anxiety, schizophrenia, and personality disorders. It defined the disorders, described the main foci of ISTT when used in the treatment of clients who have such conditions, and demonstrated the implementation of the interventive process in detail.

Chapter 10

Nonvoluntary and Hard-to-Reach Clients

There are many clients who do not seek help voluntarily but rather because they are fearful of the negative consequences of not doing so, or are mandated or ordered by legal authorities to be involved in treatment, or are required to undergo counseling in order to receive other services. And even when some clients come for help voluntarily, they nevertheless may be distrustful of the helping process and those whom they perceive as representing authority and the wider society. Moreover, because many of these clients may be overwhelmed by a lack of adequate environmental resources and multiple stressors or problems, they may have little hope, energy, or motivation to work on improving their situation.

After discussing some of the common features that these clients present, this chapter describes and illustrates the special emphases in the application of ISTT to their treatment.

COMMON FEATURES

In order to apply ISTT to work with nonvoluntary or hard-to-reach clients, workers must be aware of and be prepared to address numerous common characteristics that these clients present:

1. Often they do not want to be involved in or have difficulties making use of the interventive process because they fear the loss of self-determination and seeming control, intrusion, exposure, feelings of being powerless, and negative repercussions.
2. They may have limited expectations that anything positive can

be done to help them because of prior disappointments or the overwhelming nature of their problems.

3. They tend to distrust authority figures based on their past experiences.
4. Frequently they lack adequate material resources and social supports for even minimal subsistence and well-being.
5. They demonstrate angry and provocative behavior or apathy and indifference in order to protect themselves.
6. They may be survivors of extreme childhood and adult trauma in which they have been exploited, abused, and not protected by others, even those closest to them.
7. They may have borne the brunt of dislocation, racism, discrimination, and other forms of societal neglect and oppression that contribute to their feelings of alienation, rage, and despair.
8. They may not be verbal and able to articulate their thoughts and feelings easily.
9. They tend to act out their feelings rather than talk about them.
10. They may become easily frustrated, argumentative, or demanding when their needs are not met immediately because of their long history of deprivation.

Workers face many challenges in attempting to engage and help such clients that stem not only from the clients' nonreceptivity and antagonism to the interventive process and to the worker himself or herself, but also because of what these characteristics may stimulate in workers (Larke, 1985; Schlosberg & Kagan, 1977). It is difficult for many workers to understand what is behind the clients' presenting attitudes and behaviors and not to personalize them. Even when workers recognize what is operating for these clients, they still may react with distress, feelings of rejection, and anger when their intentions are rebuffed, not appreciated, or attacked.

A significant dilemma for workers arises in situations in which their role as an authority may conflict with their feelings about wanting to be helpful to and to remain connected with the client, for example, when workers are expected to divulge information about drug use or illegal behavior; monitor clients' adherence to treatment requirements;

make recommendations to authorities about custody, removal from, or return of children to the home; or report suspected minor or major incidents of child abuse or neglect.

The overwhelming and sometimes horrific nature of clients' difficulties, the absence or minimal amount of resources available to help them, and the limited amount of time allotted to address their problems also may lead workers to experience feelings of helplessness, impotence, revulsion, depletion, exploitation, and frustration. Moreover, because of their own values and backgrounds, which may be at great variance from or similar to those of the client, workers may be highly judgmental and critical in their attitudes toward such clients and may not wish to work with or try to impose their own values on them.

Workers and agencies are not immune from the effects of racism and other types of discrimination. Practitioners' awareness of their own negative and stereotypical views, their skill in creating a safe, respectful, and accepting environment, and their ability to help empower clients and advocate for them are crucial elements of effective intervention, and their participation in efforts to identify and modify prejudicial and nonresponsive agency policies and practices are important ingredients to effective intervention.

Despite the complex issues and worker reactions that surround the treatment of involuntary and hard-to-reach clients, workers often find the interventive process very rewarding. Many of these clients need so much, and even small improvements and changes in their lives can mean a great deal.

SPECIFIC FOCI

Although all of the components of ISTT are important in work with nonvoluntary and hard-to-reach clients, there are those that require special emphasis.

Addressing Feelings About the Helping Process

Chapter 4 discussed some of the ways of engaging nonvoluntary and hard-to-reach clients, particularly with respect to their lack of interest in being involved in the interventive process, their attitudes toward authority, and their feelings of lack of self-determination. It underscored the necessity of giving clients the opportunity to express their negative feelings about having to see the worker and to discuss their previous experiences with social workers and social service agencies, as well as other representatives of authority. It also emphasized the importance of workers' acceptance of the clients' resentment, anger, or indifference and efforts to maximize the choices that exist. In order to accomplish these tasks, it is helpful for workers to put themselves in their clients' shoes and to see the world through their eyes. Talking to these clients openly, straightforwardly, and in a nonjudgmental manner about these issues may temporarily diffuse their intensity, but it likely will be necessary to address the clients' feelings at various points in the helping process.

Educating About the Interventive Process and Available Options

Workers can provide information to clients about the nature of the interventive process by telling them what services can be provided, discussing what the process entails and mutual responsibilities, explaining how the worker can be of help, and correcting misperceptions or unrealistic expectations that clients may have.

Workers must discuss confidentiality and its possible limit with clients, such as in instances when the worker is required to provide information to others as part of the treatment arrangements. This may be necessary when clients are at risk of hurting themselves or others; when there may be child abuse and neglect; when workers are supposed to monitor clients' adherence to certain procedures, such as attendance at sessions, parent training workshops, involvement in occupational programs, appointments with medical personnel, or abstinence from substance use; and when they are responsible for making reports or testifying about the clients' functioning in order for them to get custody of their children, to get parole, or to be discharged from court-mandated treatment.

At the outset of treatment, workers must clearly articulate how information that is discussed in the course of their working with clients will be used. Not only do clients have the right to know this information, but talking about this issue builds trust and may, but not always, prevent later disruptions of the worker-client relationship should it be necessary for the worker to share information with others that clients would like to keep private and that might have negative consequences. In most instances, it is recommended that workers share with clients their intention to disclose information to others before actually doing so.

Increasing Motivation

It is necessary to help involuntary and hard-to-reach clients to identify some positive value that derives from their involvement in the interventive process, even if the only benefit is to avoid negative consequences. Additionally, the worker needs to demonstrate in a tangible way his or her interest in and capacity to help the client in even some small area of his or her life. The worker's ability to partialize clients' difficulties in order to make them less overwhelming and more manageable and to arrive at an often concrete and readily attainable goal are essential in mobilizing their sense of hope and willingness to be more active participants in the interventive process.

The Worker's Use of Self

Workers need to be available, flexible, consistent, genuine, persistent, and creative in their work with nonvoluntary and hard-to-reach clients. Speaking in ways that clients can understand, becoming familiar with the customs and mores of their cultural background, reaching out to them repeatedly, entering their life space, and participating with them by accompanying them to court hearings or medical appointments are ways in which workers can demonstrate their commitment to helping clients.

Emphasis on Strengths

Even marginally functioning clients and those in seemingly intractable situations possess some strengths, though they may not recognize them. It is crucial for workers to locate clients' strengths, help clients appreciate them, and use them in working on and ameliorating their problems. All too often, workers tend to view the client's problems and behavior exclusively from the perspective of pathology. They may neglect the impact of oppression, discrimination, stigmatization, dislocation, and marginalization and how clients have adapted to stress, deprivation, and adversity.

Building Self-Confidence and Self-Esteem

Since helplessness and powerlessness are so pervasive among nonvoluntary and hard-to-reach clients, an important focus of the interventive process is to help clients increase their sense of personal responsibility and control over their lives, feel positive about themselves, and develop a sense of self-efficacy. The use of more active and role-modeling techniques that help clients improve their reality testing, judgment, and impulse control and to learn new, more effective behaviors should accompany other types of interventive efforts. Workers should involve clients in identifying tasks that they can accomplish and in practicing being more assertive, getting their needs met, managing their impulses and behavior, and handling certain aspects of their lives.

Environmental Intervention

A crucial aspect of the interventive process with involuntary and hard-to-reach clients is linking them to services, entitlements, and other forms of material assistance. Workers must both locate appropriate resources and assist clients in accessing them. They may have to help clients with application and intake procedures, eligibility requirements, and waiting lists and deal with agency personnel and bureaucratic red tape. Additionally, it may be necessary for the worker to mediate and advocate for clients.

Case Management

Because nonvoluntary and hard-to-reach clients often are involved with several agencies and a multitude of services, it may be important for workers to oversee and coordinate these diverse resources. Collaboration is essential and requires considerable skill because of the differing priorities, agendas, and personalities of the participants.

The Use of Adjunctive Services

Vocational training, parent guidance, self-help and other types of support groups, tutoring, after-school programs, mentoring, and health services often are important adjuncts in work with nonvoluntary and hard-to-reach clients. Such experiences help clients to decrease their isolation; strengthen their identification with others who share common concerns; increase feelings of acceptance, self-esteem, and self-efficacy; develop their problem-solving and other skills; learn new options for dealing with their feelings and problems; and gain support from others.

Balancing Empathy with Confrontation and Limits

Because of their frequent use of denial and other maladaptive defenses and coping mechanisms, it may be necessary to use confrontation in the treatment process. The timing of this intervention is important; too much confrontation early in treatment may lead clients to feel attacked or threatened, rigidifying defenses, escalating acting out, and increasing resistance. When workers decide to address clients' self-defeating or destructive behavior or maladaptive defenses, it is generally preferable to do so in ways that show an understanding of what the client may be feeling and the reasons behind his or her behavior. This can be accomplished through empathically relating to the client's urgent needs and feeling states and through pointing out the negative consequences of behavior that the individuals may have learned in order to survive early neglect, abuse, or other kinds of trauma.

While the setting of limits and the use of behavioral contracts may be helpful with some clients, many nonvoluntary clients are unable to keep to the terms of the contract and may experience slips and repeated crises. There should be sufficient flexibility in the treatment structure to help them through these without their being discharged or terminated from treatment.

THE INTERVENTIVE PROCESS

Work with the following homeless woman illustrates many of the issues that arise in the treatment of nonvoluntary and hard-to-reach clients.

THE CURTIS CASE

Mrs. Curtis, a 30-year-old African American, reluctantly entered a homeless shelter when the weather turned bitterly cold. She had been living on the streets for several weeks following an eviction from her apartment for nonpayment of rent. Although the shelter allowed residents to stay for two months and offered services such as counseling and housing assistance, Mrs. Curtis only wanted a "place to sleep and a hot meal" until the weather cleared. She initially avoided all contact with the staff and other residents and appeared sad, tired, and sullen.

Mrs. Curtis was angry and hostile when the worker first approached her, stating that she just wanted to be left alone. The worker said she could see that the client wanted her privacy but that there was some information that the city required of all the residents. The worker explained that her questions were not meant to invade her privacy but were a means of determining what services the client might want or need. Mrs. Curtis commented bitterly that everyone always wanted to get into her business but never really wanted to help her. When the worker said she wanted to be of help but that it seemed the client had some bad experiences with others, the client began complaining about welfare workers, hospital personnel, and other people in general. She then blurted out, "I don't know why I'm telling you all this. It's none of your fucking business!" The worker was taken aback but didn't counterattack. She replied that she did not wish to force anything on Mrs. Curtis, would be available if she needed or wanted anything, and would stop by the next day just to see how she was doing.

When the worker sought out the client the following day, the worker inquired how she was adjusting. She said, "Fine but I can't stand living with all of these women." The worker took this opportunity to explain that one of her jobs was to help clients apply for housing if they were in-

terested. The worker inquired if Mrs. Curtis had any plans for when she left the shelter.

Mrs. Curtis: I haven't thought about it. I don't care what happens to me. I'll just go back to the streets.

Worker: You seem tired and sad.

Mrs. Curtis: I am tired of everything. Nobody gives a shit, not even my family.

Worker: You seem to have given up hope that anyone will come to your aid. I hope you will give me a chance to help.

Mrs. Curtis: Go away! I just came here to get out of the cold.

Worker: Okay. But I'm still here, and I want to help you. I'll check in again tomorrow.

The worker persisted. The next day, she found the client sitting alone on her cot. When she saw the worker, she immediately launched into a litany of complaints about the shelter and the other residents. The worker listened patiently and commented that life in a shelter was difficult and wondered how the client had come to be homeless. The client sighed and replied, "You seem okay, so I might as well tell you what's going on." She proceeded to recount in a somewhat disjointed fashion that up until a year earlier, when she found out that she was HIV positive, she and her teenage daughter had lived with her two sisters and their children. When she informed her sisters of her illness, they angrily told Mrs. Curtis that she was just like their mother, who had died of AIDS two years previously, and they didn't want their children exposed to her. They were so unsympathetic and made her feel so uncomfortable that she left the house immediately. Because she had nowhere else to go, she moved in with her boyfriend, a drug addict. When Mrs. Curtis tried to contact her daughter, her sisters threatened to report her to the Administration for Children's Services (ACS) as a neglectful mother. About two months later, her boyfriend, Lenny, said he didn't want to be with her anymore and took off. She stayed in the apartment until the eviction.

Worker: You have had a very hard time since learning of your diagnosis. Your sisters really attacked you, and your boyfriend abandoned you. No wonder it's difficult for you to believe that anyone would want to help you.

Mrs. Curtis: This has been the worst experience of my life.

Worker: Have you been receiving medical treatment?

Mrs. Curtis: What does it matter? Why bother? Nothing really matters. I wish I never told anyone about my condition. I have no one. I can't even see my child.

The worker determined that Mrs. Curtis could not plan for her future or take care of herself until the rejection by her family and her inability to see her daughter were addressed. The worker recognized that the client's attachment to her daughter was an important strength that could be used to help her to care more for herself. When the worker suggested that she might try to reestablish contact with her sisters and daughter, Mrs. Curtis said she missed all of them but said she doubted her sisters would ever talk to her again, let alone allow her to see her daughter. The worker offered to intervene by calling them. The client warned the worker that her sisters could be pretty tough. The worker and client both smiled, and the worker said she could be pretty tough too. The client then asked the worker if the shelter provided any clothes for the residents because she didn't have much that was clean. The worker suggested that they go through the closets together and find some suitable clothes.

In their fourth meeting, which occurred about four days later, the worker told Mrs. Curtis that she had made contact with her sisters, and they had reluctantly agreed to meet with the worker. Mrs. Curtis was not optimistic about the outcome but thanked the worker for her efforts. Since Mrs. Curtis had nothing particular on her mind, the worker suggested that they return to discussing her HIV status. The client became angry, saying the subject upset her and that she didn't want to talk about it. In pressing her further, the worker learned that Mrs. Curtis blamed herself for her condition because of her previous drug use. The worker then explored the client's history and learned that she was the youngest of three girls. Until age 17, Mrs. Curtis had resided with her mother, a postal employee, and her older sisters, who were both single parents. Then she became pregnant, dropped out of high school, and left home to live with the baby's father. She started using drugs, her boyfriend left her when the baby was six months old, and she placed her daughter informally with her mother and sisters.

For the next eight years Mrs. Curtis moved from relationship to relationship and tried numerous drug programs, unsuccessfully. She did maintain contact with her family and visited her daughter regularly. Five years ago, the client's mother became ill with HIV-AIDS. Mrs. Curtis's father, who had lived apart from the family for many years, also had died of the disease. Mrs. Curtis and her sisters were devastated by the mother's illness. Although the client did not stop using drugs, she took control of her problem and moved back in with the family to help out with caretaking. They told friends and relatives that the mother had cancer. When she passed away four years ago, only Mrs. Curtis and her sisters knew the truth. The client said she never wanted her daughter to know she was HIV positive.

Upon learning the client's history, the worker felt touched by her sadness and plight and distressed about how AIDS had devastated the family and how they felt they had needed to hide the illness. She was upset further after she visited the client's sisters, who were less than sympathetic to Mrs. Curtis's problems. They felt she had brought them on herself because of addiction, were embarrassed by her, were tired of bailing her out of trouble, and, most important, did not want any of the children to know about Mrs. Curtis's condition because they feared the children would be stigmatized at school and by their friends. Despite her disappointment that they were not more forthcoming in their willingness to help, the worker communicated that she understood how angry and overburdened they felt by Mrs. Curtis's problems. She assured them that Mrs. Curtis also did not want the children told about her condition but did want to see her daughter, Dawn, whom she missed terribly and about whom she was very concerned. When the worker asked how Dawn was doing, the sisters admitted that she was having a hard time, particularly at school, where her grades were slipping. They said they recognized that it was not easy for a 14 year old to be separated from her mother, but they had been fearful that if Mrs. Curtis saw her, she and the others would learn about her mother's condition. They believed they were acting in everyone's best interest. The worker agreed they were doing the best they could under very difficult circumstances. They were becoming concerned about Dawn but did not want any involvement with city agencies because they feared Dawn would be taken away from them. The worker thought that letting Mrs. Curtis see Dawn might help the girl and the situation and said she could arrange a meeting if the women did not wish to be involved. The sisters said they would consider it but gave no promises.

Over the next two weeks, the worker acted as a mediator between Mrs. Curtis and her sisters, and eventually a visit was arranged at the shelter between Mrs. Curtis and Dawn, who was initially distant and reticent. With the worker's encouragement, Dawn expressed her anger at her mother for not seeing her sooner. The worker had prepared Mrs. Curtis for how Dawn might feel, and the client was able to accept Dawn's feelings. When the visit was over, both Dawn and her mother looked visibly relieved and happier.

With the sisters' permission, the worker was also in touch with a number of preventive service programs in the community in order to get some help for the family in coping with the children and in dealing with the family secret about the multiple illnesses and deaths from AIDS. One program agreed to do family counseling in the home. The sisters agreed to meet with the family counselor, but not with Mrs. Curtis present. The worker brought the family counselor to the home and stayed for the interview with the children and Mrs. Curtis's sisters. The meeting went reasonably well, and the sisters agreed to meet with the counselor alone.

By the sixth week after coming to the shelter, Mrs. Curtis was much more responsive to the worker. After seeing Dawn, she showed some motivation to plan for her future and care for herself. The goals of the remaining three weeks became: (1) accessing medical services, (2) working on housing, (3) discussing the psychological impact of her condition, and (4) motivating her to seek additional counseling that would support her coping.

The worker, through a colleague's help, arranged for a medical evaluation, obtained and forwarded Mrs. Curtis's medical records, and accompanied Mrs. Curtis to the appointment. The client was nervous about the exam; she talked about her fears that she was going to die soon and discussed her concerns about Dawn, whom she felt was the only good thing in her life. She said she hadn't wanted Dawn to be hurt by the way she was living and that was why she let her sisters and mother care for her. The worker commented that Dawn was a lovely youngster, that Mrs. Curtis could be proud of having kept Dawn safe, and although Mrs. Curtis had some serious difficulties, her life was hardly over.

At Mrs. Curtis's request the doctor met with both the client and the worker. Although HIV positive, Mrs. Curtis did not have AIDS. The doctor carefully explained the difference, and the worker asked for recommendations as to how to proceed. They discussed efforts that Mrs. Curtis could undertake to help her condition, and the doctor also recommended a nutritional plan for Mrs. Curtis to follow. When they left the clinic, Mrs. Curtis was relieved and seemed more hopeful. She and the worker discussed the possibility of applying for housing for people with special needs, and the worker told Mrs. Curtis about a vocational and counseling service for HIV-positive clients.

The next morning the worker looked for Mrs. Curtis at the shelter. The security guard said that the client had left the evening before. Five days later, she returned, looking disheveled, unkempt, and tired. As the worker approached, Mrs. Curtis told her to get away and leave her alone.

Worker: It looks as if you have had a rough time. Do you want to tell me about it?

Mrs. Curtis: No!

Worker: I don't think you really want me to give up on you.

Mrs. Curtis: I'm just ashamed. Lenny came to the shelter to look for me. He offered me drugs, and I felt so lonely that I went with him. We got high for a few days, and then he took off. I don't know why I keep doing these things. What's the matter with me?

Worker: You have been doing really well. Maybe it all seemed too much. Sometimes it seems easier to go back to what we know.

Mrs. Curtis: It's just too hard to change. There are so many things that I have to do. I don't know if I have the energy to get a new apartment, take care of myself, stop the drugs, stay away from men like Lenny, and get a job. I don't even have a high school diploma.

Worker: That is a lot to have to deal with. You don't have to do it all at once and totally by yourself.

The worker and client got back on track, and over the next two weeks they focused on her housing applications and connecting her with an outpatient substance abuse program. Mrs. Curtis made a positive connection with the worker at the drug program and began attending Narcotics Anonymous meetings. Unfortunately, at the point that Mrs. Curtis had to leave the shelter, her housing approval had not come through, her sisters would not let her return to their home, and the client had to move to a single-room-occupancy (SRO) building that was a known hang-out for drug addicts. The worker and client discussed at length how difficult it would be for the client to sustain her progress in the face of the environment she would be living in. The worker and client together met with the counselor at the substance abuse program, who suggested that Mrs. Curtis increase her attendance at the NA meeting she was attending, encouraged her to get a sponsor, and strongly suggested that she try to get involved with the other people in the program who were struggling with the same issues.

At their last meeting together, which was difficult for both the worker and the client, the worker went over the progress that Mrs. Curtis had made. She was seeing her daughter regularly, was attending the substance abuse program and NA meetings, and was staying away from Lenny. Although her sisters had not changed their minds about her returning to the family home, they were continuing to work with the family counselor. The client was hopeful that in time her sisters would see her progress and be more open to involvement with her. They agreed that the client would return to see the worker in three weeks.

Discussion

The worker maintained a patient and empathic stance and persevered in the face of the client's anger and unwillingness to cooperate initially. She encouraged her in sharing her past negative experiences with other authorities and tried to be attuned to the client's feelings and needs. The worker built on the client's attachment to her daughter in order to motivate and engage the client and offered to mediate between the client and her sisters so that the client could reestablish contact with her daughter. Despite her disappointment in the sisters' reaction, the worker was able to relate to their needs, link them to a community resource that could provide them with assistance, and succeed in arranging a visit for Dawn and her mother. The worker was then able to help the client concretely with her medical and housing needs.

In the face of Mrs. Curtis's temporary setback, the worker remained consistent, reached out to the client, and showed understanding of the pressures on the client. She was able to mobilize the client's hopefulness. In the final phase, there was considerable use of collaboration and adjunctive services. Although the client's future was uncertain, the worker felt she had made a real difference in the client's life.

The following example shows the beginning work with a client who was less overtly resistant to the interventive process than Mrs. Curtis but whose overwhelming internal and external problems presented other kinds of obstacles to her becoming engaged in the helping process.

THE WATERSTON CASE

Mrs. Waterston, a separated mother of four children, ages 8, 6, 3, and 5 days old, was referred to a community-based foster care agency by her son's day care provider. The client told her that she felt nervous and overwhelmed about caring for her newborn daughter, who had remained hospitalized because of jaundice and was scheduled to be discharged the following day. She was temporarily living in a one-bedroom apartment with her elderly aunt and three other children. She realized that she could not take care of her baby and wanted to place her in foster care.

The worker supported Mrs. Waterston's efforts to reach out for help and wondered what had led her to her decision about her new daughter. The client said she just felt overwhelmed and guessed she hadn't thought that far in advance when she was pregnant about what it would be like to have an infant given everything else that was going on. She said she just thought it would work out, but she became very frightened when she thought of taking the baby home: "I don't even have a *place for her to sleep or any baby clothes. I haven't even decided on a name."* In exploring what the client meant when she said that so much had happened, the client said that her life had been going downhill for the past year. Her mother had died a year earlier and she still thought about her constantly. Then she learned that she was pregnant, and her husband, who did not believe he was the father, left her for another woman. Mrs. Waterston and her three children recently moved in with her aunt because the building in which the client resided was scheduled for demolition. The client had high blood pressure and migraine headaches; she was depressed, lethargic, and very nervous.

In hearing this account, the worker commented that the client certainly was under a great deal of stress and asked how she was doing. She responded that it was very hard but her aunt tried to help out, and when she felt too tired or jittery, she would take a nap and make the children lie down even if they weren't tired. When the worker inquired about the client's income, she learned that prior to her move, she had received public assistance and food stamps. Although she said she had informed the welfare worker of her change of address, she had not received any of her checks and had not gone back because she was looking for an apartment, taking the kids to school and day care, and then giving birth. Her aunt gave her some money for food. The client thought that it might be better for everyone if she placed her new infant in foster care until she could find housing, feel calmer and stronger physically and emotionally, and resolve her problems with welfare.

The worker agreed to assist the client with foster care placement, contacting the welfare department, and filling out her housing application, but she also suggested that she might help the client with some of her sad and anxious feelings as well. The worker called the welfare department and resolved the bureaucratic problem and was assured that the check would be sent the following day. She also went over the procedures, policies, rights, and responsibilities, including weekly visiting, associated with voluntary foster care placement, had the client sign the necessary consent forms, and arranged for her and the client to pick up the baby at the hospital the next morning in order to take her to the foster family. The client concluded by saying she would name the baby Marie, after her mother.

The following day, Mrs. Waterston never appeared at the hospital, and the worker transported the baby herself. The foster mother, who had raised three children of her own, was delighted to care for the baby, and the worker explained the situation, including the infant's medical needs, and helped the foster mother get settled. When the worker contacted the client and inquired about what had happened, Mrs. Waterston said that one of her other children was sick and she couldn't leave him. She never asked about the baby. The worker said she had filed the necessary papers, and the baby was with the foster family. She said she would like to visit the client as they had discussed, and a time was set.

When the worker arrived the next afternoon, Mrs. Waterston looked quite upset. She said she'd had a terrible morning. Her son, Johnny, was still sick with a virus, she had had to get the older two off to school, and her aunt had walked out of the house after telling the client she was a bad mother for putting her daughter into foster care. The worker listened patiently while the client explained that she was doing the best she could, and now she was having one of her headaches. The worker asked if the client thought it might be related to all the stress she was under and the client said, "Definitely." When the worker inquired about Johnny, the client said she had called the doctor, and when she described his symptoms, the doctor assured her it was only a virus. The worker asked if she could see Johnny and the rest of the house. The worker noted that the apartment was small but well kept, there were toys for the children, and Johnny, who was playing quietly with some blocks, immediately smiled when the worker went to him. He readily told the worker his name and age and then sat in his mother's lap. The worker noted that Mrs. Waterston seemed gentle and caring with her son.

> Worker: Let's talk a little more now about the baby. I wondered what you were feeling about the placement because you didn't ask about the baby.
>
> Mrs. Waterston: How can I think about her? Look at everything that's happening to me.
>
> Worker: Yes. There does seem to be a lot going on. You told me yesterday that your life started to go downhill when your mother died. Can you tell me more about that?

The client explained that she was an only child and that she and her mother had always been very close. When her father died seven years ago, her mother moved in with her and her husband. She was glad to have her mother, who helped out with her son. Her mother and husband fought a lot, and after a particularly acrimonious interchange, her mother moved into her own apartment in the same building. Mrs. Waterston continued to spend a lot of time with her mother, who helped her with the children. Her mother had a fatal heart attack in the client's home. The client said she still couldn't believe her mother was gone.

Mrs. Waterston: She was my whole world. Nothing is the same since she died. I've never taken care of the kids by myself.

Worker: This was a terrible loss for you. How did you manage after her death?

Mrs. Waterston: My husband was helpful for a while and seemed to understand how much she meant to me. After a couple of weeks, he told me to get over it and start taking care of him and the kids. He worked all day, and when he came home and dinner wasn't ready and the house was a mess, he would start yelling and screaming. He told me I was a lazy, good-for-nothing wife. I would cry, and he would storm out of the house. It got so that he didn't come home for days at a time. Then I got pregnant. He said he couldn't take it anymore and left to move in with his girlfriend.

Worker: It sounds as if it was an awful time for you, particularly when you had to take care of the children by yourself.

Mrs. Waterston: I have trouble taking care of myself right now. My aunt tries to help, but she's old and not my mother. My mother would not have blamed me for putting the baby in a foster home.

The worker explained that the baby could stay in temporary foster care for three months, and at the end of that time they would have to make permanent plans for her. The client said that she wanted to straighten everything out by then so that she could take her baby home. The worker stressed that it was important for the client to visit regularly with the baby and that they would set up a weekly visiting time. The client agreed, and they set up a visit. The client signed release forms so that the worker could talk to her aunt, the school, and the day care provider about how the other children were doing.

The next day, the worker visited with the children's teachers and learned that the two oldest were functioning well. They arrived on time each day, seemed healthy, related well, and were achieving at grade level. Johnny's day care provider, however, said that although he appeared to be in good health and was affectionate with her, he was aggressive with the other children when she gave attention to them and was easily distracted. She added that his mother often appeared tired and overwhelmed and did not bring him consistently. Mrs. Waterston's aunt indicated that although she could not understand why her niece placed the baby in foster care, she thought that overall the client was good to the children. Nevertheless, she described her as having been immature and too dependent on her mother.

The worker determined that the client's mother had been a major source of support and that the client appeared to need her help in order to take care of her children adequately. The loss of her mother not only was a blow but also left her to manage on her own. Additionally, the loss of her husband and her apartment, her pregnancy, and her problems with welfare overtaxed her coping capacities. Mrs. Waterston clearly cared for the three other children and was trying to meet their basic needs but was overburdened and could not get her life organized and under control. The worker also thought the client was ambivalent about taking care of the new baby.

Mrs. Waterston did not come to the scheduled visit with her daughter, nor did she call to cancel. When the worker telephoned, she apologized for missing the visit and explained that after dropping the children off that morning, she had taken a nap and overslept. She did not ask about the baby or request another visit. The worker said it was important for them to schedule another appointment, and the client agreed to come in the next day. Mrs. Waterston was a half-hour late for her appointment; she had lost track of the time, she explained. She was having difficulty doing everything she had to do. The worker said that she could see that the client was struggling and that maybe together they could try to see what was going on and how to help her. The client said the most important thing was getting an apartment. The worker agreed *and said that they needed to fill out housing applications and explained that she would get priority because her obtaining an apartment was one of the requirements necessary for her daughter to leave foster care. The worker also informed her that a court hearing was scheduled for the following week to review the voluntary placement.*

Mrs. Waterston: Why do I have to go to court?

Worker: It's routine. The judge will ask you your reasons for placing the baby and what your future plans for her are.

Mrs. Waterston: I plan to take her home but not right away.

Worker: With all you have been through, it would be understandable if you had doubts about taking care of another child.

Mrs. Waterston: Why are you saying that? Do you think I am a bad mother?

Worker: You seem like a very good mother to your other children. I've had positive reports from the children's teachers, I saw how sensitive to Johnny you were when he was sick, and I sensed your pain about having to place Marie. But you are still having a lot of stress, and I wondered if your not visiting Marie or asking about her reflected some mixed feelings about taking her home.

Mrs. Waterston: I don't know. Sometimes I think the baby would be better off with somebody else who could take care of her and give her a good home. Why should I get to know her and love her and then have to give her back to the foster family? It would be too painful.

Worker: This might be very hard. How did you feel about the baby during your pregnancy?

Mrs. Waterston: I thought about an abortion, but my parents were religious, especially my father, and I couldn't go through with it.

Worker: You haven't mentioned him before.

Mrs. Waterston: I loved him but he was very strict, required total obedience, and would frequently beat my mother and me when I was a kid. He always accused her of cheating on him, would not let me have friends, and when I met my husband, I had to lie about my whereabouts. I married my husband to get out of the house, but then found that he was just like my father. I had to obey him and never talk back. He wanted everything his way. I just did what I was told. Now that I am on my own, I don't even know how to make decisions.

Worker: It's understandable that you don't feel sure of yourself or capable of making a firm decision about the baby right now. There is time for you and me to sort out what is in your best interests and what is best for your daughter. The first thing we need to do is get you through the court hearing. I will accompany you when you have to talk to the judge. After that, we will work on the housing application, and I will try to locate a program near you that will send someone to help you with the kids temporarily. You and I can continue to meet together to talk about what bothers you, how I can help you to feel better, and the ways in which you can establish more control over your life. Because you are not sure what you want to do about taking your daughter home, it is important to keep your options open. It will be necessary for you to visit her on a regular basis, and we can try to figure out how you can do this without feeling more pressured. We also can discuss your feelings about the visits. You will need to promise me that you will try to keep your visiting appointments and the ones we set up for the two of us and that if problems arise that interfere with your ability to keep your promise, you will tell me so that we can find ways of working them out. I've said a lot. What do you think about all this?

Mrs. Waterston: It's sounds as if you know what you're doing and that you want to help me. I need some direction.

Discussion

Although the client came for help voluntarily, she had difficulty cooperating fully with the plan because of her stressful life situation, underlying depression, feelings of inadequacy and dependence on others, and difficulty organizing herself and problem solving. The worker was empathic and patient with the client, reached out when the client did not follow through with the plans they had agreed to, to cooperate initially, encouraged and gave permission to the client to share her thoughts and *feelings, and acted as an auxiliary ego who helped the client do things that she could not do for herself. In a nonjudgmental and accepting way, the worker also helped the client to recognize her ambivalent feelings about her new daughter. The worker supported the strengths and capacities of the client and took responsibility for formulating a step-by-step plan aimed at relieving the client's stress and depression and helping her to take more control of her life. The case also involved helping the client to access needed adjunctive services and resources and collaboration.*

SUMMARY

This chapter discussed many of the common features shown by non-voluntary and hard-to-reach clients that have important implications for the interventive process. It described the specific foci of ISTT in work with such clients and illustrated the interventive process with two different types of clients.

Chapter 11

Family-Oriented ISTT

O ften it is the family rather than the individual that becomes the focus of treatment. Many families request help in acquiring necessary resources; improving parent-child relationships; coping with illness, emotional problems, disability, life stage issues, losses and separations, and other types of stressful situations; and dealing with acute or chronic conflict and disharmony. Sometimes the worker determines that intervention with the family as a whole is indicated because the presenting problem seems to be linked to or affecting all family members.

Although family systems work generally derives from a unique constellation of theoretical concepts and principles and has generated numerous treatment models (Hartman & Laird, 1983; Nichols & Schwartz, 1995; Walsh, 1997), it is beyond the scope of this chapter to consider these developments. Instead, it will show how ISTT can be adapted to work with families. It will discuss four specific foci of family-oriented ISTT and illustrate the interventive process.

SPECIFIC FOCI

The overriding consideration in using family-oriented ISTT is the broadening of focus that accompanies the move from an individual approach to a family-centered one. Although all of the components of ISTT are applicable to family work, their use necessitates emphasizing and modifying certain aspects of the framework.

Problem Identification and Engagement

Because family members may define the problem differently, the worker must elicit each person's view of the problem and its causes, its implications and consequences, and how it has been addressed. Major tasks in the beginning phase are to enable family members to hear one another; help them accept that when one person in the family has a problem, it affects everyone; and facilitate family members' agreement on the difficulties on which they want to focus jointly. The worker's efforts at fostering communication and consensus regarding goals and foci are especially important when there is family conflict or when one or more family members are reluctant to participate in the interventive process.

Sometimes family members may appear to be in agreement that one person is the sole problem. This view may reflect a scapegoating process and fail to encompass how everyone is contributing to or affected by the problem. In order to engage the family in such instances, the worker initially may need to accept the family's definition of the difficulty. It is likely, however, that relatively quickly, it will be important for the worker to help the family to identify and accept their role in contributing to the identified client's problems.

In certain instances, families may not recognize the impact of certain events, role transitions, or life stage issues on their functioning and sense of well-being. In these situations, the worker may need to help the family to recognize the presence and effects of certain stressors.

Although it often is suggested that family intervention deal exclusively with here-and-now attitudes and behavior and disregard family-of-origin issues, ISTT addresses both the present and past if indicated. Adult family members bring values, characteristic ways of relating, and conflicts from their own family of origin and personal development to their current family interactions. These may play a significant part in the family's presenting problems.

Assessment of Individual Family Members and the Family System

It is necessary to assess not only each individual family member and the issues that arise from his or her family of origin but also the current family system itself. This assessment should take into consideration the family's structure and development; patterns and styles of communication; cultural background and degree of acculturation; relationship to others and to the community; environmental conditions, stressors, and resources; strengths; and problem-solving capacities. (See Chapter 3 for more detailed guidelines.)

Because families show different types of structure, have varying cultural backgrounds, and display a range of communication and coping styles, the worker must understand and accept the family's unique way of organizing itself in order to adapt to the environment and its own particular strengths.

The fact that families overtly display their communication patterns and characteristic ways of functioning and dealing with stress and conflict in the presence of the worker, their behavior in treatment sessions is a crucial source of data. Thus, an important aspect of the assessment process in working with families is the worker's observations of and attempts to clarify family interaction, including what is displayed in family meetings with the worker.

Activity of the Worker

The worker not only uses the family's relational patterns for the purposes of assessment but also intervenes directly in their interactive process. In the beginning, family members often direct their communications to the worker, but the worker must balance eliciting and responding to each person with trying to help family members listen and talk to one another directly. The worker may need to take an active role in pointing out, tracking, and interrupting dysfunctional interactions; structuring more optimal ways of behaving; and role modeling better ways of relating.

In family-oriented ISTT, the worker employs the full range of verbal and environmental interventions, but it is especially important for workers to use what is occurring in the sessions themselves in order to help involve family members in experimenting with new ways of communicating and behaving. For example, a worker might instruct an adolescent boy and his father, who are having problems talking to and understanding one another, to switch roles and interact on the basis of their assigned parts. The worker might ask family members to reenact a problematic situation and use what transpires as a basis for introducing new behavior. In addition, the assignment of tasks and homework to the family that they can do on their own may be helpful in moving the process forward.

Maintaining the Focus and Monitoring Progress

The presence of multiple family members, each with individual concerns, may affect attendance at treatment sessions, result in the emergence of new and distracting problems, or influence the focus of a family meeting. Although workers need to show some flexibility, they must be direct about the need for full participation and consistency where feasible and in maintaining a clear focus on the problems that the family has agreed to address.

Because family members may have different needs and goals that can be in conflict at times, it is helpful if the worker regularly asks for feedback about the process. This inquiry will enable the worker to address any dissatisfaction or frustration that develops before it disrupts the treatment and to make any necessary modifications. Moreover, change can be frightening for many people, and this is true for families too. Change may be perceived as threatening to the preservation and survival of the family unit rather than as beneficial. Consequently, families often need considerable help in identifying and overcoming their fears.

Worker Reactions

Although individual intervention stimulates reactions in workers that they need to identify, understand, and manage, family intervention is even more likely to engender complicated and hard-to-manage feelings. It is difficult (and not even advisable) for workers to remain detached from the family interactive process, so they are prone to become immersed in the family process, sometimes losing their objectivity and separateness. Workers also bring their own family-of-origin values, expectations, ways of relating, issues, and conflicts into the treatment, and this may lead to their overidentification with certain family members, difficulties in accepting and appreciating the family, attempts to make the family over into the worker's ideal, or intense reactions that are related to difficulties with their own families. Workers may be experiencing similar problems to those of their clients making it hard to be objective or optimally involved. And the sometimes overwhelming and disturbing nature of family interactions, lack of the most basic resources, and presence of outright abuse or neglect may leave workers feeling overwhelmed, fatigued, discouraged, frustrated, and inadequate.

THE INTERVENTIVE PROCESS

In the following example, which shows the beginning work with the Diegos, the family sought help for problems centering on their childrens' school difficulties, which were related to underlying marital conflict that affected everyone in the family.

THE DIEGO CASE

Juan and Rosa Diego, ages 34 and 32, and their two children, Pedro and Maria, ages 9 and 7, were referred to a family counseling agency by the children's guidance counselor. During the past few months, Pedro was having academic and social problems, and Maria seemed withdrawn, sensitive, and given to crying over minor frustrations. Married for 10 years, the Diegos and their children resided in a two-bedroom apartment near their families. Mr. Diego was employed as a limousine driver, and his wife worked as a claims adjuster in an insurance company.

All four family members attended the first session at the worker's request. After the introductions and some polite conversation, the worker inquired why the family was coming to the agency. Mrs. Diego took the lead and responded that she was surprised when the school called her because there had never been any complaints about the children before and she did not understand why the children were having problems. She reported that they were a close family who spent a good deal of time with the children and gave them everything they wanted or needed. Mr. Diego coached Pedro's soccer team, and Maria enjoyed cooking and shopping with her mother. In response to the worker's questions, Mrs. Diego indicated that, like other children, the kids sometimes fought with each other at home. She said that she and her husband wanted to do everything they could to help their children, which is why they agreed to come for help even though they did not believe in counseling.

The worker observed that Mr. Diego and the children listened intently while Mrs. Diego spoke. The worker said she sounded very concerned but also unclear about what was happening. Turning to Mr. Diego, she asked if he had any thoughts about the situation. He said no, and as his wife had said, there were not any problems at home except that like all other kids, Pedro and Maria sometimes got in fights with each other.

Mr. Diego: My son is very active and enthusiastic. He has a lot of energy and stands up for himself. Maybe the school mistook that for bad behavior. I'm sure he doesn't mean to hurt anyone.

Mrs. Diego: Maria has always been sensitive because she's the baby. She's used to getting her way, and she gets over her crying if I comfort her.

Observing that the Diegos were trying to assure the worker that they were good parents and that the children were normal, the worker commented that she could see that the parents were concerned and giving people and that her questions were related to learning more about the situation. She asked if there had been any recent changes in their lives over the past few months.

When the parents said they couldn't think of anything, the worker turned her attention to Pedro and asked him if he could tell her a little about what had been going on at school. He looked at his father, who told him to go ahead and answer the worker.

Pedro: Sometimes the other kids pick on me, and I fight.

Mrs. Diego: (Glaring at her husband) I told you, you shouldn't be telling him to fight!

Mr. Diego: Let's not get into that now. This isn't the time.

At this point Maria started fidgeting, and Mrs. Diego told her to sit still. Maria responded that she was bored and didn't want to stay here. The worker intervened, gave Maria some paper and crayons, and returned to Mr. Diego's comment.

Worker: Mr. Diego, I can see that your wife's comment bothered you. Can you talk a little about your reaction?

Mr. Diego: Sometimes my wife and I disagree about how to handle the children. I think Pedro needs to know how to take care of himself. She doesn't believe in fighting.

Mrs. Diego: What good is fighting? You just want him to be like you.

Mr. Diego: As his father, I know what's best for my son.

Worker: Do you also disagree about how to handle Maria?

Mrs. Diego: He always tells me that I baby her. She's a little girl, and she needs me. He just doesn't like it when I give her attention. He thinks I don't give enough attention to Pedro, but Pedro is a big boy now.

Mr. Diego: You never took care of him the way you take care of Maria.

The worker pointed out that they did seem to have some disagreement about how to handle the children and commented that when they differed during the session, Maria started fidgeting and distracted them for a moment. The worker wondered if this ever happened at home. Mrs. Diego responded that Maria did not like to see them argue and didn't understand that their fighting didn't mean that they didn't care about each other. Although she was drawing, Maria was also listening to the interchange, and the worker asked her if she got upset when her parents argued. Maria first shrugged her shoulders and then nodded.

Worker: What upsets you?

Maria: They yell so loud.

Mr. Diego: Sometimes adults fight. It doesn't mean anything. I told you not to worry about it. It's between your mother and me.

Mrs. Diego: We love you.

Worker: You do love the children, and what you say about adult fighting may be true. Nevertheless, your arguments still may upset the kids. Has there been more fighting lately?

Mr. Diego: I don't think so.

Pedro: (Making a face) All you and Mommy seem to do lately is yell.

The worker asked what Pedro did when his parents fought, and he responded that he went into his room, shut the door, and played video games. When the worker asked Maria what she did, Maria went over to her mother and put her head in her lap. Mrs. Diego gently caressed her daughter's hair and said that she and her husband tried not to fight when the children were around.

Mr. Diego: So we argue. What does that have to do with the kids' problems at school? Parents fight and argue. They have to understand that.

Maria now asked to go to the bathroom, but when her mother offered to take her, Pedro said he would do it. When the children left, Mrs. Diego acknowledged that the parents' fighting got very intense sometimes, but she didn't see why that should affect their school performance.

Mrs. Diego: We love them and want the best for them.

Worker: Of course, you do. The fact that you are willing to come for help is evidence of that. It also seems that you have some strong differences with one another about how the kids should be treated. Even though it is not unusual for parents to disagree at times, your arguing may upset the children more than you realize. Kids often show their distress at school rather than at home because they want to protect their parents or not make the situation worse. This doesn't mean that the kids are bad or that there's anything wrong with them or you.

The children then reappeared. Maria was crying and said Pedro had punched her. Mrs. Diego started to reprimand Pedro, but Mr. Diego interrupted and accused her of not finding out Pedro's side of the story before blaming him. Pedro said that Maria called him a name and *that's why he hit her. Mrs. Diego said he shouldn't hit her even if she did call him a name. Mr. Diego responded by telling his wife that Maria knew how to provoke her brother. By this time, the children were both quiet, but the parents were arguing. The worker interrupted to point this out.*

Worker: *We have only a few minutes remaining, and maybe it is a good time to discuss where to go from here.*

Mr. Diego: *We will do whatever is necessary to help the kids. What do you think the problem is?*

Worker: *Is there anything that has come out today that seems important?*

Mrs. Diego: *I know the kids don't like it when we fight, but I never thought that our arguing would make the kids have problems at school.*

Mr. Diego: *I'm not sure that our fighting is causing their problem at school, but I am tired of our arguments. They are getting worse.*

Worker: *How would all of you feel about returning so that we can try to understand what is causing your fighting, and I can help you with it so that the kids can do better? Meanwhile, I can also visit the children's school and speak to their teachers.*

Pedro and Maria said they wanted to come back, and Mr. and Mrs. Diego made another appointment. The worker explained the clinic policies and that they could meet for 10 sessions once weekly. Mr. Diego thought that was too much. The worker responded that 10 was the most sessions that they could have, but it was not necessary to use them all. She suggested that they meet for 4 additional sessions and then reevaluate whether to continue.

The worker observed that although they were caring parents, the Diego's marital relationship seemed strained, and it was unclear what areas of harmony existed other than that they both wanted their children to do well. The worker also wondered if anything in the school setting could be impacting on the children.

It seemed that the couple argued with one another through the children rather than directly. Although both were upset about their in-

creasing conflict, Mrs. Diego appeared to be more open than her husband to the possibility that their fights were influencing the children negatively.

A few hours before the second appointment, Mrs. Diego called to cancel due to illness. She sounded upset but when the worker commented about this, Mrs. Diego said she was fine and the family would be in the following week. In visiting with the children's teachers, the worker learned that both were well liked and well thought of. The teachers were concerned because they could find no explanation in the school setting to account for the children's changes in behavior.

At the next appointment, the worker began by asking how Mrs. Diego was feeling. She looked at her husband and said it wasn't right to lie. She recounted how they had had a bad argument that led to their pushing and shoving each other. As her mother spoke, Maria started to cry and went over to her mother, who tried to comfort her. Pedro turned his chair around to face the wall. Mr. Diego looked exasperated.

Mr. Diego: Do you see how she pays attention to Maria and not to Pedro? This is what happens at home all the time and why we fight! What am I supposed to do? When I try to talk to her, she doesn't pay any attention to what I am saying. Then I get mad. Do you blame me?

Mrs. Diego: Do you expect me to push her away if she comes to me?

Mr. Diego: What about Pedro? He needs you too.

Mrs. Diego: He is more independent and doesn't like me to mother him too much. I don't know why you can't just go along sometimes instead of arguing with me. You only seem to talk to me when it's about something I'm doing wrong.

Worker: I'm not sure whether your fighting is about the children or your both feeling that the other doesn't understand or appreciate you. For example, Mrs. Diego, you just said that your husband doesn't talk to you except to criticize you, and Mr. Diego, I wonder if you need more attention from your wife than you feel you get. Perhaps it is hard to say what you need directly to one another. What do you think?

Mr. Diego: I don't want her to ignore me and my wishes.

Mrs. Diego: You don't want me to ignore you? What about me? Do you ever show an interest in what I'm doing or feeling? We don't even go out together anymore! You do your thing with Pedro, and I turn to Maria. We're not close any more the way we used to be.

Worker: Tell me what it used to be like and what changed.

The Diegos gave the following background. They knew each other as children in Mexico and immigrated to New York with their families when they were teenagers. Mr. Diego, the oldest of five children, came from a family in poor economic circumstances. His father worked long hours as a laborer, and Mr. Diego was responsible for helping his mother take care of his younger siblings. He left school at age 12 to earn money to help the family and worked hard. When he was 17, his mother's brother, who lived in New York City, arranged for the whole family to immigrate. Mr. Diego got a job in a local bodega while his siblings attended school. Eventually the family moved to a larger apartment, where Mr. Diego resided until, at age 24, he married his wife.

Mr. Diego's parents had had a stormy marriage and argued about money, the raising of the children, and the father's explosive moods. Although generally a devoted father, he would frequently drink to excess, rage about his inability to provide better for his family, and take out his frustrations on his wife and children. Mr. Diego's mother, a religious woman, was devoted to her children and often neglected her husband, which added to his feelings of inadequacy. Mr. Diego still contributed money to the family whenever he and his wife had a little extra.

Mrs. Diego was the middle of three children. Her family lived in somewhat better financial circumstances than her husband's family. Her father worked in a grain factory and brought home regular paychecks. When Mrs. Diego was 10, her oldest sister died in an automobile accident. The family was devastated by the loss, and Mrs. Diego's father remained depressed and angry, often criticizing her for not measuring up to her older sister. There was little pleasure after that. The family moved, hoping that a change of location would help the father's depression. Her mother found work caring for other people's children, *and her father continued to be unemployed. Mrs. Diego went to work after graduating from high school.*

The Diegos saw one another at a dance and became reacquainted. They came from the same background and enjoyed music, dancing, going to the beach, and seeing movies and friends. They dated for four years and married when they had saved enough money to secure their own apartment. Although they had not planned on having children right away, Pedro was born a year later and Maria two years after that. When the children were born, the Diegos took their child rearing responsibilities very seriously and gradually relinquished their own interests in favor of family activities.

Almost from the beginning, Mr. Diego was very attached to Pedro and wanted him to have the life that he did not have as a child. As time went on, he spent more and more time with Pedro. Maria, who resembled and was named for Mrs. Diego's sister, was born prematurely and required extra care. Mrs. Diego felt left out of her husband and son's relationship and sought comfort and companionship in her relationship with Maria. Mr. Diego was feeling more trapped by family and work responsibilities, and Mrs. Diego was feeling more alone and getting less enjoyment from life. In talking about their histories, the Diegos both were surprised at how much they had to put their needs aside as children and adolescents because of their family situations.

> *Worker: It seems that both of you were forced to take on a great deal of responsibility at an early age and that your own needs may have been neglected. It also appears that there was not much time for having a good time.*
>
> *Mr. Diego: I had to take care of my family. I missed out on a lot of things. My mother was so busy herself. It's not her fault, but I want my son to have a different kind of life.*
>
> *Mrs. Diego: It was so difficult when my sister died. It changed everything. I was very frightened when Maria was born that something might happen to her.*
>
> *Worker: Do you think there's any connection between your early family experiences and what is going on now?*
>
> *Mr. Diego: What do you mean?*

Worker: Sometimes couples repeat things that have happened to them earlier in their lives. For example, both of you take your current family responsibilities very seriously and feel burdened and alone in ways that are similar to how you felt when you were growing up.

Mrs. Diego: That's true.

Worker: It is possible, Mr. Diego, that doing things for Pedro is a way of making up for what you did not get as a child and that when your wife seems not to pay attention to you or Pedro, it reminds you of how your needs were put aside in the past. And Mrs. Diego, perhaps your concerns about Maria are intensified by what happened to your sister. And when your husband criticizes your parenting, this makes you feel guilty and reminds you of how your father found fault with you.

Mr. Diego: I don't know. I am a little too critical of her. Sometimes I do wish she would pay more attention to me.

Mrs. Diego: I know my husband did a lot for his family when he was younger, and he still does. Maybe I don't always see that he needs me too. What can we do now?

Worker: You seem to care about one another. It would help if you could try to talk to each other directly about what you do need, try to listen to one another, and begin to have some pleasure together without the children, as you did earlier in your relationship. This also will relieve the children.

The worker suggested that they could begin by trying not to criticize each other during the week even if they felt like doing so and that they try to think about what they wanted from one another.

In the third and fourth sessions, the worker met with the Diegos without the children present. The worker focused on improving the couple's communication, particularly around letting the other know what they needed and wanted. This was difficult because they invariably started fighting about the children again in the sessions, and the worker needed to intervene to help them identify why the other was upset by what had transpired. The worker helped the Diegos to talk more about what their early experiences were like for each of them. On one occasion the following interchange occurred:

Worker: Mr. Diego, you are complaining about how much time your wife spent Saturday afternoon with Maria, but I wonder if what you really wanted was for your wife to spend more time with you.

Mr. Diego: I don't think she wants to be with me.

Mrs. Diego: But he never asks me. He just goes off with Pedro.

Worker: Mr. Diego, it seems hard for you to ask your wife for companionship. It seems important that she know what you want without your having to say it. Do have any thoughts about why this might be?

Mr. Diego: Sometimes she just seems so busy.

Worker: It reminds me of what you said about your mother. You must have learned not to bother her but still hoped that she would pay attention to you. Could you talk directly to your wife right now?

Mr. Diego: I know you have a lot to do and I don't want to burden you. Sometimes I would like you to think about me.

Worker: Mrs. Diego, how do you feel about what your husband is saying?

Mrs. Diego. Sometimes I don't know what to do to make him happy.

Worker: That reminds me of what you said about your father and how no one could make him feel better. That must have been very painful. Perhaps there are things you can do to affect your husband. Maybe you can ask him now.

Mrs. Diego: Is there something I can do?

Mr. Diego: I'd like to have some fun. We don't see people or go away or go out together.

Mrs. Diego: I thought you wanted to be with Pedro.

Mr. Diego: He doesn't need me as much as he did.

Worker: It is really good that you are talking to and trying to hear one another tonight. Do you think that you could make some plans to go out together during the week?

Mrs. Diego: Maria needs to me to do her homework with her.

Worker: Mrs. Diego, even though what you are saying may be true, do you see how your husband might feel that you prefer to be with Maria than with him?

Mr. Diego: You took the words right out of my mouth.

Mrs. Diego: You're right. I'm so used to my ways. It's hard to change.

Worker: It's good that you can acknowledge that. Change is difficult.

The Diegos agreed to continue for the remaining six sessions because they saw that their children were experiencing some relief, and they also recognized that they had ignored their relationship. In the time left, the worker focused on helping the couple stop the escalation of their arguments by identifying what was bothering each of them in terms of their own needs. Sessions were used to continue to help them talk more directly to one another. The worker supported the couple's efforts to reach out to others and to plan activities together and have the children spend more time with relatives. By the end of the treatment, the children's behavior in school improved markedly, and the Diegos were fighting less and socializing more.

Discussion

The worker learned that each member of the family had a different view of the problem. Although they were doubtful that their problems were contributing to the children's school difficulties and that their involvement in the interventive process would result in their children's doing better, the worker used their interest in and commitment to their children to help motivate them to continue coming for help. Had the children not been present at the early meetings, the worker would not have learned of the parental fighting and its effects on the children because the parents were not forthcoming about the true nature of their interaction. In learning about the individual backgrounds of the parents and the history of their marriage, the worker was able to see some of the main dynamics that led to their current stalemate. Using this information, the worker was able to intervene in their here-and-now interactions in sessions to lessen their fighting, improve their communication about their needs, and connect their relationship difficulties to their early life experiences. She suggested and supported the parents' participation in joint activities that might bring them pleasure and enhance their closeness.

In the following case, which shows the beginning work with the Sevinos, the family showed more severe difficulties and rigidity than did the Diegos and were less motivated to seek help.

THE SEVINO CASE

The Sevinos, a religious Pentecostal family, were referred to a preventive service program by the state division of child protection after an allegation of abuse was deemed unfounded but the family nevertheless was thought to be at risk. The family lived together in a rented house in a deserted industrial neighborhood and consisted of the father, Jack, age 45, a maintenance worker at his daughters' school; the mother, Diane, age 45, a housewife; and two daughters, Chris, age 17, and Lisa, age 15, both high school students. During the past several years, Chris had telephoned the child abuse registry on numerous occasions to complain that her father was using excessive physical force to discipline her. Each time there was an investigation, Chris would admit that her complaint was not true but based on her anger at her father for being rigid and controlling. Finally, the state investigator told the family that they had to get counseling. They sought out their pastor, who had known them a long time, but they never kept their scheduled appointments with him and were then referred to the protective services program.

The first meeting was scheduled to take place at the family's home because the mother, Diane, said she was too frightened to leave the house. When the worker arrived, the family was not home, so she waited. After about 20 minutes, the family arrived and made no explanation about their lateness.

Jack: Why do we have to see you? We just want to see our pastor.

Worker: You can still see him if you like, but because you have not followed through with your appointments, the state has determined that it will be necessary for you to work with our program. What are your concerns about my involvement?

Jack: We don't think our family life is any of your business.

Diane: We don't want to talk to a stranger.

Worker: I can understand your feelings about your privacy and about your not knowing me. What is it like for you to be in this situation?

Chris: I'm glad you're here so you can hear my side of the story.

Jack: You're not from our church. No offense. We would prefer to have someone who knows our ways.

Worker: That might be more comfortable, but I will be open to learning about you. Perhaps it might help to see me as someone who can be a resource to you in order to free you from further involvement with protective services.

Diane: Jack, maybe we should look at it that way.

Worker: When did the problems you are having begin? Who wants to start?

Chris: I will. My father does not like my 21-year-old boyfriend, Tony, and does not allow me to see him outside of church. It's his way or no way.

Jack: (Interrupting and yelling) That's not true! You know that's not true!

Worker: You need to give one another a chance to talk without interrupting, and I will make sure that everyone has his or her say.

Chris: He thinks he can leave whenever he wants and that we're supposed to obey him when he decides to return. He leaves without telling us and comes back without an explanation and starts his usual control shit. No way! It doesn't work like that.

Jack: Watch your mouth. We don't talk like that!

Chris: Who are you to tell me? You have an ugly mouth when you get started. You weren't even here for six years.

Amid many interruptions and blaming comments between Jack and

Chris, the following story emerged. Jack had left the family 12 years earlier for another woman. After no contact, he reappeared 6 years later and wanted to start anew. He moved the family to a southern state, but after a series of relocations, they returned to their original neighborhood. Before the father returned, the family was on welfare and the mother did her best to care for the children. When Jack came back, he took over all of the decision making and discipline, pushed Diane aside and disregarded her wishes, and imposed strict rules on the children, whom he thought were in need of control.

Worker: It sounds like a difficult time for everyone. What was it like for you, Diane, and you, Lisa, when your father returned?

Lisa: I was 3 years old when he left, and I was 9 when he came back. I was glad to have a father. I just don't want him to punish me the way he does. I'm 15. I don't do anything wrong. I'm sick of the fighting. I wish everyone could get along

Diane: Jack and Chris do fight a lot.

Worker: What kind of punishment do you believe in?

Jack: They need to learn how to behave.

Chris: (Interrupting) He makes us stay home and confines us to our room. We can't watch TV. We can only listen to religious music. He took the telephone out of the room. He lectures us all the time. If I call to say I'm going to be late, he accuses me of lying and calls me a slut and a sneak.

Jack: (Interrupting) You are a sneak! I have to watch you all the time. Both of you think you're adults, but you're not. You have an attitude problem. You can't do everything you want. You have to obey me. I know best.

Diane: Jack, maybe you should stop.

Jack: Why should I stop? There's nothing wrong with what I'm saying. I just want what's best for the kids.

Worker: I can see that you feel very strongly about your beliefs about what your children need, but it is a problem for everyone that Chris and Lisa feel so strongly about their needs. What is happening is not good for anyone. If we can find a way to help all of you with *the fighting, then it will be easier to live together without Chris's having to make official complaints. I have a few more questions before we stop because I have to fill out some forms. Does anyone have any medical problems?*

Whispering back and forth to one another, Diane finally told Jack to tell the worker the truth. Jack revealed that both he and his wife were HIV positive, he for nine years and she for five years. They were both taking medication and doing well. The worker was surprised by this revelation at the end of the session, when she did not have time to discuss this subject with them at greater length. She did ask them about what it was like for them to have told her. Jack and Diane said that they had not told anyone else, even their pastor, because they were concerned about being judged. The worker said that she was glad that they felt able to share this information with her. The session ended with the family's agreeing to do see the worker on a weekly basis in their home for 20 meetings.

Amid canceled appointments and threats of quitting, the worker persevered. She tried to relate to the parents' anger at what they perceived as the worker's intrusion in their personal lives and to point out that she was trying to help them to get along better so that they could prevent further intrusion by social agencies.

What emerged in the next several meetings was a considerable amount of overt conflict between the father and Chris, who seemed to act as the spokesperson for her mother and sister. The main subject of the arguments was Chris's relationship with her boyfriend, Tony, whom her father disliked intensely because he was not religious. Jack feared that Chris would get pregnant, marry Tony, go on welfare, contract AIDS, and die. Jack let them see one another only under very specific conditions, and he always remained in sight on these occasions. He was concerned that Lisa was becoming like Chris and growing up too fast. Jack spied on Chris and Lisa when they were at school and would repeatedly ask their teachers about whom they spoke to and about their behavior in class. Although Jack would not allow the girls to see friends other than at school or church and demanded that they spend their weekends at home, the family never did anything together. Jack and Diane often slept until noon and did solitary activities the rest of the time, leaving the girls to occupy themselves. Jack complained that Diane would not have sex with him, was a poor housekeeper, and was too lax with their daughters. Diane, who had never been an outgoing person, became increasingly withdrawn after Jack returned to the household. Although she disagreed with his handling of the girls and resented his possessiveness and criticism of her, she found it too hard to fight with him and submitted to his demands and need for control. She was fearful that the worker's involvement would cause Jack to become even angrier and more relentless in his criticism. Depressed and isolated, she had no family nearby or friends and rarely left the house except to attend church and shop for groceries and other essentials.

In exploring why Jack was so fearful about Chris and Lisa, the worker learned that Jack, even as an adolescent, had been sexually active with numerous women whom he never really cared about and whom he would discard once he had tired of them. He continued to be a womanizer all though his adult life, fathering numerous children whom he never supported or saw. He believed that if he did not keep his daughters safe, they would be subjected to men like him. He turned to religion after learning about his HIV status and felt that his behavior would not have changed if he had not embraced the church. The worker also learned that Jack had been abandoned by his own father and raised by his mother. He grew up on the streets, had little education, and was determined that his children would have a better life, including a college education.

In discussing the background and implications of Jack and Diane's HIV status, the worker learned that Jack did not know the source of his infection but imagined that it resulted from a visit to a prostitute. He transmitted the virus to his wife. Knowing this because of the recriminations that followed Diane's diagnosis, the girls blamed their father for giving HIV to their mother and also had many concerns about the parents' becoming ill and dying. Sometimes Chris would yell that she couldn't wait for him to die but then would become extremely upset because she did not want to lose her mother. In addition to blaming Jack, Diane blamed herself for getting HIV because she knew her husband had the infection and sometimes did not use any protection when they did have sexual relations. Significant in her history was the fact that she had been raped repeatedly as an adolescent by a family friend. When she told her family, they told her to try to forget about it and broke off contact with the perpetrator. Although her father and siblings were alive, they lived in another state. They never liked her husband, and she was not close to them.

Despite the worker's feelings of frustration with and dislike of Jack's rigid, controlling, and destructive behavior and her dismay at Diane's passivity, compliance, and lack of self-protection, she was able to contain her feelings by recognizing that helping the family required her to find a way of understanding what was behind their disturbing actions and attitudes. The worker recognized that Jack truly believed that he was doing the right thing for his family and wanted his daughters to do well in life and that this would make the task of trying to help him to ease his controlling behavior very difficult. She realized that he did not know any other way of relating to them and might be feeling some sense of urgency because of his HIV status. The worker saw that Diane cared about her daughters but had little energy or internal and external resources to oppose her husband effectively or leave him. Additionally her HIV status undoubtedly made her feel more dependent on him.

The worker decided that it was important to (1) validate Jack's wish to help and protect his daughters and not to challenge his beliefs and excessive fears; (2) appeal to Jack's better interests by helping him to see that his efforts to control his daughters and make them obey him, rightly or wrongly, might be successful temporarily but that he could not go on doing this indefinitely without alienating them further and causing them to rebel, run away, and get in to the very trouble that he feared the most; (3) help Chris and Lisa talk more concretely about what they wanted and needed and see that it was in their better interests to refrain from screaming and yelling at Jack and try to show him greater respect; (4) provide Diane an opportunity to express her feelings and opinions without being criticized by Jack; and (5) help all members of the family problem-solve about ways that the daughters could have a little more freedom while still adhering to the father's values. Although the worker knew that the parents' HIV status was making the system more vulnerable, it did not seem to be affecting the presenting problem directly. Nevertheless, it would need to be addressed eventually. Because of Diane's depression and relative isolation, the worker also recognized that she needed a medication evaluation and that connecting her to outside resources eventually was indicated in order to help her self-esteem, offer her a support system, and strengthen her coping capacities.

In the initial phase of the interventive process, the worker was active in structuring the family's communications, which were chaotic, filled with verbal abuse, accusations and threats, and interruptions. She was successful in building an alliance with Jack. He was able to see the worker as helping him to forward his goals with his daughters and became somewhat more amenable to lessening his control of them. Concurrently, the worker was able to establish an alliance with the three women without alienating Jack. She helped them to acknowledge his good intentions while expressing their needs and wishes. The worker educated Jack and Diane about the fact that much of Diane's upsetting behavior that angered Jack resulted from depression and might improve with medication. Although he was skeptical, he agreed to take her to the doctor, who prescribed Paxil, an antidepressant.

The work was arduous, but the family made progress in talking to and hearing one another. It then became possible to problem-solve about and implement ways of permitting more freedom and spending some time together in more pleasurable activities. Although Jack remained overly controlling, he was less extreme and volatile; Chris and Lisa were less confrontative and somewhat happier; and Diane felt more energetic and became less withdrawn. These small successes gave the family members some confidence that they could work on other issues in later sessions.

Discussion

The Sevino family was involuntary and resistant to intervention. Because they disagreed on the nature of the problem and what to do about it, the main tasks of the worker were to help the family to accept her involvement with them, develop an alliance with the healthy parts of the family, and find some common ground that they could work on together. Once this was accomplished, it became possible to use family *sessions to help each family member identify his or her needs and possible courses of actions that might be acceptable to everyone.*

SUMMARY

This chapter discussed the application of ISTT to work with families and illustrated the interventive process with two case examples. It emphasized the importance of individualizing family members as well as relating to the family as a system and of using family sessions to help families listen to and hear one another, understand the connection between past family-of-origin issues and current problems, and experiment with new ways of communicating and behaving.

Chapter 12

Group-Oriented ISTT

Social work and other mental health professionals are using groups increasingly as a major treatment modality. In addition to the economic factors that make group intervention appear potentially more attractive than individual intervention, there are numerous clinical indicators for the use of this method. Groups can be a significant vehicle for offering clients acceptance, reassurance, and encouragement; providing an opportunity for clients to share their concerns with others who have similar experiences and thereby decreasing isolation and stigma; promoting problem solving; mobilizing strengths; enhancing and developing ego capacities; developing common interests and skills; enhancing a sense of mastery and competence; providing information and education; facilitating mutual aid; changing attitudes and behavior; and developing new ways of relating to others.

Although group intervention has a long and rich tradition in social work that has its roots in the settlement house movement of the late nineteenth century, it asserted its importance after World War II. Social group work and group psychotherapy have generated different models and draw on a variety of theories (Budman & Gurman, 1988; Garvin, 1997; Mishne, 1993, pp. 111–132). It is beyond the scope of this book to review all of these. Instead, it will consider the application of group-oriented ISTT, which is consistent with aspects of each of the major social work group models: the mediation model that emphasizes the role of group process and experience, the remedial model that focuses on the individual within the group, and the task-centered model that stresses the use of tasks and activities (Garvin, 1997, pp. 316–317). After discussing the indicators for the use of group-oriented ISTT and its special foci, this chapter will illustrate the process of intervention.

INDICATORS FOR THE USE OF GROUPS

Although there is an unfortunate tendency on the part of many agencies to place clients into short-term groups indiscriminately without attention to their individualized problems and capacities, there are many indicators for deciding to use group-oriented ISTT. These include situations in which clients are:

1. Experiencing similar life transitions, such as retirement, widowhood, geographic relocation, leaving home, or hospital discharge.
2. Going through similar developmental phases, such as adolescence or middle age.
3. Occupying the same social or occupational roles or statuses or sharing common interests or concerns, such as neighborhood violence and safety, environmental protection, school programs and personnel, and community resources.
4. Coping with similar life crises such as childhood illness or disability, loss and death, surgery, domestic violence, rape, or psychiatric hospitalization or the need for ongoing adjustment to caretaking burdens or chronic illness and disability.
5. Requiring help in developing specific interests and skills such as socialization, daily living, parenting, or finding employment.
6. Needing assistance in enhancing problem solving or building ego functions such as impulse control, reality testing, or self-esteem.
7. Showing similar types of maladaptive patterns, problems, emotional disorders, substance abuse, or antisocial behavior.
8. Demonstrating the effects of similar kinds of past trauma such as childhood sexual abuse.
9. Coping with a family member who has a significant impairment

such as schizophrenia, manic-depressive illness, alcoholism, or gambling.

10. Showing the need for prevention and early intervention.

SPECIFIC FOCI

Although all of the components of ISTT are applicable to group work, their use necessitates emphasizing, modifying, and expanding certain aspects of the framework.

Balancing Individual and Group Assessment

A major task of group-oriented ISTT is balancing a focus on individual and group assessment. A group is more than the sum of its parts and has a life of its own. It is characterized by certain here-and-now processes that involve the nature of communication, the assumption of roles, the establishment of leadership, the formation of subgroups, and the allocation of power. Group intervention emphasizes the facilitation and use of the group process to achieve group goals. Concurrently, group members bring their unique backgrounds, personalities, problems, needs, strengths, capacities, and ways of relating to their group interactions, and individualization is necessary.

Engagement

In order to facilitate engagement, it is crucial for workers to elicit clients' diverse feelings and expectations about being part of a group. These reactions may stem from their membership in their family of origin, school and peer group experiences in childhood and adolescence, and adult group interactions. When past experiences with family and group membership have been generally positive, the individual is likely to be optimistic, hopeful, and comfortable in participating in a group. Other individuals, however, may have had decidedly negative family and group experiences in which they were rejected, neglected, abused, demeaned, humiliated, marginalized, exploited, or attacked. Consequently, they may be fearful and distrustful of being in a group.

Individuals differ too with respect to the value they place on privacy, exposing their concerns to others, and speaking openly about certain topics, so some clients may have more difficulty with the expectation that they participate in a group.

Contracting

Although group members may share common types of concerns, each may have different needs. It is necessary for the worker to explore each group member's view of what he or she wants from the group and help all members arrive at what they are going to focus on and how they are going to structure their work together. Major tasks in the beginning phase are to help group members discuss their feelings about being in a group; enable group members to hear one another; identify common concerns; set ground rules or group norms regarding such matters as attendance, confidentiality, participation, behavior, communication, and outside interaction; and facilitate agreement on the goals and focus of the group.

Building Group Cohesion

A collection of individuals does not necessarily function as a viable group, even when they share similar concerns and problems. Workers must intervene in ways that create an atmosphere of acceptance, respect, safety, and trust; promote mutuality and reciprocity; and foster joint problem solving. In addition to facilitating verbal interaction, involving group members in shared activities, tasks, exercises, and role plays sometimes is a good way of promoting group cohesion.

Facilitating Group Interaction

Although groups have different goals and foci—some are supportive, educative, or organized around activities and some are change oriented—workers must always intervene to encourage group interaction. In the beginning, group members often direct their communication to the worker, who must balance eliciting and responding to each group member with trying to help group members listen to and respond to one another. Groups differ in the degree to which they are able to interact freely and constructively. The worker may need to take an active role in structuring group interaction and modeling optimal ways of relating, problem solving, and setting limits.

Resolving Conflict

Inevitably conflicts arise when people come together to work on their problems, and they arise from a variety of sources: differences in point of view, needs, priorities, or styles of relating; misinterpretations of certain aspects of the group process; insensitive or hurtful remarks; violations of confidentiality or other group rules and norms; disruptive behavior; erratic attendance; nonparticipation of a member; or rivalry and envy among members. Helping group members to identify the reasons for and to address and resolve group conflicts is essential to maintaining a positive group experience and may enable group members to learn new ways of resolving conflict and relating to others.

Worker Roles and Interventions

Workers may use themselves in a variety of ways based on the goals and focus of the group and the capacities and problems of its members: providing information, guidance, education, validation, and support; building on strengths; discussing and modeling alternative ways of problem solving, thinking, feeling, and behaving; helping group members to support and validate one another; establishing tasks, activities, and exercises that improve the group members' ability to relate to others and their ego functioning, problem solving, and socialization and others skills; enabling group members to reflect on the group process; interrupting potentially destructive interactions; helping group members to see the relationship between their group behavior and their current life problems; and enabling them to make connections between past experiences and current problems. It also may be appropriate for workers to help group members locate and access necessary resources and services and to act on their behalf with others.

Worker Reactions

Leading a group can stimulate complex reactions in the worker. Workers, like clients, bring their own backgrounds, positive and negative family and group experiences, and preferred ways of relating to the interventive process. Some workers may be vulnerable to becoming enmeshed in or detached from the group process so that they cannot lead the group effectively. Group interaction can be quite intense, and some workers may personalize group interactions, become intimidated by the group, and have difficulty managing their reactions. Workers may overidentify with or feel more empathy with some members of the group than others, and this may result in their showing such attitudes as favoritism, insensitivity, nonprotectiveness, and scapegoating. And the sometimes overwhelming and disturbing nature of group members' problems, group interaction, or lack of necessary resources may result in workers' becoming overwhelmed, drained, depleted, or depressed.

Termination Issues

What makes termination in group-oriented ISTT different from completing individual or family treatment is that group members must deal with ending with one another and the group as a whole. Workers must elicit and relate to the full range of reactions that group members experience during the termination process. Although groups are formed to carry out an overall purpose or to help members address individual problems and issues, participating in a group may have its own benefits, such as a sense of belonging and feelings of mutuality. Group members may form meaningful relationships with one another that may be difficult to give up or maintain without the structure of the group.

Not everyone in a group derives the same benefits, establishes the same meaningful relationships, or makes the same progress as other participants. Consequently clients who have not had as positive an experience as other members may feel disappointed, deprived, or envious as they make inevitable comparisons.

THE INTERVENTIVE PROCESS

The example that follows shows excerpts of the interventive process of a 12-session group for adult survivors of childhood sexual abuse that was given under the auspices of a hospital outpatient department. Because issues that are addressed in such a group are emotionally charged and clients who are survivors often are fragile, participation in the group required that each member also be involved in treatment.

THE ADULT SURVIVORS' GROUP

In addition to the worker, Gail, a 48-year-old Caucasian woman, the group consisted of the following six members: Cissy, a 42-year-old married African American woman with three children; Joan, a 27-year-old Caucasian single woman; Denise, a 20-year-old African American woman; Alice, a 30-year-old Caucasian woman; Millagros, a 24-year-old Hispanic woman; and Terry, a 55-year-old Caucasian woman.

Each client was referred by his or her treating therapist, who submitted a description of the client, the presenting problem, and a brief history. The group leader met with each of the women individually to ascertain their suitability for the group, share information about how the group would be organized and led, and make a beginning connection to each prospective group member. The following information was gathered from these two sources.

Cissy had begun individual treatment three months earlier for help with the effects of early sexual abuse. She told her therapist that a day did not go by without her thinking about the abuse. Three months earlier, she had had an argument with her mother because the client did not want to leave her 7-year-old daughter alone with her grandfather. Her mother was hurt and angry and could not understand her daughter's behavior. Cissy realized that she was becoming increasing fearful that someone would harm her children and that her fears were related to her early sexual abuse. She called agencies to see if there were any groups for incest survivors. When she learned that a prerequisite was individual treatment, she reluctantly sought help. She had sought treat-

ment earlier in her life but stopped after a few sessions. The referring therapist described the client as quiet, uncomfortable talking to the therapist, but highly motivated to be in a group with other women who had similar experiences.

An only child, Cissy grew up in an intact southern family. At age 9, her favorite uncle forced her to have oral sex. They had spent the day together at the zoo and had gone back to his home. He swore her to secrecy and told her he would kill her if she ever told anyone. During the next year, he molested her twice more when he was taking care of her. When her father got a new job and the family moved to New York, she never saw the uncle again. She never told her parents or anyone else, including her husband, about the incidents.

Joan had been in individual treatment for a year for her depression and problems sustaining relationships before being referred to the group. She had conflicts on the job and had limited social interactions. Although she had been dealing with her sexual abuse in her individual treatment, her therapist thought Joan could benefit from a group experience that would help her with her interpersonal problems. The therapist described Joan as angry, suspicious, and given to occasional binge drinking. Although hesitant, she was willing to try a group.

From ages 10 to 16, Joan was sexually abused repeatedly by Greg, her older brother, when he was 15 to 21 years of age. The abuse, which started as playful exploration of each other's genitals, led to his forcing her to have oral sex and intercourse. She said she knew there was something wrong with what they were doing but did not want him to be angry with her. She looked up to him and depended on him because their alcoholic parents were physically and emotionally neglectful. When Joan was 13 years old, Greg threatened to abuse her younger female siblings if Joan did not have sex with three of his friends. She submitted. At 16, however, she told him she would kill him if he ever touched her again or went near the younger children.

Alice had been in individual treatment for seven months because of an alcohol problem before coming to the group. She had been attending AA for a year after losing her automobile license following a car accident that left her and two passengers hospitalized. Alice entered treatment to help her maintain her sobriety. Her therapist thought the group *might help her with her belief that her feelings and experiences were unique. Alice was open to entering group treatment. Her therapist described Alice as flamboyant, full of energy, pseudo-independent, and engaging but with underlying guilt and anger.*

Alice grew up in a well-to-do midwestern Irish Catholic family. Her prominent family often "displayed" the children at parties, where she was introduced to alcohol. She reported feeling that she did not matter to her parents, who were concerned only with appearances. Her parents had their own real estate business, and she described them as cold, detached, and rarely home. The client and her siblings were pushed to do well academically, athletically, and socially. When Alice was 13, her mother developed multiple sclerosis; she quickly lost her eyesight and was confined to a wheelchair. Alice reported that the father would come to her bedroom at night seeking comfort and solace after having been drinking heavily. He told her he was lonely and needed her. He had sexual relations with her for over a year. She did not want to hurt her mother or the rest of the family and told no one. The incest ceased when her father started an affair with another woman. Alice felt relieved but also guilty because she was angry and hurt when the father stopped coming to her room. She felt alone and abandoned. Subsequently, she had a life filled with drinking and disappointing relationships with men who left her. She worked steadily.

Denise, who had been in foster care for seven years, was receiving individual counseling from the agency social worker in order to prepare her to leave the system at age 21. She got along well with the foster family, was attending a local community college, and had a number of friends. At one meeting with her worker, Denise shared the contents of her private journal, which was filled with sexually explicit material, ranging from romantic musings to sadistic and masochistic fantasies. The worker, who knew about Denise's early sexual abuse, became frightened and referred her to the group. The worker described Denise as intelligent and verbal once she felt safe and accepted.

Denise had been placed voluntarily in care when she was 13 by her mother because Denise was out of control, refused to go to school, and stayed out all night. There had been reports of sexual and physical abuse and neglect. Two years later, the mother was arrested on drug charges and jailed. Denise has been in seven different foster homes since her initial placement. The worker learned that Denise had been sexually abused by one of her mother's boyfriends when she was 9. When she told her mother what had happened, her mother accused her of trying to steal her boyfriend and beat her for lying. Denise also reported being sexually abused in one of her foster homes and was removed, but when the police investigated the incident, no charges were filed.

Millagros entered couples treatment with her boyfriend for two months to work on their communication and sexual difficulties. They wanted to be married, but Millie was concerned that Tom was "not a talker" and he was concerned because she seemed "uninterested in sex." In the couples treatment, Tom was making progress in sharing his thoughts and feelings with Millie, but she was having difficulty exploring her sexual problems with two men. Because the worker thought there was a connection between her sexual problems and her early sexual abuse, he thought a women's group might help Millie to talk more openly about her early experiences and help her separate the present from the past. The worker described Millie as a serious young woman whose many strengths were evident and who had succeeded despite her family's reactions to the sexual abuse.

From ages 13 through 15, Millie's 20-year-old cousin had repeatedly forced her to have sex with him while he was living with her family. When she told the school guidance counselor, the cousin was arrested, Millie pressed charges, and he was jailed for two years. Her family was angry with her and blamed her for the cousin's incarceration and for exposing what had happened. Millie felt estranged from her family, and when she graduated from high school she got a job and went out on her own. She had reconciled somewhat with her family after her cousin was released from prison and apologized for what he had done. When Millie met her boyfriend, she began to have more intrusive thoughts when they were physically intimate and resisted sexual involvement.

Terry had been in treatment for a year when her therapist strongly urged her to attend a survivors' group. She had come for treatment because of intrusive thoughts and fragmented memories of past sexual abuse when she was 6 to 12 years of age. Terry, who had been married for 30 years and had four grown children, had worked in the business field all of her adult life. About a year before entering treatment, an incident occurred at work in which one of her male employers became enraged and yelled at her. While this was happening, she thought the walls were closing in on her, and she became terrified. Later, she had her first memory of having been sexually molested by her father. She became panic stricken and very depressed over the subsequent months and eventually had to stop working. She felt suicidal and almost was hospitalized but seemed to improve somewhat when her family doctor prescribed an antidepressant. She sought treatment because she could not cope. The therapist described Terry as a soft-spoken, somewhat reticent and serious woman who had many strengths and a good support system but who needed help in dealing with the consequences of her recent memories.

Terry was the oldest of two sisters born into a poor family who had emigrated to this country when they were adolescents. Her father was a hard worker who hated his job and took out his frustrations on the family. He was a frightening figure but was often away from home. Her mother was quite passive and submissive. Terry began to recall that starting when she was about 6 years of age, the father would repeatedly come into her room and lie on top of her and force her to perform oral sex and engage in other sexual behaviors. From what she recalled, she hated him and couldn't tolerate being around him. She thought that her now-deceased grandmother found him in Terry's room on at least one occasion, but her mother has denied any knowledge of the abuse. Her sister also did not believe her when she told her about these events recently, and her sister's attitude, along with the mother's denial, were major sources of stress to Terry.

Based on this information, the worker determined that all of the women seemed appropriate for the group because they were continuing to experience issues related to their early sexual abuse, seemed to have the capacity to deal with the impact of the abuse, and showed reasonably intact ego functioning. Although showing different levels of motivation for the group and somewhat different needs, all were willing to attend, and it seemed likely that some common goals could be identified. The worker thought it was helpful to have some age and cultural diversity represented in the group. She did wonder whether Alice would become a leader, what impact Joan's angry approach to others would have on other group members, whether Denise would overcome her suspiciousness and negative feelings about female authority, and how Terry would fit in because of her only recent memory of her sexual abuse and her age and life experiences.

The worker began the initial session by introducing herself and asking the members to do the same. They did so, and Cissy and Alice, the most lively, verbal, and motivated members of the group, volunteered some additional information. Cissy indicated that she was glad to be in the group because for a long time she had wanted to talk with other women about "things" that had happened and Alice said she had a lot she wanted to share. She told the group that she attended AA, liked it, but hoped that she would get more feedback in the group than she received at AA meetings. As the women introduced themselves, Denise's body language and tone of voice reflected considerable apprehensiveness and suspiciousness. Her eyes darted back and forth and watched the worker's reactions when Cissy spoke. Joan looked annoyed and seemed to be sizing everyone up. Millie seemed the most comfortable, to the point of being rather nonchalant, and Terry appeared fearful and hesitant. The worker picked up on Cissy's and Alice's comments.

Worker: It seems that you want to be able to share your feelings and get feedback from others who have had similar experiences. What might the rest of you want? (There was no response.) It is natural that some of you might feel uncomfortable because you don't know one another, what to expect, or how others will react.

Alice: I don't know why people aren't saying anything. I'll break the ice and tell my story. I'm used to talking from my AA meetings.

Alice recounted the basics of what had happened between her and her father in an affectless way while the others listened intently. When Alice finished, Joan looked irritated.

Joan: She doesn't sound like she has any feelings about what happened to her.

Worker: It's not always easy to feel painful emotions or to share such feelings with relative strangers.

Joan: Isn't that why we're here?

Worker: It's important that everyone feels safe. It takes time for people to feel secure that what they say will be accepted.

Joan: I do get upset when I try to talk about what happened to me. I don't know if I will ever feel safe.

Worker: Do you mean you don't know if you will feel safe with the other women in the group?

Joan: I never feel safe. I'm a private person. I don't talk to people too much. I only came here because my therapist thought it was a good idea.

Worker: You don't have to talk if you aren't ready. You can just listen for a while. What do the rest of you think about being here?

Millie: I'm not sure if the group can help me. I've been having problems with my boyfriend, and we have been seeing a male therapist. He thinks my abuse has something to do with the problems we're having and that it might help me to talk to other women about what happened to me when I was younger.

Worker: Can you share what happened to you?

Millie: (After telling her story) What upset me the most was the way my family handled the situation. They got mad at me and made me feel like something was wrong with me, not my cousin. He was the one who did it! He belonged in jail.

Denise: That was what happened to me. My mother didn't believe me when I told her about her lousy boyfriend and called me a liar and beat me.

Cissy: I never told my parents about what happened to me. No one knows. Not even my husband.

Worker: Many of you seem to be talking about similar experiences. It has been quite difficult for you when others who are important to you have not believed you or blamed you. Some of you feared telling others because harm might come to you.

Joan: How come Terry's not saying anything?

Worker: Maybe Terry doesn't feel comfortable talking yet? It's important for all of you to have some space.

Joan: But she hasn't said anything.

Worker: This seems to bother you.

Joan: I don't know what she is thinking. Maybe she thinks she's better then we are.

Worker: Why don't you ask Terry if she feels comfortable talking about what she's feeling and thinking?

Terry: I don't think I'm better then any of you. You have all had to deal with so much. It's been different for me because I only began to remember what happened to me in the last two years.

Worker: You have had a very hard time since then.

Terry: Yes, and I still can't quite believe it. My whole life feels different. Thank God, my husband and friends believe me and are supportive. But there's only so much I can say. People don't really understand or want to hear. I am having a lot of problems with my mother and sister who don't believe me and want me to keep quiet. I can't understand how my mother let my father do all the things he did to me.

Millie: (Nodding her head) Well, you aren't so different from us.

Alice: Do you mean you never had any memories of your abuse?

Terry: No. I didn't. That's why it was so shocking to me. I had to quit my job, and I wanted to die when I began to realize what had occurred.

Alice: What did happen?

Terry shared what she remembered, including the fact that she thought her mother or grandmother did know what was going on and should have done something about it.

Worker: It seems that all of you have not only had to struggle with your abuse but with how others in your life have failed you.

All of the group members related to the worker's comment, and she empathized with them. She observed that they were nearing the end of their time and asked how they were feeling about the session. All of the women except Joan said that they felt good about being able to be in a place in which everyone could understand what they had gone through. Joan was noncommittal but wanted to know what the group was going to talk about in weeks to come.

> Worker: That's a good question. As I explained previously, the group has 12 meetings, so we have 11 sessions remaining in which we can talk about your abuse experiences and how they have affected your lives. It's possible that these discussions will enable you to feel less alone and ashamed and to help one another to arrive at some different ways of thinking about and coping with the impact of your abuse.

The worker thought that the initial session had gone well. The members had interacted much as the worker thought they would. Cissy seemed very happy and comfortable about being in the group; Alice was the most talkative and helped to move the group along; Joan was the most insensitive and obstructionist; Denise, although she did speak, was wary and watchful; Millie was not clear about whether she needed the group but nevertheless participated; and Terry, who seemed somewhat isolated from others in the beginning, was more connected by the end. Gail noted that the members had begun to shift from directing most of their communication to her to addressing one another. She also observed that the women were more able to talk about others' reactions rather than about their abuse experiences, which undoubtedly would require more time and a sense of safety.

Gail began the second session by asking the members if they had any reactions or thoughts about the previous meeting.

> Terry: After we met, I thought I would try to speak to my sister again, and I called her. I felt very upset after our conversation because she told me that she didn't understand why I have to bring up the past and kept asking why I was making trouble for everyone.

> Worker: That must have been very disturbing.

> Denise: What did she mean by that?

Terry: She blames me for upsetting my mother, but my mother should have done something to stop my father.

Cissy: What really haunts me is the feeling that I should have been able to have stopped my uncle. Maybe there was something that I could have done to make him stop.

Worker: Can you tell us more about what happened?

Cissy told her story and ended by saying that she should have tried to fight her uncle off. Joan was sympathetic to Cissy and said she was too small and frightened to do that, but Joan and Millie also said that they often feel that they should have been able to prevent their abuse.

Worker: Feeling that you should have been able to do something to prevent the abuse seems to be a common feeling for many of you.

Because Joan's remark was the first indication that she was connecting positively to another member, the worker attempted to draw Joan out by asking her to talk more about what she was feeling.

Joan: (Directing herself to Cissy) I know just how you feel. I should have killed myself. That would have stopped the abuse. I should have done whatever it would have taken to end it. Why didn't I? Does that mean I wanted it? I thought I was trying to protect my younger sisters. You don't know what happened.

Alice: Maybe you can tell us now.

After Joan finished, Terry said that she had wanted to kill herself too because she felt that she had done something unspeakable and was ashamed. She added that she still felt suicidal sometimes but she didn't believe that suicide was the answer.

Worker: Does anyone else want to add something?

Millie: I don't understand why you would want to commit suicide. I didn't want to kill myself. I wanted to hurt my cousin for what he did to me.

Terry: I can't seem to feel anger at my father. He must have been a very sick man to have done such a thing to me. I feel angrier at my mother for not stopping my father.

Denise: I know what you mean. My mother never protected me,

and I hate her for everything she did to me. I ended up in a foster home and was abused there too, but no one did anything about it. I had to leave.

Worker: What you all had to go through was terrible, and you were not protected. It is understandable that you would want to hurt those who hurt you so badly or who didn't protect you. Sometimes instead of putting the responsibility on the perpetrator, where it belongs, children protect the perpetrator and blame themselves. This is very common among children who have been sexually abused.

Joan: Why?

Worker: When we are young, we need and depend on our parents, and it is too hard to think that our parents would hurt us. It is easier to think that we are at fault.

Cissy: Maybe there was something I could have done.

Worker: Children are helpless when the adults whom they depend on hurt them or do not protect them.

In the next several sessions, the women spoke more about their actual abuse experiences and expressed a range of intense feelings. It was clear that the members were connected to one another.

In the seventh session, the women began to bring up problems that they were having in their current lives. Some spoke of their conflictual feelings about sex. Millie described feeling either angry or numb when her boyfriend approached her physically. She often found herself pushing him away, and although he tried to be understanding, he was becoming frustrated. She didn't know what to do.

Alice: I used to drink in order to have sex. I'd get myself so drunk nothing bothered me. It's hard for me now, but I have been trying to practice telling myself that it is all right to have pleasure, that the man I'm with is not my father, and that I have some control in the situation. Talking to myself doesn't always work, but it has made it easier.

Millie: What do you mean about control?

Alice: I don't know if I can explain it, but I know I never felt that I had any say in what happened to me as a child and that I carried this feeling with me into relationships with men. I have realized that I am not a child anymore and can have control. I don't have to do what I don't want to.

Worker: Millie, does this seem to connect to what you are experiencing?

Millie: It's true that I usually feel that I don't have a say with my boyfriend. I feel like I'm supposed to do what he wants. He doesn't make me feel that way. I just can't help it. I don't know what to do.

Worker: Does anyone have any ideas that might help Millie?

Terry: Perhaps you could decide where you would like to be touched and what might feel good and tell your boyfriend to let you lead the way at your pace. Maybe this would give you more of a feeling of control.

Alice: I still think it is good to try to talk to yourself and give yourself permission to have some pleasure. Maybe it would help you to relax more.

Millie: I'm afraid I'll feel guilty if I don't do what my boyfriend likes.

Worker: Have you thought that he would feel good if he knew you were feeling better? He is not the only one who deserves pleasure and satisfaction.

Joan: I have a problem I want to talk about. I am due for a gynecological examination because I have a condition that needs to be checked. My doctor retired, and I have to go to someone new. It took me so long to get used to my old doctor. I just feel so frightened to see someone else. I'm avoiding taking care of this.

Terry: It's strange that you brought this up. I have to see my doctor, and I have been putting it off too. I don't know what I'm afraid of. It doesn't make sense. I have a woman doctor. I'm not afraid she's going to do anything to me.

Denise: I've been examined like that only once, years ago, when I was abused by my foster father. It was a horrible and humiliating experience. I hated it. I know I should go because I need some birth control, but I can't face it.

Worker: What do you think being examined stirs up?

Joan: I think it reminds me of being helpless and violated in some way. I just don't like being in that position.

Terry: I'm afraid I will have more bad memories.

Cissy: I'm afraid I'm going to panic and scream.

Worker: What has helped some of you to go through with these exams?

Alice: I used to have a friend accompany me, and I asked the doctor if my friend could stay in the examining room with me.

Joan: That's a good idea, but there is no one that I can ask to do that.

Alice: I'll go with you. In fact, you can go to my doctor, who is very understanding.

Joan: No one ever offered to help me like that.

Cissy: Maybe we can all do this. That would be a way we could help one another.

In the eighth session, the women were talking of the disturbing thoughts and fantasies that they had about sex. Denise said that for many years she had kept a journal of her sexual preoccupations.

Joan: No one wants to hear about that!

Denise: I have a right to bring it up.

Joan: Why did you bring it up now?

Millie: Don't interrogate Denise.

Joan: I wasn't talking to you. Why are you protecting Denise?

Worker: Let's stop and try to understand what's happening here.

Joan: I only asked a simple question. What's the big deal, and why does Millie have to get involved? Who's she! She's not in charge!

Denise started to cry, and Terry, who was sitting next to her, put her arm on Denise's shoulder. Joan got even more annoyed.

Joan: Why are you babying her. Can't she take care of herself?

Worker: Wait a minute. We need to calm down and talk about what is happening here. Joan, something clearly is upsetting you, but I don't think you realize that your questioning Denise about bringing up her journal seemed attacking and made Millie want to protect Denise.

Joan: I didn't think I was doing anything wrong.

Worker: It's not a matter of whether you did anything wrong. It seems more important to try to understand how you might have come across and what you were feeling, as well as to understand what was going on for Millie and Denise.

Joan: I didn't mean to hurt Denise, but I do feel upset that everyone feels sorry for her. I know she's been through a lot, but so have I. No one seems concerned about me.

Terry: We do care about you. Last week, when Alice offered to go with you to her doctor, you seemed quite pleased.

Joan: I was happy, and I made an appointment with the doctor. I wanted to tell you all about it.

Worker: Maybe you were disappointed that the group didn't ask about what happened after the last session and that Denise introduced something she wanted to discuss. Instead of saying what you needed, perhaps you showed your disappointment by being angry.

Joan: I didn't realize I sounded angry. I was disappointed. I feel that way a lot of the time.

Denise: It hurt my feelings when you spoke to me as you did. It didn't make me want to be nice to you.

Millie: I felt upset for Denise. I've always tried to defend other people whom I feel are being mistreated.

Worker: Is it possible that you came down a little hard on Joan?

Millie: Maybe. Other people have said that about me. I'm always sticking up for people when it may not even be necessary.

Joan: My therapist thinks that I alienate people because I don't say what I need, but I get upset when people don't respond the way I want them to. I'm sorry if it hurt you.

Worker: This is a good place for you to practice saying what you do need. Is there a way we can help you to do that?

Cissy: Maybe we should start each session by asking each person what they would like to bring up or if there is anything they need from the group that day before we settle on a topic.

Joan: I need to try to be more aware of what I'm feeling and what I need.

Worker: That's a good idea for everyone. All of you have had the terrible experience of having your needs trampled on. It's understandable that you are out of touch with what you need and don't know how to ask for your needs to be met. We have four weeks left. We need to talk about how you feel about that and how you want to use the remaining time.

The women said they wanted to continue to talk about how their past abuse had interfered with their relationships with others and to get some help with deciding how open to be with others about their experiences and how to deal with the people in their lives who had let them down. They all felt that the group was very important to them and that it had helped their individual therapies. They expressed sadness and apprehension about the group's coming to an end because they had come to value the relationships and being able to be with other adult survivors. They wanted to plan for the continuation of the group on some basis without the worker in view of the fact that it was against agency policy for the worker to continue.

Discussion

The initial phase of the group centered on engagement, goal setting, facilitating group interaction, and building group cohesion. As the participants felt safer and saw their commonalities, they began to discuss their past traumatic experiences and their impact. In this process, the group members became more connected to one another and to the group as a whole. The worker found these sessions very taxing, the material was highly charged. She was struck, however, by the women's strengths in surviving their difficult backgrounds and their willingness to help one another. In later sessions, the women brought up individual issues and concerns, and the group was able to provide mutual support, feedback, and assistance. When conflict arose among several members of the group, the worker was able to help them to reflect on its meaning for each of them and to use the incident to connect their behavior in sessions to their issues outside the group. The final sessions of *the group focused on helping the members in their current lives and on the ending process, which was difficult for all of them.*

SUMMARY

This chapter discussed and illustrated some of the major foci of group-oriented ISTT. After describing some of the indicators for the use of groups, it emphasized the importance of balancing individual and group assessment, engagement, contracting, building group cohesion, facilitating group interaction, conflict resolution, using a wide range of interventions, worker reactions, and termination issues.

References

Abarbanel, G., & Richman, G. (1991). The rape victim. In H. J. Parad & L. G. Parad (Eds.), *Crisis intervention book 2: The practitioner's sourcebook for brief therapy* (pp. 93–118). Milwaukee, WI: Family Service America.

Adler, A., & Ansbacher, R. (1956). *The individual psychology of Alfred Adler*. New York: Basic Books.

Alexander, F., & French, T. M. (1946). *Psychoanalytic therapy*. New York: Ronald Press.

American Psychiatric Association. (1994). *Diagnostic criteria from DSM-IV*. Washington, DC: American Psychiatric Association.

Austin, L. (1948). Trends in differential treatment in social casework. *Social Casework, 29*, 203–211.

Austrian, S. G. (1995). *Mental disorders, medications, and clinical social work*. New York: Columbia University Press.

Baker, H. S. (1991). Shorter-term psychotherapy: A self-psychological approach. In J. P. Barber & P. Crits-Christoph (Eds.), *Handbook of short-term dynamic psychotherapy* (pp. 287–318). New York: Basic Books.

Bandura, A. (1976). *Social learning theory*. Englewood Cliffs, NJ: Prentice Hall.

Bartlett, H. (1970). *The common base of social work practice*. New York: NASW.

Beck, A. (1976). *Cognitive therapy and the emotional disorders*. New York: International Universities Press.

Beck, A. T., Emery, G., & Greenberg, R. L. (1985). *Anxiety disorders and phobias*. New York: Basic Books.

Beck, A. T., Freeman, A., et al. (1990). *Cognitive therapy of personality disorders*. New York: Guilford.

Beck, A. T., Rush, J. A., Shaw, B. F., & Emery, G. (1979). *Cognitive theory of depression*. New York: Guilford.

Bellak, L., Hurvich, M., & Gediman, H. (1973). *Ego functions in schizophrenics, neurotics, and normals*. New York: Wiley.

Brekke, J. (1991). Crisis intervention with victims and perpetrators of spouse abuse. In

H. J. Parad & L. G. Parad (Eds). *Crisis intervention book 2: The practitioner's sourcebook for brief therapy* (pp. 161–178). Milwaukee, WI: Family Service America.

Budman, S. H., & Gurman, A. S. (1988). *Theory and practice of brief therapy.* New York: Guilford.

Burgess, A. W., & Holmstrom, L. L. (1974). Rape trauma syndrome. *American Journal of Psychiatry, 131,* 981–986.

Caplan, G. (1964). *Principles of preventive psychiatry.* New York: Basic Books.

Cockerill, E., et al. (1953). *A conceptual framework of social casework.* Pittsburgh: University of Pittsburgh Press.

Craighead, L. W., Craighead, W. E., Kazdin, A. E., & Mahoney, M. J. (Eds.). (1994). *Cognitive and behavioral intervention: An empirical approach to mental health problems.* Boston: Allyn & Bacon.

Crits-Christoph, P., Crits-Christoph, K., Wolf-Palacio, D., Fichter, M., & Rudick, D. (1995). Brief supportive-expressive psychodynamic psychotherapy for generalized anxiety disorder. In J. P. Barber & P. Crits-Christoph (Eds.), *Dynamic therapies for psychiatric disorders (Axis I)* (pp. 43–83). New York: Basic Books.

Davanloo, H. (1978). *Basic principles and techniques in short-term dynamic psychotherapy.* New York: Spectrum.

Davanloo, H. (1980). *Short-term dynamic psychotherapy.* New York: Jason Aronson.

Davanloo, H. (1991). *Unlocking the unconscious.* New York: Wiley.

DeRoche, P. L. (1995). Psychodynamic psychotherapy with the HIV-infected client. In J. P. Barber & P. Crits-Christoph (Eds.), *Dynamic therapies for psychiatric disorders (Axis I)* (pp. 420–444). New York: Basic Books.

Elkin, I. (1994). The NIMH treatment of depression collaborative research program: Where we began and where we are. In S. L. Garfield & A. E. Bergin (Eds.), *Handbook of psychotherapy and behavior change* (4th ed.) (pp. 114–139). New York: Wiley.

Ellis, A. (1962). *Reason and emotion in psychotherapy.* New York: Lyle Stuart.

Ellis, A. (1973). *Humanistic psychotherapy: The rational-emotive approach.* New York: McGraw-Hill.

Elson, M. (1986). *Self psychology in clinical social work.* New York: Norton.

Epstein, L. (1980). *Helping people: The task-centered approach.* St. Louis: Mosby.

Epstein, L. (1992). *Brief treatment and a new look at the task-centered approach.* New York: Macmillan.

Erikson, E. (1950). *Childhood and society.* New York: Norton.

Erikson, E. (1959). Identity and the life cycle. *Psychological Issues, 1,* 50–100.

Fairbairn, W. R. D. (1952). *Psychoanalytic studies of personality.* London: Tavistock.

Fairbairn, W. R. D. (1954). *An object relations theory of the personality.* New York: Basic Books.

Ferenczi, S., & Rank, O. (1925). *The development of psychoanalysis.* New York: Nervous and Mental Disease Publishing.

Fischer, J. (1978). *Effective casework practice: An eclectic approach.* New York: McGraw-Hill.

Flegenheimer, W. (1982). *Techniques of brief psychotherapy.* Northvale, NJ: Jason Aronson.

Freud, S. (1905). On psychotherapy. In J. Strachey (Ed.), *Standard edition of the complete psychological works of Sigmund Freud* (Vol. 7). London: Hogarth Press, 1953.

Garfield, S. L. (1986). Research on client variables in psychotherapy. In S. L. Garfield & A. E. Bergin (Eds.), *Handbook of psychotherapy and behavior change* (3rd ed.) (pp. 213–256). New York: Wiley.

Garrett, A. (1958). Modern casework: The contributions of ego psychology. In H. J. Parad (Ed.), *Ego psychology and dynamic casework* (pp. 38–52). New York: Family Service Association of America.

Garvin, C. (1997). Group treatment with adults. In J. R. Brandell (Ed.), *Theory and practice in clinical social work* (pp. 315–342). New York: Free Press.

Gaston, L. (1995). Dynamic therapy for post-traumatic stress disorder. In J. P. Barber & P. Crits-Christoph (Eds.), *Dynamic therapies for psychiatric disorders (Axis I)* (pp. 161–192). New York: Basic Books.

Germain, C. B. (1979). *Social work practice: People and environments.* New York: Columbia University Press.

Germain, C. B. (1991). *Human behavior in the social environment: An ecological view.* New York: Columbia University Press.

Germain, C. B., & Gitterman, A. (1980). *The life model of social work practice.* New York: Columbia University Press.

Goisman, R. M. (1997). Cognitive-behavioral therapy today. *Harvard Mental Health Letter, 13,* 4–7.

Golan, N. (1978). *Treatment in crisis situations.* New York: Free Press.

Goldstein, E. G. (1990). *Borderline disorders: Clinical model and techniques.* New York: Guilford.

Goldstein, E. G. (1995a). *Ego psychology and social work practice* (2nd ed.). New York: Free Press.

Goldstein, E. G. (1995b). Psychosocial approach. In *Encyclopedia of social work* (19th ed.) (pp. 1948–1954). Washington, DC: NASW.

Goldstein, E. G., & Gonzalez-Ramos, G. (1989). Toward an integrative clinical practice perspective. In S. M. Ehrenkranz, E. G. Goldstein, L. Goodman, & J. Seinfeld (Eds.), *Clinical social work with maltreated children and their families: An introduction to practice* (pp. 21–37). New York: New York University Press.

Gordon, W. (1969). Basic constructs for an integrative and generative conception of social work. In G. Hearn (Ed.), *The general systems approach: Contributions toward a holistic conception of social work.* New York: CSWE.

Graziano, R. (1997). The challenge of clinical work with survivors of trauma. In J. R. Brandell (Ed.), *Theory and practice in clinical social work* (pp. 380–403). New York: Free Press.

Greenson, R. R. (1967). *The technique and practice of psychoanalysis.* New York: International Universities Press.

Grinker, R. R., & Spiegel, J. D. (1945). *Men under stress.* Philadelphia: Blakiston.

Grossman, L. (1973). Train crash: Social work and disaster services. *Social Work, 18,* 38–44.

Guntrip, H. (1969). *Schizoid phenomena, object relations, and the self.* New York: International Universities Press.

Guntrip, H. (1973). *Psychoanalytic theory, therapy, and the self.* New York: Basic Books.

Hamilton, G. (1940). *Theory and practice of social casework*. New York: Columbia University Press.

Hamilton, G. (1958). A theory of personality: Freud's contribution to social casework. In H. J. Parad (Ed.), *Ego psychology and dynamic casework* (pp. 11–37). New York: Family Service Association of America.

Hartman, A., & Laird, J. (1983). *Family-centered social work practice*. New York: Free Press.

Heller, N. R., & Northcut, T. B. (1996). Utilizing cognitive-behavioral techniques in psychodynamic practice with clients diagnosed as borderline. *Clinical Social Work Journal, 24*, 203–215.

Hill, R. (1958). Generic features of families under stress. *Social Casework, 39*, 139–150.

Hollis, F. (1949). The techniques of casework. *Journal of Social Casework, 30*, 235–244.

Hollis, F. (1963). Contemporary issues for caseworkers. In H. J. Parad & H. Miller (Eds.), *Ego-oriented casework*. New York: Family Service Association of America.

Hollis, F. (1964). *Casework: A psychosocial therapy*. New York: Random House.

Hollis, F. (1972). *Casework: A psychosocial therapy* (2nd ed.). New York: Random House.

Hollis, F., & Woods, M. E. (1981). *Casework: A psychosocial therapy* (3rd ed.). New York: Random House.

Holmes, F. H., & Rahe, R. H. (1967). The social readjustment scale. *Journal of Psychosomatic Research, 11*, 213–218.

Iodice, J. D., & Wodarski, J. S. (1987). Aftercare treatment for schizophrenics living at home. *Social Work, 32*, 122–128.

Jacobson, G. F., Strickler, M., & Morley, W. E. (1968). Generic and individual approaches to crisis intervention. *American Journal of Public Health, 58*, 338–343.

Janis, I. (1958). *Psychological stress*. New York: Wiley.

Kaplan, D. M. (1962). A concept of acute situational disorders. *Social Work, 7*, 15–23.

Kaplan, D. M. (1968). Observations on crisis theory and practice. *Social Casework, 49*, 151–155.

Karasu, T. B. (1990). *Psychotherapy for depression*. Northvale, NJ: Jason Aronson.

Klein, M. (1948). *Contributions to psychoanalysis: 1921–1945*. London: Hogarth Press.

Kohut, H. (1971). *The analysis of the self*. New York: International Universities Press.

Kohut, H. (1977). *The restoration of the self*. New York: International Universities Press.

Koss, M., & Shiang, J. (1994). Research on brief psychotherapy. In S. L. Garfield & A. E. Bergin (Eds.), *Handbook of psychotherapy and behavior change* (4th ed.) (pp. 664–700). New York: Wiley.

Langsley, D., & Kaplan, D. (1968). *Treatment of families in crisis*. New York: Grune & Stratton.

Larke, J. (1985). Compulsory treatment: Some practical methods of treating the mandated client. *Psychotherapy, 22*, 262–268.

Laughlin, H. P. (1979). *The ego and its defenses* (2nd ed.). New York: Jason Aronson.

Lazarus, A. A. (1971). *Behavior therapy and beyond*. New York: McGraw-Hill.

Lazarus, A. A. (Ed.). (1976). *Multimodal behavior therapy*. New York: Springer.

Lazarus, R. S. (1966). *Psychological stress and the coping process.* New York: McGraw-Hill.

Le Masters, E. E. (1957). Parenthood as crisis. In H. J. Parad (Ed.), *Crisis intervention: Selected readings* (pp. 111–117). New York: Family Service Association of America.

Lindemann, E. (1944). Symptomatology and management of acute grief. *American Journal of Psychiatry, 101,* 7–21.

Linehan, M. M. (1993). *Cognitive-behavioral treatment of borderline personality disorder.* New York: Guilford.

Luborsky, L. (1984). *Principles of psychoanalytic psychotherapy: A manual for supportive-expressive treatment.* New York: Basic Books.

Luborsky, L., Mark, D., Hole, A. V., Popp, C., Goldsmith, B., & Cacciola, J. (1995). Supportive-expressive dynamic psychotherapy of depression: A time-limited version. In J. P. Barber & P. Crits-Christoph (Eds.), *Dynamic therapies for psychiatric disorders (Axis I)* (pp. 13–42). New York: Basic Books.

Mahler, M. S., Pine, F., & Bergman, A. (1975). *The psychological birth of the human infant.* New York: Basic Books.

Malan, D. (1963). *A study of brief psychotherapy.* New York: Plenum.

Malan, D. (1976). *The frontier of brief psychotherapy.* Cambridge, MA: Harvard University Press.

Mann, J. (1973). *Time-limited psychotherapy.* Cambridge, MA: Harvard University Press.

Mann, J. (1991). Time-limited psychotherapy. In P. Crits-Christoph & J. P. Barber (Eds.), *Handbook of short-term dynamic psychotherapy* (pp. 17–43). New York: Basic Books.

Marmar, C. R. (1991). Brief dynamic psychotherapy of post-traumatic stress disorder. *Psychiatric Annals, 21,* 405–414.

McFarlane, A. C. (1990). Post-traumatic stress syndrome revisited. In H. J. Parad & L. G. Parad (Eds.), *Crisis intervention book 2: The practitioner's sourcebook for brief therapy* (pp. 69–92). Milwaukee, WI: Family Service America.

McNew, J. A., & Abell, N. (1995). Posttraumatic stress symptomatology: Similarities and differences between Vietnam veterans and adult survivors of childhood sexual abuse. *Social Work, 40,* 115–126.

Mayer, J., & Timms, N. (1970). *The client speaks.* New York: Atherton Press.

Meyer, C. H. (1970). *Social work practice: A response to the urban crisis.* New York: Free Press.

Mishne, J. M. (1989). Individual treatment. In S. M. Ehrenkranz, E. G. Goldstein, L. Goodman, & J. Seinfeld (Eds.), *Clinical social work with maltreated children and their families: An introduction to practice* (pp. 38–61). New York: New York University Press.

Mishne, J. M. (1993). *The evolution and application of clinical theory.* New York: Free Press.

Mor-Barak, M. E. (1991). Social support intervention in crisis situations: A case of maritime disaster. In H. J. Parad & L. G. Parad (Eds.), *Crisis intervention book 2: The practitioner's sourcebook for brief therapy* (pp. 313–329). Milwaukee, WI: Family Service America.

Nichols, M. P., & Schwartz, R. C. (1995). *Family therapy: Concepts and methods* (3rd ed.). Boston: Allyn & Bacon.

Noonan, M. (1998). Understanding the "difficult" patient: From a dual person perspective. *Clinical Social Work Journal, 26,* 129–142.

Parad, H. J. (Ed.). (1958). *Ego psychology and dynamic casework.* New York: Family Service Association of America.

Parad, H. J. (Ed.). (1965). *Crisis intervention: Selected readings.* New York: Family Service Association of America.

Parad, H. J. (1971). Crisis intervention. In R. Morris (Ed.), *Encyclopedia of Social Work* (16th ed.) (Vol. 1, pp. 196–202). New York: NASW.

Parad, H. J., & Caplan, G. (1960). A framework for studying families in crisis, *Social Work, 5,* 53–72.

Parad, H. J., & Miller, R. R. (Eds.). (1963). *Ego-oriented casework: Problems and perspectives.* New York: Family Service Association of America.

Parad, H. J., & Parad, L. G. (1990a). Crisis intervention: An introductory overview. In H. J. Parad & L. G. Parad (Eds.), *Crisis intervention book 2: The practitioner's sourcebook for brief therapy* (pp. 3–68). Milwaukee, WI: Family Service America.

Parad, H. J., & Parad, L. G. (Eds). (1990b). *Crisis intervention book 2: The practitioner's sourcebook for brief therapy.* Milwaukee, WI: Family Service America.

Patten, S. B., Gatz, Y. K., Jones, B., & Thomas, D. L. (1989). Post-traumatic stress disorder and the treatment of sexual abuse. *Social Work, 34,* 197–203.

Perlman, H. H. (1957). *Social casework: A problem-solving process.* Chicago: University of Chicago Press.

Perlman, H. H. (1979). *Relationship: The heart of helping people.* Chicago: University of Chicago Press.

Philips, L. J., & Gonzalez-Ramos, G. (1989). Clinical social work practice with minority families. In S. M. Ehrenkranz, E. G. Goldstein, L. Goodman, & J. Seinfeld (Eds.), *Clinical social work with maltreated children and their families: An introduction to practice* (pp. 128–148). New York: New York University Press.

Piaget, J. (1951). *The child's conception of the world.* London: Routledge & Kegan Paul.

Piaget, J. (1952). *The origins of intelligence in children.* New York: International Universities Press.

Pruett, H. L. (1990). Brief crisis-oriented therapy with college students. In H. J. Parad & L. G. Parad (Eds.). *Crisis intervention book 2: The practitioner's sourcebook for brief therapy* (pp. 179–192). Milwaukee, WI: Family Service America.

Rapoport, L. (1962). The state of crisis: Some theoretical considerations. *Social Service Review, 36,* 211–217.

Rapoport, L. (1967). Crisis-oriented short-term casework. *Social Service Review, 41,* 31–43.

Rapoport, L. (1970). Crisis intervention as a mode of brief treatment. In R. W. Roberts and R. H. Nee (Eds.), *Theories of social casework* (pp. 267–311). Chicago: University of Chicago Press.

Reid, W. J., & Epstein, L. (1972). *Task-centered casework.* New York: Columbia University Press.

Reid, W. J., & Shyne, A. (1969). *Brief and extended casework*. New York: Columbia University Press.

Richmond, M. L. (1917). *Social diagnosis*. New York: Russell Sage Foundation.

Ripple, L. (1964). *Motivation, capacity, and opportunity: Studies in casework theory and practice*. Chicago: University of Chicago Press.

Robinson, V. P. (1930). *A changing psychology in social casework*. Chapel Hill: University of North Carolina Press.

Schlosberg, S. B., & Kagan, R. M. (1977). Practice strategies for engaging chronic multiproblem families. *Social Casework, 58*, 29–35.

Scott, M. J., & Stradling, S. G. (1991). The cognitive-behavioural approach with depressed clients. *British Journal of Social Work, 21*, 533–544.

Selye, H. (1956). *The stress of life*. New York: McGraw-Hill.

Sermabekian, P. (1994). Our clients, ourselves: The spiritual perspective and social work practice. *Social Work, 39*, 178–183.

Seruya, B. B. (1997). *Empathic brief psychotherapy*. Northvale, NJ: Jason Aronson.

Shear, M. K., Cloitre, M., & Heckelman, L. (1995). Emotion-focused treatment for panic disorder: A brief, dynamically informed therapy. In J. P. Barber & P. Crits-Christoph (Eds.), *Dynamic therapies for psychiatric disorders* (AXIS I) (pp. 267–293). New York: Basic Books.

Shechter, R. A. (1997). Time-sensitive social work practice. In J. R. Brandell (Ed.), *Theory and practice in clinical social work* (pp. 529–550). New York: Free Press.

Sifneos, P. (1972). *Short-term psychotherapy and emotional crisis*. Cambridge, MA: Harvard University Press.

Sifneos, P. E. (1979). *Short-term psychotherapy: Evaluation and technique*. New York: Plenum.

Sifneos, P. (1987). *Short-term dynamic psychotherapy* (2nd ed.). New York: Plenum.

Siporin, M. (1975). *Introduction to social work practice*. New York: Macmillan.

Skinner, B. F. (1953). *Science and human behavior*. New York: Macmillan.

Smalley, R. E. (1970). The functional approach to casework process. In R. W. Roberts & R. H. Nee (Eds.), *Theories of social casework*. Chicago: University of Chicago Press.

Sokol, B. (1983). Intervention with heart attack patients and families. *Social Casework, 64*, 162–168.

Solomon, A. (1992). Clinical diagnosis among diverse populations: A multicultural perspective. *Families in Society, 73*, 371–377.

Stadter, M. (1996). *Object relations brief therapy*. Northvale, NJ: Jason Aronson.

Stamm, I. (1959). Ego psychology in the emerging theoretical base of social work. In A. J. Kahn (Ed.), *Issues in American social work* (pp. 80–109). New York: Columbia University Press.

Stern, D. N. (1985). *The interpersonal world of the infant*. New York: Basic Books.

Straussner, S. L. A. (Ed.). (1993). *Clinical work with substance-abusing clients*. New York: Guilford.

Strean, H. (1978). *Clinical social work*. New York: Free Press.

Strickler, M. (1965). Applying crisis theory in a community clinic. *Social Casework, 46*, 150–154.

Strupp, H. H., & Binder, J. L. (1984). *Psychotherapy in a new key: A guide to time-limited dynamic psychotherapy.* New York: Basic Books.

Sullivan, H. S. (1953). *The interpersonal theory of psychiatry.* New York: Norton.

Sullivan, W. P., Wolk, J. L., & Hartmann, D. J. (1992). Case management in alcohol and drug treatment: Improving client outcomes. *Families in Society, 73,* 195–204.

Tabachnick, N. (1991). Crisis and adult development: A psychoanalyst's perspective. In H. J. Parad & L. G. Parad (Eds.), *Crisis intervention book 2: The practitioner's sourcebook for brief therapy* (pp. 192–208). Milwaukee, WI: Family Service America.

Taft, J. (1937). The relation of function to process in social casework. *Journal of Social Process, 1,* 1–18.

Taft, J. (1950). A conception of growth process underlying social casework. *Social Casework, 31,* 311–318.

Thyer, B. A., & Myers, L. L. (1996). Behavioral and cognitive theories. In J. R. Brandell (Ed.), *Theory and practice in clinical social work* (pp. 18–37). New York: Free Press.

Towle, C. (1949). Helping the client to use his capacities and resources. In *Proceedings of the National Conference of Social Work, 1948* (pp. 259–279). New York: Columbia University Press.

Towle, C. (1954). *The learner in education for the professions.* Chicago: University of Chicago Press.

Turner, F. J. (1996). *Social work treatment* (4th ed.). New York: Free Press.

Tyhurst, J. S. (1958). The role of transitional states—including disaster—in mental illness. In Walter Reed Army Institute of Research, *Symposium on Preventive and Social Psychiatry.* Washington, DC: U.S. Government Printing Office.

Walsh, F. (1997). Family therapy: Systems approaches to clinical practice. In J. R. Brandell (Ed.), *Theory and practice in clinical social work* (pp. 132–163). New York: Free Press.

Weick, A., Rapp, C., Sullivan, W. P., & Kisthardt, W. (1989). A strengths perspective for social work practice. *Social Work, 34,* 350–354.

Wells, R. A. (1990). *Planned short-term treatment* (2nd ed.). New York: Free Press.

Wells, R. A., & Phelps, P. A. (1990). The brief psychotherapies: A selective overview. In R. Wells & V. Giannetti (Eds.), *Handbook of the brief psychotherapies* (pp. 3–26) New York: Plenum.

White, R. F. (1959). Motivation reconsidered: The concept of competence, *Psychological Review, 66,* 297–333.

Wilson, G. T. (1981). Behavior therapy as a short-term therapeutic approach. In S. H. Budman (Ed.), *Forms of brief therapy* (pp. 131–166). New York: Guilford.

Winnicott, D. W. (1965). *Maturational processes and the facilitating environment.* New York: International Universities Press.

Wolberg, L. R. (Ed.). (1965). *Short term psychotherapy.* New York: Grune & Stratton.

Wolberg, L. R. (1980). *Handbook of short-term psychotherapy.* New York: Thieme-Stratton.

Wolpe, J. (1958). *Psychotherapy by reciprocal inhibition.* Stanford, CA: Stanford University Press.

Wolpe, J. (1969). *The practice of behavior therapy*. New York: Pergamon.

Woods, M. E., & Hollis, F. (1990). *Casework: A psychosocial therapy* (4th ed.). New York: McGraw-Hill.

Woods, M. E., & Robinson, H. (1996). Psychosocial theory and social work treatment. In F. J. Turner (Ed.), *Social work treatment*. (4th ed.) (pp. 555–580). New York: Free Press.

Wright, J. H., & Borden, J. (1991). Cognitive therapy of depression and anxiety. *Psychiatric Annals, 21*, 424–428.

Yelaja, S. A. (1974). *Authority and social work: Concept and use*. Toronto: University of Toronto Press.

Yelaja, S. A. (1986). Functional theory for social work practice. In F. J. Turner (Ed.), *Social work treatment* (3rd ed.) (pp. 46–68). New York: Free Press.

Index